SELF–RELIANCE AND SOCIAL SECURITY

1870 – 1917

KENNIKAT PRESS
NATIONAL UNIVERSITY PUBLICATIONS
SERIES IN AMERICAN STUDIES

General Editor
JAMES P. SHENTON
Professor of History, Columbia University

Hace Sorel Tishler

SELF–RELIANCE AND SOCIAL SECURITY 1870 – 1917

NATIONAL UNIVERSITY PUBLICATIONS

Kennikat Press, Inc.

Port Washington, N.Y. ● London

Library of Congress Catalog Card Number: 79–139361
ISBN 0–8046–9012–X

Manufactured in the United States of America

Published by
Kennikat Press, Inc.
Port Washington, N.Y./London

To My Wife

PREFACE

On the eve of the First World War, Americans took their first steps toward social security. For some, the passage of the state workmen's compensation laws and the state mothers'.pension acts marked a regrettable departure from time honored national values. For others these events were merely a beginning gesture to the masses whose patience with charity was fast running out. Although welfare reformers considered the new measures shamefully overdue, they were in fact truly inspired about the possibility for reform in America. "You may call it Socialism, Communism or what you like," declared Robert McDonough, former labor commissioner of New York State, "it is what we are coming to and you may as well face it."[1] Like the progressive movement as a whole, the new social welfare movement appeared to have reached the legislative phase with unexpected suddenness. A few of the advocates even feared that the movement would get out of hand, that the yearning for social justice would become a clamor for silly and reckless panaceas.

Actually the movement had been in the making for a generation. If what happened during the progressive era can be called a "birth," the years between the Civil War and 1900 can be referred to as a period of gestation. The nation was suffering its first pains from an industrial revolution and many segments of society were diagnosing the social ills in such a way that social security, albeit by no means widely prescribed, was at least a logical remedy, and one that seemed less and less alien as late nineteenth-century society enacted social reforms, conservative and ineffectual as these were.

More than likely, were the intelligent layman asked to pinpoint the birth of social security, he would answer with a reference to the early days of the New Deal. His belief is reinforced not only by the election reminders of the Democrats (and the still occasional accusations by the Republicans) but by the authoritative voice of written history as well. Unfortunately, historians, preoccupied with national legislation, have left the impression that before 1935 social welfare reform was inconsequential, and that the American commitment to individual self-reliance somehow remained virtually unchanged for three hundred years. There is, of course, abundant and not entirely unconvincing evidence that can be marshalled to support this picture. By contrast with many western industrial nations, America was indeed a laggard in developing public welfare programs. There are, in addition, enough valid distinctions between the social security measures of the Progressive Era and those of the New Deal, so that the former could be regarded as unworthy of any great celebration or censure. They were, for example, designed for and limited almost exclusively to persons of low income, and coverage was neither comprehensive nor adequate. In addition, progressive reformers achieved success only in the area of workmen's compensation and pensions for dependent mothers.

The progressive legislation, nonetheless, incorporated the basic principle of any modern social security system: the assurance by the government that relief be provided as a right and not as a charity when a disability hampers the normal earning of income. And however imperfectly these principles were carried out in practice the measures did in fact change an essential part of our social fabric. They not only challenged the sanctity of "laissez-faire" as did much of the reform legislation of the period, they represented a significant reinterpretation of that other American shibboleth, "self-reliance."

That the social welfare reforms constituted a reinterpretation of self-reliance rather than a rejection of it is, perhaps, an obvious but nonetheless important point. To miss it is to miss both the continuity and the changes in American social welfare history. To measure social welfare change in terms of outright rejections of self-reliance (particularly if one makes an analysis of the rhetoric) is to find little or no change at all. Were it not for the archaic language of the late eighteenth-century lectures on thrift, sobriety and hard work, and the promise of American life, one could easily mistake them for twentieth-century pronouncements. It is certainly significant that most Americans have felt compelled to reassure themselves that every new acceptance of the welfare state will enhance rather than weaken the individual's self-reliance. Yet equally significant is the fact that somehow we have managed, in spite of the remarkable constancy of our professions of faith in the Protestant ethic, to make accommodations which to an earlier generation would have seemed like a betrayal.

In a sense this work is an attempt to describe and analyze this process of accomodation. Since the demands for self-reliance have historically been applied with less rigor to the disabled poor, I have dealt almost exclusively with the able-bodied, for whom self-reliance has been a more relevant and controversial question. By "able-bodied" I mean to include those persons who at some time in their adult life prior to an accidental injury, sickness or debilitating old age, enjoyed the kind of physical and mental health that would not have precluded their making some provision for a future disability. Although this paper focuses upon the movement for public-compulsory programs, some attention must be paid to the development of the private-voluntary efforts, for these too represented a departure from the more pristine concepts of individual self-reliance. Moreover, the meaning of the public compulsory programs cannot be fully appreciated unless we see them as having been both encouraged by and hindered by the rise of the private voluntary systems of relief.

Even among the more recent histories that have acknowledged and examined the transformations in the public and private welfare during this period, certain historical problems remain. With minor exceptions here and there, their story of social welfare begins with a nation strongly committed to the Protestant ethic of thrift, industriousness and self-reliance. As they see it, failure to remain financially independent was commonly regarded as a sign that the individual had fallen victim to his own vices and weaknesses. "To the nineteenth century," writes Robert Bremner, "few crimes were more reprehensible than inability to make a living."[2] The individual's thriftlessness, improvidence, laziness and drunkenness were, therefore, to be eliminated by morally recharging him through some form of discipline. As time passes, so the story goes — as charity workers, politicians, journalists actually begin to enter the homes of the poor and more realistically survey the social scene — the penchant to blame the individual for his plight diminishes and the preoccupation with moral reform of the individual gives way to a concern for reform of the environment.

By the Progressive Era some discernably new stage of collective responsibility was reached. Though historians differ in characterizing the extent of the advance at any point in time, their conception of individual and collective responsiblity and of the rather tight inverse relationship presumed to exist between them are such that the advance is minimized. Thus in his discussion of the charity workers' capacity for "radical reform" in the late nineteenth century, Professor Roy Lubove writes that their focus upon the individual case and upon the moral roots of dependency precluded any such possibility."[3] Robert Bremner agrees with this view and although his assessment of the progressive contributions to welfare is more generous than Lubove's, it is scarcely a vote of confidence in the capacity of the American public to change. After noting that the health insurance movement met with strong opposition from employers and taxpayers associations, organized labor and insurance companies, Bremner declares that "the success with which such groups employed ideological arguments against public health insurance revealed that despite the adoption of accident compensation, the notion of individual responsibility was deeply rooted in the public mind."[4]

Now there is considerable value and truth in this picture, even taking into account the disservice done to it by so brief a summation. There are some problems with it, however. In the case of Bremner's reference to the defeat of public health insurance as a manifestation of the tenacity of individual responsibility, the absence or presence of direct governmental participation in a social welfare measure appears to be the feature that distinguishes the individualistic from the collectivistic approach. This is no place to enter into an extended discussion of the argument, but it should be pointed out that many of the opponents of health insurance favored employer and union benefit plans that required collective and cooperative ventures among workers or between workers and their employers. This is not to suggest that these private schemes should be equated with public social insurance, but they were a far cry from the kind of individual responsibility that required the worker independently to put his savings under the rug or in a bank.

Lubove's *The Struggle for Social Security* provides a brilliant corrective on this score. For in dealing with the voluntary welfare systems as one of his central themes, he manages to bring the social insurance debate down to earth – as a struggle between various vested and collective interests – without losing sight of the loftier issues of individualism, freedom, democracy, paternalism, etc. There is a problem, though. Essentially he is attempting to explain the failures and weaknesses of the social insurance movement. He persuasively supports the case for a kind of stacked deck against the movement: "the inhospitable environment" into which social insurance was introduced; its identification as an alien system; and the uneven match in having to compete with private systems offering something other than economic efficiency. Lubove further notes that the supporters of the "voluntarism" called the tunes, thwarting health insurance and adapting workmen's compensation to their own ends.[5] Much of this is indisputable. But it begs what in America is the really critical question: How in such hostile territory did the social insurance movement achieve even the limited success that it had? What were its strengths? And on this count Lubove's treatment is less satisfying. Not so much because he discounts the movement's achievements – though in the case of Workmen's Compensation, his claim that "it did not signify the emergence of new convictions about the role of the secondary income distribution system in a capitalist society"[6] — would have left the converts to social insurance a bit puzzled. More important, he reduces the social insurance argument to "an elaborate rationale based almost exclusively on objective economic need". And given that kind of a movement, there would of course be little to say about its strengths.

Far from being a scientific and technical answer to an objective condition, the social insurance movement was from its inception a broadly conceived response to the problem of the individual's security and responsibility and to the problem of society's security and responsibility. And by making the connection between the twin concerns — in what was a strikingly dualistic approach to welfare — the social insurance advocates could and did present their case in the name of old-fashioned thrift, economic independence, and mobility, and could and did as well promote social insurance as a means of preserving the social order, enhancing the national prestige, preventing class conflict, and assimilating the foreigner.

This is not to signify that the dual theme in the social insurance movement was merely a propaganda device. On the contrary, the individual — social ethic was present long before the progressive social insurance movement and indeed helps to explain its rise within a group apparently too pre-occupied with individual moral reform.

For in the late nineteeth century, a number of those engaged in the crusade against pauperism and public out-door relief to the able-bodied were also among the few who showed any interest in social insurance.

NOTES

[1] Minutes of Compensation Department, December 8, 1911, NYP, National Civic Federation MSS, #125.
[2] Robert Bremner, *From the Depths: The Discovery of Poverty in the United States* (New York: 1956), p. 71.
[3] Roy Lubove, *The Professional Altruist* (Cambridge: 1965), p. 11.
[4] Bremner, *From the Depths,* p. 259.
[5] Roy Lubove, *The Struggle for Social Security* (Cambridge: 1968), Chapter I.
[6] *Ibid,* p. 45.

CONTENTS

SELF–RELIANCE AND SOCIAL SECURITY

1870 – 1917

INTRODUCTION

We shall never fully know how many Americans in the late nineteenth century lost the struggle for economic independence. Records of relief recipients were grossly inaccurate, if kept at all; and even had the records been accurate, knowledge of the actual plight of the poor would have been snuffed out by their silence or their pride. Undoubtedly vast numbers of the poor came desperately close to "official" dependency, being saved from it only by falling upon their relatives or neighbors, or preferring hunger to a handout.

It was perhaps natural that a country heretofore so wrapped up in national self-praise and currently in the midst of a remarkable economic boom should have been disarmed by scenes of widespread poverty and class antagonisms. Reactions were understandably strong and mixed. Fear, anger, disgust, disillusion, guilt, and sympathy – all the primitive human emotions – played a very large role, as they usually do in critical times, even in the most sober analyses of the problem. In spite of the reactions, or perhaps because of them, positive action in the form of progressive social welfare reform was meager.

The failure to respond with programs of social justice has often been attributed to, or cited as evidence for, a traditional and enduring commitment on the part of Americans to individual "self-reliance" or "rugged individualism". Yet there were significant changes taking place in these years without which the progressive social insurance movement as we know it could not have occurred. In part, our tendency to write off the late nineteenth-century welfare activities as "more of the same" is an extension of our failure to see that for all the harshness and continuity of our approach to welfare in the preceding 200 years, self-reliance had neither absolute nor fixed meaning.

In its most ruggedly individualistic formulation – when general conditions were perceived as allowing a minimum of blame on forces beyond the individual's control – certain kinds of public aid were regarded as doing no violence to the doctrine of self-reliance. They were respectable, legitimate aids without a connotation of welfare or charity. Moreover, in responding to poverty with its traditional weapons of charity, however inadequate and inappropriate they may have been, American society tempered its

3

individualism with the belief that the community had an obligation to care for those who could not care for themselves. Public relief, though believed to be fraught with dangers to the spirit of self-reliance was nonetheless justified on the grounds that helping the weak was nobler than letting them starve on the alter of individual responsibility, or that an act of altruism, while temporarily doing violence to self-reliance, might ultimately create a stronger individual.

* * * * *

The welfare institution that the earliest settlers brought with them was already hundreds of years in the making and would serve Americans even longer than it would continue to serve the English. In the Elizabethan Poor Law of 1601, which for its day was a progressive measure, the state assumed responsibility for assigning direct responsibilities for the provision of the poor. Where an individual could not take care of himself, the public held his family legally liable for support, and when this line of defense fell, the public directly assumed the burden for his care. The law placed the taxing power and administrative authority with the local community. The Poor Law, in addition, classified the cases of dependency and set forth the appropriate handling for each class. It made a distinction between adults and children and for the latter prescribed apprenticeship. Insofar as it applied to adults, it divided the poor into two categories — those who were physically or mentally incapable of caring for themselves and those who were able-bodied and consequently expected to be self-supporting. For the disabled (the sick, feeble-minded, aged) the law provided for their care in an almshouse. The able-bodied were given relief, and until they returned to the labor market, were forced to work on the "stock of wool, hemp, flax, iron, or other stuff" supplied by the community. Should the able-bodied be unwilling to work, they were to be sent to the house of correction.

The final piece in the Poor Law system, the Settlement Act of 1662, reflected both the traditional fear of the roving unemployed and the desire of the local communities to confine their recently required obligations to the support of their own residents. The law thus enabled the local officials to refuse settlement and to return to his last legal residence any newcomer who paid less than a yearly rental of 10£ and who within forty days gave evidence of becoming a public charge.[1]

The process of transplantation to American soil undoubtedly had an effect upon the operation and interpretation of the Poor Law. In a society where regional and local differences were pronounced, a locally controlled and administered relief system was bound to reflect these variations. In the American setting, where migrations of labor were far more common than in

England and where frontier conditions required a mobile labor force, the restrictions of the settlement laws were neither as consistently nor as rigidly applied as in England.[2] It would also be safe to say that American conditions turned the able-bodied dependent into a more contemptible figure than was true in the mother country. Given a general economic setting in which any surpluses were jealously reserved for productive reinvestment, the relief of the able-bodied poor was reserved for only the most urgent and most deserving applicants. Further, given the general scarcity of labor and the relatively high wages of the average worker, it is not surprising that Americans perpetuated and even more strictly interpreted all those assumptions about the able-bodied poor that underlay the English poor laws. And nothing in the American experience compares with the experiments inspired by Thomas Firmin or the later Speenhamland system of wage supplements.[3]

Notwithstanding certain adaptations to American conditions, the English poor law not only survived the transatlantic journey with few alterations; it endured for more than two hundred years with its basic structure intact. For the most part, the major developments in public welfare from the colonial period to the Civil War had to do with the implementing of a framework that remained relatively stable. The setting up of formal machinery, the creation of specialized functionaries, the growth of institutional relief, the elaboration and proliferation of settlement laws or other protections against tramps and vagrants were in essence accomodations made for the sake of efficiency and convenience. Thus, in 1870, every state required the adults to take care of the needy members of their own family. The scope of this obligation ran the gamut from New York's law which imposed reciprocal responsibility on adult children and their parents, to the California example, in which all members of the family — including brothers and sisters — in a direct line from grandparents to grandchildren were liable for each other's support.

With some exceptions in the south and west, the majority of states continued to rely upon settlement laws as a legal protection. In many instances settlement was acquired simply by having resided in the community for a specified time, usually shorter in the western states than in those of the northeast. In a number of cases, however, established residence was necessary but not sufficient. Generally in the northeast, additional safeguards in the form of property qualifications and proof of ability to remain off the pauper rolls were required to gain settlement. In addition, many of the laws prohibited the transporting of paupers into the states as well as into towns and counties.[4]

Only minor changes in administration and financing were in evidence by 1870. The states had increased their direct expenses by assuming the costs for the "State Poor", i.e. for those who for one reason or another had no settlement, and by setting up or supporting institutions which were economically unfeasible on a local level. Yet even in Massachusetts, New York, Ohio, and Pennsylvania, which had recently created state boards of charity, the business of public welfare rested with the towns and counties. As yet there existed no private organization, let alone any federal body, that gave national direction to the American welfare system.[5]

This is not to say that public welfare policies or philanthropies either embodied some pristine notion of self-reliance for more than 200 years, or that they remained static in their impact upon the poor. Here, as in England, the Poor Law remained an assertion of collective responsibility for those in need as well as for the protection of society. It was a blending of altruism and repression. And while the public clearly reserved most of its compassion for the impotent poor and most of its discipline for the able-bodied poor, even as it pertained to the latter, the welfare system can be construed as having endorsed an idea of rugged individualism only when taken out of its social and economic context.

In the 17th century, for example, when entire communities barely scratched out a living, the Poor Law not only extended a helping hand in the form of relief, but the economic system of the day held on to the medieval concept of the "just" price and the "just" wage. Indeed, in the Puritan communities the entire social system remained under the spell of medieval social ethics. As John Winthrop described the values of his society:

> We must entertain each other in brotherly affection; we must be willing to abridge ourselves of our superfluities, for the supply of others' necessities; we must uphold a familiar commerce together in all meekness, gentleness, patience, and liberality. We must delight in each other, make others' conditions our own, rejoice together, mourn together, labor and suffer together: always having before our eyes our commission and community as members of the same body.[6]

What we have come to regard as the "traditional" notion of self-reliance — with all of the icy attitudes toward the poor that it conjures up — was more accurately a highly abstract concept that evolved over centuries, partly by circumstance, partly by design.

Some of the refinements within the Poor Law structure, e.g. without necessarily implying a conscious change of policy, worked a hardship on the poor. The disabled and the aged for whom there was no remedy but affection and personal attention were probably better off in the seventeenth century under the care of a friend reimbursed by the town than in a 19th-century county or state supported institution. Even outdoor relief to the poor became cold and impersonal as the size of the welfare enterprise increased and the procedures were formalized. Most communities in the 17th century were small enough so that an appeal to the town council was in reality an appeal to one's neighbors, and where public responsibility was recognized, it was often carried out as a neighborly amenity. In the larger towns and cities of the 1800's, where applicants were not so well known, they were more vulnerable to the suspicions of the relief officials and consequently suffered more humiliating experiences in the attempt to prove themselves worthy of the dole. Some areas developed the practice of forcing the relief recipient to advertise his indignity on a publicly posted pauper dole and required him to wear the pauper's badge, a letter "P" on the right shoulder.[7]

To a considerable extent, however, the refinements in welfare certainly represented a stricter interpretation of self-reliance in keeping with the steady growth of individualism in all phases of American life. As American society emerged from its hard and precarious existence of early colonial times into a position of stability and affluence, the 17th-century notions of pre-ordained success and failure and of religious and economic order were giving way to the freer spirit of 18th-century rationalism with its emphasis on free will, benign self-interest, progress, and human perfectability. As a result of these greater expectations, the welfare system was becoming less of a holding operation for incurables and more of an instrument for individual reform. The atmosphere of the early nineteenth century economic liberalism and romanticism invested the ideal of self-reliance with an even greater purity. A prime article of faith in this new age of democracy held that by removing economic and political regulations and by destroying the vestiges of favoritism, the natural blessings of the American environment would enable the "common man" to be the "self-made man".

Without necessarily subscribing to all the democratic tenets of the Jacksonian era, philanthropists of the period reinforced many of its individualistic precepts. The welfare investigations of Josiah Quincy of Massachusetts and J.V.N. Yates, Secretary of State of New York in the 1820's, along with the persuasive Royal Poor Law Commission Report in 1834, unleashed a steady stream of criticism against public outdoor relief to the poor as an expensive and highly pauperizing form of charity. For many years thereafter the states made concerted efforts to replace it with the cheaper and allegedly less harmful insitutionalized relief and to limit this form of public charity to children and the disabled.[8]

In a complementary fashion, the expansion of the private welfare system in the early decades of the nineteenth century not only relieved some of the pressures upon the public authorities but also rather clearly illustrated the ever growing desire to keep public responsibility at a minimum. With the formation of agencies like the New York Society for the Prevention of Pauperism (1817) and the Union Benevolent Association in Philadelphia in 1831, charity reformers signaled their determination to foster a preference for voluntary relief, which in their view did more honor to the donor and, more important, less damage to the recipient. The New York Association for Improving the Condition of the Poor (1843) and similar associations in several other cities carried the concern for prevention of pauperism a step further by attempting to curtail the abuses that it found resulting from the indiscriminate uncoordinated efforts of many private societies, particularly those set up to meet temporary needs of the recession unemployed.[9] In the aftermath of the 1858 recession, the New York AICP confidently reported that it was a "matter of demonstration and grateful record, that in order to meet such trying situations, we need no special municipal aid, no public parades, no truckling politicians — for all these have been tried, and proved themselves not only worthless but positively injurious."[10]

By 1870 little in the philosophy of this welfare system had changed. The disabled poor were still receiving the lion's share of the public's sympathetic attention. But the record here was a dismal one. Many of the disabled were either auctioned off to the highest bidder who garnered whatever services he could from them in return for room and board, or they were placed in an institution leased out by the government to the lowest bidding private contractor. In neither case were the interests of the poor likely to be protected. The government-run institutions were hardly better. They had already come under suspicion as a source of political corruption, a breeding ground for pauperism, and a place unlikely to comfort or aid the inmates. Here one saw men and women lonely and destitute in their old age, adults in their prime of life but too sick or mentally disturbed or feeble-minded to care for themselves; able-bodied adults with "stifled consciences" or criminal tendencies, and children cast off by their parents or born out of wedlock within the walls of the institution. Only in their lack of care, their degradation, and their poverty did they share anything in common.[11]

In some cases, the situation in the almshouse reflected the willingness to allow the primary obligation of providing custodial care for the deserving to be perverted by a desire to deter the nondeserving. "Care has been taken," proclaimed a New York relief official, "not to diminish the terrors of this last resort of poverty, because it had been deemed better that a few should test the minimum rate at which existence can be preserved, than that the many should find the poor house so comfortable a home that they would brave the shame of pauperism to gain admission to it."[12]

If the divergence between the law and custom left the disabled poor in an ambiguous position, the able-bodied poor had an even less concrete claim upon public beneficience. Many Americans in 1870 obviously invested self-reliance with a severity that would have made modern usage seem more a synonym for dependency. For them, the abundance of the American soil and the opportunities for employment left little excuse for poverty or dependency. Barring some unforeseen natural tragedy like flood, fire, or storm, only a personal weakness could explain the failure to live a comfortable life. Having failed in the midst of affluence, the poor were confronted with a popular social psychology dictating that an environment of struggle and discipline offered the best cure for weak wills. Outside help would therefore be limited by the perceptions of need and desireability that flowed from the conventional assumptions.

Although poverty, dependency, and pauperism were frequently seen as going hand in hand, as stemming from similar personal faults, and as deserving of similar general treatment, important distinctions were made between them. Poverty was the inability through ignorance, improvidence, or other bad habits to triumph over the economic struggle, but it was a personal rather than a social problem until it led to a request for charity or what was worse, until it meant that the struggle was forsaken. Neither of these contingencies, however, were generally regarded as the result of poverty, per se. Indeed, it was believed that poverty might be a blessing in disguise by stimulating the individual to greater efforts. Further, there were many "virtuous" poor who, despite other failings, remained self-supporting; and there were rich people who sought "something for nothing". It was the spirit of getting something for nothing that defined paupersim and set it apart from poverty. However much Americans might drum upon the theme, "the Poor ye shall always have with you", they could not abide the presence of the pauper. The poorly fought battle of simple poverty could be ignored. The occasionally lost battle of temporary dependency could be grudgingly tolerated. But the deserted battle of pauperism had to be faced as a monstrous social evil.[13]

Although a considerable number of able-bodied found their way into the almshouse, for the most part they received temporary outdoor relief under conditions and in amounts least calculated to encourage the practice. Like the disabled, the able-bodied might have lost the right to vote or the freedom to move from place to place; in addition, they were subjected to constant reminders that they were not really entitled to the aid.[14]

To speak of the "rights" of the poor was, therefore, virtually a contradiction in terms. Although public relief was talked about as an "obligation" and a Christian duty, and though contributions came from tax funds, the poor law could at best be regarded as a charity; that is, an act of love performed at the discretion of the donor rather than an act of justice that could be demanded by the recipient. Society, through its elected and appointed Poor Officers, retained the discretion to give or not to give, and to give only if the applicant were truly needy, morally deserving, and in some cases, properly contrite. In some instances, the courts somewhat strengthened the position of the poor by forcing the overseers to dispense relief. In other cases, however, the courts declared that the frustrated applicant had not even the right to bring his complaint into the courts. But whatever the theories, the realities of the poor law system militated against recognizing that the poor had a certain and definite claim upon the public treasury.[15] "Common humanity" might require that no one should starve and that those unavoidably destitute should receive some aid; but it was feared that to emphasize the "rights" of the poor, and particularly of the able-bodied poor would simply incite them to mouth the already too prevalent dictum, "The world owes them a living". It was, therefore, in keeping with the ritual of the whole public relief system that the "failures" appear before the "successes" and humbly prove themselves worthy of a gift.

Notwithstanding the steady trend toward a more rugged individualism, it would be somewhat misleading to portray the American welfare policies as having developed into fixed and rigid patterns or as having developed out of a total lack of sympathy for the plight of the poor. It was one thing to have envisioned an ideal society in which the average individual, without the handicap of restraints or special privileges, would be expected to thrive by dint of his own efforts. It was quite another to have claimed that American society already offered these freedoms and equal opportunties. While many of the champions of laissez-faire made this claim, others rejected it. Their prescription for the prevention or cure of poverty may have overlooked the real impediments to success, but their analysis of the problem obviously placed part of the blame on forces beyond the individual's control. Moreover, the attachment to laissez-faire did not in practice rule out the legitimacy of non-charitable governmental assistances in the form of cheap credit, cheap land, free land, or Civil War pensions.

Insofar as charity is concerned, it should be remembered that almshouses were initially conceived as, among other things, a means of providing facilities and professional services unavailable through outdoor relief. In spite of the wretched conditions that eventually prevailed in most, some of them managed to carry out the intent of the law with fair success. And to the degree that society was reminded of its neglected responsibility for the disabled, some of the credit must go to the same reformers who railed against the public's indiscriminate charity to the able-bodied. Secretary Yates, of New York, whose report in 1824 called for the abolition of public outdoor relief also exposed the cruelties and abuses heaped upon the poor who were auctioned off like slaves or placed under the not-so-tender mercies of the private almshouse keeper. He recommended that these practices be eliminated in favor of a county-run almshouse system.[16] By the early decades of the nineteenth century, some states were beginning to make headway in the direction of setting up the specialized institutions such as hospitals, homes for the blind, insane asylums, and orphanages; and these efforts continued through the 1840's, 50's, and 60's under direction of reformers like Samuel Gridley Howe and Dorothea Dix. While the critical veto by President Pierce in 1854 of legislation providing support for mental institutions is often cited as a characteristic American response, too often overlooked is that the bill, sponsored by Miss Dix, won the endorsement of both houses of Congress.

Even in the case of the able-bodied poor, there were some ameliorating influences. The very looseness of the system made an inflexible stance all but impossible. Not only were there variations from state to state, but within these jurisdictions laws were variously implemented and interpreted by poor relief officials who, for good or for evil, were guided by their own prejudices, by prevailing local customs and conditions, and by political temptations. It is a mistake to take the stern views of the charity reformers as typical, when the practices against which they directed their reforms were apparently widespread. No doubt they exaggerated the "evils", but the persistence of outdoor relief to the able-bodied and the steady growth of public expenditures for welfare suggest that in practice communities maintained a certain sensitivity to the problems of a society with liberal immigration policies and one just beginning to feel the pinch of industrial expansion and urbanization. In periods of severe economic distress, emergency relief committees, soup kitchens, and breadlines appeared in spite of attempts of the reformers to curb or abolish them. Some reformers even acknowledged that hard times brought to the relief offices people who ordinarily would not be supplicants of charity. Some were even aware that in normal times the bounties of American life did not extend to all equally.[17] The Freedman's Bureau, however inadequate, testifies at least to a flexibility — a recognition that individuals were not always in control of their destinies.

NOTES

[1] Karl de Schweinitz, *England's Road to Social Security*, (New York: 1943), Chap. III and IV.

[2] Marcus W. Jernegan, *Laboring and Dependent Classes in Colonial America, 1607-1783,* (Chicago: 1931), Ch. XII; Ralph Pumphrey and Muriel Pumphrey, (Ed.), *The Heritage of American Social Work,* (New York: 1961), pp. 1026; Sophonisba P. Breckenridge, *Public Welfare Administration in the United States,* (Chicago: 1935), pp. 16ff; Arthur P. Miles, *An Introduction to Public Welfare,* (Boston: 1949), Ch. IV.

[3] Breckenridge, *Public Welfare,* p. 16; De Schweinitz, *England's Road,* Chaps. VI & VII.

[4] Walter Friedlander, *Introduction to Social Welfare,* (New Jersey: 1955), pp. 71-89; H.A. Millis, "The Law Relating to the Relief and Care of Dependents, I", *American Journal of Sociology,* Vol. III, pp. 631-648; Pumphrey and Pumphrey, *Heritage,* pp. 10, 137.

[5] See for example David M. Schneider, *The History of Public Welfare in New York, 1609-1866,* (Chicago: 1938); for Rhode Island, Margaret D. Creech, *Three Centuries of Poor Law Administration,* (Chicago: 1936); and William Clinton Heffner, *History of Poor Relief Legislation in Pennsylvania, 1682-1913,* ([Cleona] Pennsylvania: 1913).

[6] John Winthrop, "A Model of Christian Charity", excerpted in Perry Miller (ed.), *The American Puritans,* (New York: 1956), p. 83.

[7] Arthur Miles, *An Introduction to Public Welfare,* Ch. IV; Creech, *Poor Law,* p. 22; Pumphrey and Pumphrey, *Heritage,* pp. 19-26.

[8] Pumphrey and Pumphrey, *Heritage,* pp. 58-70; Kathleen Woodroofe, *From Charity to Social Work in England and the United States,* (London: 1962), pp. 77-85; Breckenridge, *Public Welfare,* pp. 30-54; Friedlander, *Introduction,* pp. 72-73.

[9] Pumphrey and Pumphrey, *Heritage,* pp. 71-79; Bremner, *From the Depths,* pp. 32-41; Bremner, *American Philanthropy,* (Chicago, London: 1960), pp. 43-75.

[10] Quoted in Leah Hannah Feder, *Unemployment Relief in Periods of Depression,* (New York: 1936), p. 26.

[11] Friedlander, *Introduction,* pp. 66-93, Franklin Sanborn, "The Supervision of Public Charities," *Journal Of Social Science,* I (June, 1869), pp. 72-87.

[12] New York City Department of Public Charity and Correction, Sixteenth Annual Report, (1875), pp. viii-ix.

[13] Bremner, *From the Depths,* pp. 16-19. Provides an excellent summary of attitudes. The above is a slight modification based on my own distillation of the literature from the period.

[14] Edith Abbott, *Public Assistance* (Chicago: 1937), pp. 97-105.

[15] Boston, *Annual Report of the Overseers of the Poor,* (1874), p. 9; *Ibid.,* (1885-86), p. 37; Abbot, *Public Assistance,* pp. 99-103; New York State, *Proceedings SCSP,* XVII, (1887), p. 43; S.N. Rosenau, "Poor Law Reform", *Proceedings SCSP,* pp. 71-77.

[16] Schneider, *Public Welfare,* pp. 222-227.

[17] *Ibid.,* pp. 246-247, 264; Feder, *Unemployment Relief,* Chap. I; Banjamin J. Klebaner, "Poverty and its Relief in American Thought 1815-1861", *Social Service Review,* vol. 38, (December, 1964).

CHAPTER I

SELF–RELIANCE, 1870–1893

Given the stress and strains imposed by the early stages of industrialization, it would have been highly unlikely that the welfare system could have remained significantly unaltered by the unrelenting and in some cases accellerating pressures of a society transforming itself. The most dramatic story was contained in the fact that while population between 1870 and 1890 rose 50% – in itself an event of major proportions – national income more than doubled, rising 132%, from $18.6 billion to $44.3 billion annually. The rise in production and productivity, which by the end of the century placed America in the front rank of industrial nations, was made possible by the introduction of new machines, new types of energy (in 1870 steam had replaced water as the main source of power), and by vast improvements in communications and transportation, most notably by the extension of the railroad. Twice as much railroad track was laid in the two decades between 1870 and 1890 as in the previous five.

Impressive gains were registered in all sectors of the economy. But the advances in agriculture were no match for those in the other sectors, nor did they have quite the impact on American society, except insofar as the great bounty from the soil reduced farm prices and profits and contributed to relative increases in non-agricultural pursuits. As late as 1840, seventy per cent of all goods produced were agricultural. By 1860 the relative share of farm goods dropped to 58% and by 1890 had declined still further to a little more than a third. Similarly, in contrast to 1820, when 72% of all workers were engaged in agriculture, only slightly more than half the workforce was so engaged in 1870, and by 1890 farmwork occupied only 43% of the workers. In the meantime, manufacturing, mining, and construction had come to account for 28% of the work force and occupations in trade, transportation, and finance, 15%. An equally significant and integral phase of industrialization resulted in a shifting of population from rural to urban settings. Between 1850 and 1870 the number of towns and cities with 2500 or more population nearly tripled, and their share of population rose from 15% to 25%. Within the next twenty years, the number of such urban concentrations doubled again and contained 35% of the total population. Moreover, 15% were now living in the 28 cities with a population of 100,000 or more.

By almost any standard, this great leap into the industrial age was unquestionably a tribute to American enterprise. In human terms, however, it proved to be a mixed blessing. Although recent interpretations of rather sketchy data from the period tend to show a moderate rise in hourly and daily wages,[1] the recorded gains are meaningless unless weighed against the additional psychological, economic, and social costs borne by the workers. For the technological revolution not only changed the occupational structure, tipping the balance in favor of the non-agricultural worker, it transformed the status of the industrial laborer, the conditions under which he labored, and in a sense the very meaning of work. The needs of the machine age were such that the independent craftsman was rapidly being replaced by the wage earner or the "wage slave", and among the latter the skilled were in relatively less demand than the unskilled. In addition, with the growth of large scale business organization — made possible and necessary in the new age — the wage earners increasingly found themselves removed from direct contact with their employers.

Moreover, higher hourly or daily wages would have been reduced to insignificance for the many workers who suffered through the two recessions of the period and for those who even in better times commonly faced shortened workweeks or weeks without employment. In a number of instances, too, the wages were paid in kind or at long intervals, forcing the workers to buy the higher priced goods of the company store or to borrow money at high rates of interest. In some of the mining regions of New Jersey, where the payment of low wages in scrip was prevalent, despite the law against the practice, the wives of workmen had to walk from six to eight miles for food they could have bought more cheaply and conveniently had they had the cash.[2]

Nor could the higher wages cover the higher risks of accidental injury, occupational disease, illness, or the premature death of the breadwinner. These were the concomitants of toiling long hours over hazardous machinery in poorly ventilated and lighted mines and factories and of living in congested and polluted cities, or in cramped and unsanitary residential quarters. Precise and complete statistical information is missing, but such indices as infant mortality, which rose from 146 deaths per 1000 births in 1810 to 24/1000 in 1870 and 285/1000 in 1885, and the several partial studies made by various governmental agencies are revealing. The railroad industry, justly heralded as an essential element in American affluence, took the lives of nearly 2000 workers and injured more than 20,000 others in the year ending June 30, 1890. Out of 1269 iron ore miners studied by the New Jersey Bureau of Labor and Industries in 1889, fifty-one individuals at an average age of 33.8 years were killed, and another thirty-three were incapacitated by accident or illness. Ninety-nine others were showing signs of declining health and energy — many at an early age. The miners, more than a third of whom had begun working in the mines before they were fifteen years old, earned between 90 cents and $1.25 a day.[3]

That wages of labor neither provided for a comfortable day to day existence nor sufficiently covered the worker for the normal contingencies of life was sadly borne out by several examinations of workers' budgets. The most reliable studies were not made until the turn of the century, but earlier observations suggest that a vast chunk of the work force lived a precarious existence. Some of the earliest investigations, conducted by the Massachusetts Bureau of Labor Statistics in the 1870's, found that in 65% of the families studied, the father could not maintain the household without the support of either the wife or a child and that even skilled artisans were living in poverty.[4] The New Jersey Bureau of Labor and Industry, after reviewing the effect of working conditions upon the health of some 6000 glassworkers, hatters, potters, and miners, doubted that despite the evidence of gradual increases in per diem wages "the condition of the average wage worker has been materially improved thereby", and concluded that the higher pay was "offset by early decay and expense in doctors' bills, or supplemented by habits that more than counterbalance the higher wages".[5]

To be sure, the sufferings and dislocations induced by this phase of the industrial revolution did not automatically or swiftly lead to major reformulations of welfare policy and philosophy. Indeed, at first glance the period from 1870 to 1893 may seem an unlikely one in which the concept of self-reliance was being watered down. To those who measured progress solely in terms of steel production, railroad mileage, and aggregate national wealth, the American success story gave no pause to reconsider the conventional wisdom. The social costs absorbed by individuals went by either unacknowledged or discounted as having been calculated in the higher wage rates — or were written off as the hard price of progress. The emergent industrial capitalism, having made available so many new careers and so many opportunities for wealth, seemed to have confirmed beyond a doubt that success lay within the reach of anyone who had the initiative to strive for it. Individual success stories involving men of modest and meager means made pre-war analogues pale by comparison. If the average worker realized that he could not in all his years of effort achieve the results of a Carnegie or a Harriman, he may have secretly harbored that vain hope or vicariously lived the experience through the widely popular success literature of the day. It would have been difficult to avoid the daily preachments from the press, politicians and the pulpit that wealth was the product of individual initiative, hard work and thrift, and that poverty, except as a temporary incentive, was the hell to which moral and mental defectives were consigned.

The new industrialism not only brought to the surface the latent vulgarities of early American capitalism; it gave promise of combining with science and religion in such a way that laissez-faire and self-reliance were touted as fundamental laws of nature and God. On several thousand occasions Russell H. Conwell, a Baptist minister and founder of Temple University, preached that there was no excuse to covet another man's wealth when "acres of diamonds" lay in one's own back yard. The "lazy and unsuccessful" might accuse the wealthy of having achieved their fortunes through dishonesty, declared Conwell, but "I say, get rich, get rich!"[6] Social Darwinism was in vogue, and the disciples of Herbert Spencer echoed his warnings against artificially supporting the "unfit" because their survival would disrupt the progressive evolutionary design of nature. From the prestigious perch of the Yale Sociology Department came the pronouncements of William Graham Sumner, who carried the social Darwinian individualism to its starkly logical conclusions, proclaiming that no one owed anyone anything. "Vice is its own curse", declared Sumner.

> If we let nature alone she cures vice by the most frightful penalties . . . a drunkard in the gutter is just where he ought to be. Nature is working away at him to get him out of the way, just as she sets up her processes of dissolution to remove whatever is a failure in its own line.[7]

Sumner's position never was typical, but many of the initial, almost instinctive responses to the social ills of the late nineteenth century were harsh and repressive. Fear, perhaps more than any other sentiment, marked the behavior of those articulate and influential citizens who saw the situation as critical and demanding of national attention; a fear that rose in part from the violent strikes of 1877; a fear inspired by the wave of immigrants, some of whom saw little or nothing of America between the port of embarkation and the almshouse; a fear that American society without protection would find itself no better than European society.

In the 80's, Congress rushed to defend the American way by restricting and excluding Chinese immigrants and alien contract laborers, and forbidding the entrance of, among other undesireables, those likely to become public charges. The tramp laws of the late seventies and early eighties increased penalties, defined vagrancy more broadly, and generally gave law enforcement agencies greater power in suppressing this particular type of social parasite. Settlement laws underwent revisions, relatives were called upon to assume their share of the burden, and in many areas discussions centered around the pauperizing effects of excessive relief. When you get three or four generations in the poor house, argued one relief administrator in 1890, "that is the commencement of the commune; that is the commencement of a race that will say 'You must work and when you become prosperous then divide it up with us — we are entitled to a living and we are going to have it'."[8]

Probably no era in American history can boast such a prodigious number of weapons in defense of self-reliance nor so rich an endowment of patriots who rallied around its banner. But this in itself is a clue that the ideas of self-reliance, at this juncture, are least capable of being neatly summarized. The abrasive tone in much of the rhetoric of self-help distinctly bore the marks of a Jeremiad, warning of the decay of the old system. There were ample signs that the warnings were justified.

For one thing, the industrial revolution was sufficiently damaging to have forced reappraisals of the basic assumptions upon which the strict interpretation of self-reliance rested. The most eloquent and articulate came from the pens of Henry George, Edward Bellamy, and Jacob Riis, from the pulpits of Social Gospel Ministers, from the forums and journals of the newly formed American Economic Association and the American Social Science Association, and from the reports of various governmental labor bureaus and commissions. Perhaps more important were the signals sent up by the direct victims of industrialization, who pointed to the barrenness and inequities in their environment as the cause of their distress. Surely there is little in the literature of agrarian protest to suggest that the farmers blamed themselves for their poverty. Nor does there appear to be much evidence that industrial wage earners subscribed to the theory that individual personal weaknesses accounted for mass poverty and insecurity.

To the hundreds of thousands of men who joined the labor union movement in its precarious beginnings in this period, the fault lay variously with the wage system itself, or simply with low wages, long hours, machines, working conditions, or exploited and vulnerable cheap immigrant labor. The point was made more emphatic by the many thousands willing to participate in militant action. The great railroad strikes of 1877, traumatic in their impact upon a society unaccustomed to this sort of behavior, were only the beginning of a long, drawn out struggle between labor and capital. Between 1881 and 1892 there were more than 12,000 recorded strike actions.[9] Although for a majority of American workers the union movement had little or no appeal, their discontents with the economic system were brought to the attention of the public. Well before General Coxey's army of the unorganized unemployed marched in the 1894 depression, tens of thousands of non-union men had made earlier recessions an occasion to take to the streets or to gather in meeting halls to protest the reduction in wages or the loss of their jobs.[10]

Even in more stable times and under less emotional circumstances workers made known their dissatisfactions, as in 1878—79 when the Massachusetts Bureau of Labor Statistics conducted a rare survey by mail of workingmen's opinions. Some of the testimony obviously referred to conditions during the last year of the recession: one hundred and fifty-five out of the two hundred and thirty answering the questionnaire reported some period of unemployment for an average duration of ninety-four days. But much of the testimony bore witness either to the lingering effects of the hard times or to the normal difficulties of a return to prosperity. Nearly half the respondents regarded their work as dangerous, unhealthy, or both — citing poor ventilation, excessive heat, sudden changes in the temperature, the inhalation of noxious gases and the dusts from emory, iron, steel, and stone, and unsafe machinery as among the more common menaces to health and safety. Nearly half the men reported an illness that kept them away from work on an average of twelve and a half days per year, amounting to an average loss of $52.48 for the year. More than half considered themselves underpaid, and many of the men complained in general and specific terms about unfair treatment at the hands of the employers. A large number scored the irregularity or infrequency of the paycheck over periods of steady employment. Forty-three workers claimed an average of $141 in wages uncollected in the previous five years. Perhaps the most poignant and revealing answers came in response to questions concerning the workers' progress and prospects for the future. Of the 223 men who replied to the question, "Do you live as well as you did five years ago?", only four said "better". Sixty-two returned a definite "yes". Thirteen replied either "nearly the same" or "not quite so well", and the rest, or 144, were unqualifiedly negative. When asked to assess their chances of laying by enough to support themselves in their old age, only forty-three responded positively, while 159 were pessimistic or thought the chances were uncertain. One worker replied, "With present conditions of business, I don't want to live to sixty-five".[11]

The industrial revolution struck another blow at the old-fashioned virtues of self-help and frugality by fostering a new style of life in which they were unwittingly undermined — and most effectively by the standard bearers of self-reliance. Mark Twain called the period the "Gilded Age", and it has been frequently referred to as the Great Barbecue. With due allowance for the literary effect, both figures were apt, and taken together they convey a picture in which the making and dispensing of money was a kind of game, the rules of which were quite fluid, but the quintessential trick was to gain as much for nothing and spend as ostentatiously as possible.

Businessmen and particularly railroad entrepreneurs took, without the slightest concern for their self-reliance or the cherished ideal of laissez-faire, millions of dollars from the Federal Treasury. And with equal grace they accepted, indeed begged their government to save them from the competition of foreign goods. Businessmen may have played the game more efficiently and for larger stakes but they were not alone. In the spirit of the age, there was something for everyone. When the Congress passed the Arrears Act of 1879, with virtually no debate, the government invited still more hands to dip into the public purse. If there were many Americans who, while eligible for the Civil War pension, refused it for fear of losing their independence, their murmurs of protest would probably have been buried in the thunder of stampeding pension seekers. By liberalizing the Civil War pension and making the new eligibility requirements retroactive, the legislation nearly doubled the expenditure for the following year and within a decade the cost of the program tripled and the number of veterans and survivors receiving payments more than doubled. By 1890 the Federal Government was spending $106,000,000 on 538,000 survivors and dependents.[12] Thousands more reaped the benefits of state Civil War pensions and disability payments. There were, of course, complaints about the way the pension was handled but many of these issued from those who were not fortunate enough to be among the several hundred-thousand pension recipients. The Secretary of the Interior, who handled complaints from the decisions of the Bureau of Pension, remarked that appeals were increasing so rapidly that it was difficult to keep up with them. The number had risen from 479 in 1881 to nearly 3,000 in 1886.[13]

Even the poor shared in the spoils though it was not their good fortune to be able to take the money with the dignity of one expanding the American economy or one being rewarded for patriotic service rendered to the nation for the great philanthropic movement of the nineteenth century was now in full swing. It was nourished by the charitable impulses unleashed during the Civil War, by the economic distress of the 1870's, by the accumulation of wealth and by the new ethic that placed conspicuous charity not too far below conspicuous consumption. Never before had the well-to-do been so eager to give. Thousands of "ecstatic Christian ladies" experienced in wartime philanthropies now redirected their energies to the victims of the economic battle. The husbands competed with each other, with much the same spirit as in their businesses, to found more and more enterprises devoted to more and more specialized forms of incapacity. Homes for the aged, the blind, the deaf; institutions for the insane, and the idiotic; orphanages for children; lodges for wayfarers; societies for widows; societies for working girls who needed fresh air — all flourished as charity directories grew fatter and obsolete almost immediately upon publication.[14]   New York City even boasted a home for aged couples "whose lives have been passed amidst surroundings which make their present poverty and want harder to bear than if they had never known the comforts and luxuries of life."[15] Many of these societies were fly-by-night organizations, whipped together to meet some temporary emergency, only to fold up with the end of the crisis. Other lingered on for years, buoyed up by the philanthropic atmosphere, and some are still going strong today.

The generosity of the period pervaded the offices of public relief, too. In violation of the laws, poor relief officials fed and clothed the tramps at public expense. In New York overseers of the poor would "disobey the word of the law" in order to give pensions to the aged infirm rather than send them to the almshouse. Similarly in Massachusetts, overseers of the poor, out of special consideration for the children supported families in their own homes instead of forcing them into the poorhouse.[16]

One observer's reference to "the lavish public charity becoming a custom" was probably the inflated language of hostile criticism.[17] In many instances the humanitarian touches actually proved less expensive than the technical requirements of the law.[18] Nonetheless, relief expenditures were on the rise and especially during the hard times of the early 70's cities and states met unemployment with increasing outlays of direct relief or some form of makework.[19] For example, in the eight years prior to 1873 the average number of partial relief recipients in Massachusetts was 25,000. In 1874, 35,000 were receiving this type of relief; in 1875, the number rose to 56,591; in 1876 it was 65,988 and by 1877 reached the peak of 74,384.[20] Although soaring relief expenditures were reported in the midwest, the northeastern cities of Buffalo, Philadelphia, Baltimore and New York were achieving a certain notoriety for their loose welfare policies. In 1864, Brooklyn welfare officials dispensed $26,000 to some 21,000 persons. A year later the expenditure nearly tripled. By 1877 outdoor relief amounted to $141,000 and recipients numbered more than 46,000 or roughly ten per cent of the population. It was estimated that public expenditures were triple that of the private societies.[21]

Individual men of great wealth and politicians were not the only ones responsible for the style of Gilded Age philanthropy. Up to a point their actions were condoned and even encouraged by the masses of anonymous donors. Street beggars flourished, in part, because countless citizens put pennies in their cups. The life of the tramp and the itinerant job seeker was made easier by the people who gave them shelter on the back porch or, according to the Michigan State Board of Charities, because of "a reluctance almost universal in this country, to refuse food at least to anyone who asks."[22] In addition, attempts to reduce or eliminate public outdoor relief to the able-bodied, and the endeavors to eliminate the "tramp menace" by repressing it, were thwarted in many cases by pressures of public opinion. County Superintendents of the Poor in New York complained that public outdoor relief could not be abolished as long as it remained popular among the taxpayers and particularly among the merchants who "want to be accommodated by trade."[23] "I think," declared the Superintendent of Genessee County, "the present state of public opinion and public sentiment had been dominant in almost every county. The sympathetic people have the ascendancy over the people of judgment."[24] Scarcely had the ink dried on the New Hampshire law when one of its strong supporters was already predicting its demise because of its severity.[25] "Such measures will always fail of execution," commented the Michigan Board of State Commissioners, "because people will not deny themselves from the impulses and the offices of charity, even though there be danger of aiding imposters; nor will they be deterred therefrom by the enactment of severe penalties to be visited upon themselves."[26]

Although it may be unfair to place the "ecstatic Christian ladies" in the company of common folk or of men whose reputation is a bit unsavory, these private and public alms dispensers approached the problem in much the same way. Without disavowing their loyalty to the principle of self-reliance, many of the dole givers demonstrated little or no concern for it. They offered free food, clothing and shelter without making investigations into the applicant's needs, without requiring work tests, without checking into previous requests for aid – in short, without most of the safeguards that were supposed to protect society from the pauper and the pauper from himself. The common way of dealing with tramps, vagabonds and the migrant unemployed best exemplifies the way in which public authorities enforced self-reliance. Most states, rather than rely upon the corrective and repressive elements in the tramp laws, merely indulged in what was called "passing on." The migrant was put up for the night, given breakfast and then ordered out of the county. On many occasions he was given money for transportation, thereby regaining through a crude sort of justice, a measure of the mobility he might have lost through the settlement laws.[27] But "passing on" did little or nothing to curb whatever real or imagined appetites he may have had for freeloading. Further, "passing on" nor most of the other forms of gilded age philanthropy constituted an attempt to solve the problem of poverty; they were rather a sentimental and palliative response to it. Most of the persons shut away in the almshouse failed to benefit; but the destitute and maimed who roamed the streets, the poor whose faces could not be avoided, the unemployed whose street rallies could not be muffled — these were acknowledged with breadlines, soup kitchens, "bundle" drives, shelters and all manner of benevolent enterprises. A portion of what the philanthropists had denied in the way of higher wages, steady employment and healthful working conditions, they gave with unprecedented amounts in the form of charity and particularly in the symbol of the age, money. This is not to say their activities were entirely wasted. Much good work came from their efforts and if nothing else, the rampant materialism in the enterprise nourished the notion that money brought salvation as well as damnation to the poor.

Far more constructive and purposeful were the new cooperative strategies that were rendering the old individualism obsolescent. If the new age seemed to have unleashed a rather primitive type of self-interest reminiscent of the jungle metaphors so popular among the Social Darwinists, it was overshadowed by the release of collective energies to combat the waste, inefficiency and futility of individual competitive actions.

Businessmen themselves, in addition to violating their frequent denunciations of artificial support by demanding subsidies and protective tariff, also sought protection through corporate structure, mergers and employers' associations.

Some of the efforts by the less fortunate merely dramatized the desperate and fruitless search for security. In Massachusetts, for example, thousands of workers ostensibly investing in insurance merely indulged their fantasies in a forerunner of the pyramid clubs, risking a few dollars on the hope they could persuade several other people to take an even greater risk.[28] On somewhat more solid ground, workers in ever increasing numbers took their chances with commercial companies offering a new form of life insurance. In what amounted to provision against a pauper burial, industrial insurance enabled the poor to take out small policies and to pay the premiums over many installments. In 1876 the only company doing this form of business had fewer than 5000 policies in force with a combined face value of less than $500,000 and had paid out less than $2000 in benefits. In the same year, however, foreshadowing the spectacular growth in the years to come, it had written close to 7000 new policies valued at more than $700,000. By 1892 eleven companies were in the field with more than 5,000,000 policies valued at $600,000,000 and were distributing $9,000,000 in benefits.[29]

Fraternal insurance, long a fixture on the American scene, enjoyed a comparable expansion in these years. While less markedly attuned to the needs of the working class, the several hundred new fraternal societies of the post war era were modeled on the Ancient Order of United Workmen, founded in 1868 by a wage earner, and, in contrast to the older societies like Oddfellows and Freemasons, placed somewhat greater emphasis on insurance rather than fraternalism. By 1893 the fraternals claimed a membership of 3,700,000 carrying over $3 billion worth of insurance.[30]

Still others were seeking relief in the proliferating mutual benefit societies organized along racial, religious, and ethnic lines. The numerous black societies along with those of the foreign born may very well have contained a larger proportion of their respective peoples than did the native American white groups. The local mutual aid societies were among the first institutions set up by newcomers, in some cases even predating their churches, and flourished wherever the immigrants clustered — in the small towns as well as in the large cities.[31]

On a smaller scale but no less important a sign of the times were the societies that developed out of occupational interests. Some, like those organized by railroad employees, formed the foundations for the union movement, in itself an obvious move in the general direction of collective security.[32] Other mutual benefit systems covering only those workers within a certain plant or corporation were encouraged or initiated by the employers. Only a handful of these "establishment funds" were known to exist prior to this period. Of the 461 funds uncovered by the Bureau of Labor statistics in 1908, only five were set up before 1871. Twenty-one dated back to the next decade while one-hundred came into existence between 1881 and 1890.[33]

All of these programs brought the individual into some kind of cooperative or collective relationship — either with his comrades in the union and fraternal society, or with his employer, or even in the case of private insurance, with men about whom he knew nothing. It would be easy to exaggerate the differences between the individualistic and the cooperative form of saving. Nonetheless, in light of the conventional faith in the penny savings bank, the newer collective form represented a further step in the direction of redefining self-reliance when economic dysfunctions had rendered the purely individualistic efforts useless — except in the moral sense. And in certain instances, it represented a re-evaluation of the morality of old fashioned thrift.

The case of private insurance, rarely associated now with anything un-American, posed a serious dilemma at first because many regarded it as a form of gambling and as such virtually synonymous with "getting something for nothing" or theft. One commentator frankly labeled it a game of chance, and took the position that it was justifiable "according to the necessities of the person." If the beneficiary suffered no pecuniary loss by the death of the insured, then the insurance would be unjustified; on the other hand for the poor or families "that are saved from suffering by it, it is gambling made useful".[34]

A little less soul searching was required to justify the cooperative ethic of the fraternals. "Thrift alone is not enough," asserted John Tunis. "There is a kind of thrift such as New England thrift, which is a mean egoism, and which leads a man to seek his own good, careless and even at the expense of others. The thrift which the Friendly Societies encourage is mutual; it is seeking each man's good through others. . . . The savings bank is a purely individualistic society, and as such, is outside the truly social development of modern life."[35]

In a parallel movement new strategies against the problem of poverty were being worked out by reformers working within traditional institutions created by society to deal with economic failures. There were in reality two philanthropic currents in the late nineteenth century; the sentimental-palliative and the scientific-reformist. Although the two types of philanthropy were not always easy to distinguish and although both developed out of roughly similar circumstances, the scientific-reformist philanthropy was to a considerable extent a reaction against the sentimental-palliative variety, particularly against its blatant materialism, its taint of political corruption, and its haphazard style.

Unlike the Gilded-age philanthropists, the reform philanthropists approached their tasks as problem solvers. And like many businessmen and labor leaders, they devoted much of their energies to bringing order out of chaos. In public welfare, the reformers promoted the rise of agencies that permitted the state to tighten its supervision or control over local welfare administrators and to unify the various divisions of welfare activity already under its authority. In 1863 Massachusetts took the lead in this direction with the creation of the Board of State Charities. Within a decade several other states had followed suit: New York (1867), Ohio (1867), Pennsylvania (1869), Rhode Island (1869), Illinois (1869), Michigan (1871), Wisconsin (1871), and Connecticut (1873). None of the Boards performed precisely the same functions. With the exception of the Rhode Island Board which from its inception had administrative control over the state's charitable and correctional activities, the eastern boards began largely as investigative or supervisory bodies and never fully attained the powers of the boards in western states. The trend, however, was clearly in the direction of enhancing the powers of the boards.[36]

In private welfare the two most influential new developments — the charity organization and the settlement house movements — were in the broadest sense efforts at community organization. Elements of the charity organization program had been tried much earlier in Europe and in America under the auspices of the various Associations for the Improvement of the Condition of the Poor. Yet the new societies were directly inspired and closely modeled on the London Charity Organization Society founded in 1869. The first city-wide agency in America, in Buffalo, New York, was established by an English immigrant, Reverend Humphrey S. Gurteen, who had been a worker in the London Society. The Charity Organization Societies (or Associated Charities, as they were called in some cities) were not originally conceived of as relief giving agencies; they were supposed to impose the standards of science and business on the already existing relief societies in order to avoid duplication of effort and conflicts in policy.[37]

The settlement house idea, like charity organization, was also essentially an English transplant. The movement began in 1886 when Stanton Coit, who had spent a year in residence at Toynbee Hall (the first English settlement house), established the Neighborhood Guild in New York City. Within a few years, settlement houses were springing up in most of the major cities of America. Although each house had a character of its own, and most of them performed a variety of functions, two purposes appear common to all. One was to organize a genuine neighborhood out of mere conglomerations of urban residents. "The settlements are able to take neighborhoods in cities," declared Robert Woods of Andover House in

Boston, "and by patience bring back to them much of the healthy village life, so that people shall again know and care about each other."[38] Closely related was a desire to integrate the neighborhood with the entire city and to create a common bond among people of all social classes. Young people of comfortable means thus lived as residents among the poor to help and instruct them in the ways of cooperatively utilizing their own and community resources, and so that each class would come to a better understanding of the other. The "armed peace" that existed between the "tremendous combinations of money and men," declared Julia Lathrop of Hull House, was better than warfare, but better still was the ideal of "social democracy."[39]

Significant developments were appearing on the national scene, too. The decade of the '70's ushered in a striking birth and growth of such nationally organized groups as the American Prison Association, the American Public Health Association, the American Academy of Medicine, the National Women's Christian Temperance Union, the American Association for the Study of the Feeble Minded, and, most important, the National Conference of Charities and Correction.[40]

The latter group had begun as an appendage of the American Social Science Association when, in 1874, the Section on Social Economy convened a meeting of representatives from several of the State Boards of Charity. Within five years the Section had independently organized as the National Conference of Charities and Correction and expanded its field of operations and personnel, ultimately becoming a catch-all for the many private as well as public philanthropic reform endeavors.[41]

Many of the reform philanthropists were men of wealth, yet unlike the sentimental philanthropists, they had respectability. The best known families — in Boston, the Lees, the Cabots, and the Lowells, and in New York, the Roosevelts and the Schuylers — filled the various unpaid posts of the public and private agencies. Nearly every member of the New York State Charities Aid Association was listed in the Social Register. The founder of the organization, Louisa Lee Schuyler, was a descendent of Alexander Hamilton and General Philip John Schuyler. Miss Schuyler whose philanthropic work began in 1861 as chairman of the United States Sanitary Commission (a forerunner of the American Red Cross) was influential in bringing about many of the reforms close to her heart: the removal of children from the almshouse, the separation of the epileptics from the mentally ill, and the erection of state institutions for the insane. It was a result of her energy and zeal, too, that a number of women were encouraged to continue in reform philanthropy.[42] One of her assistants on the Sanitary Commission was a very young newlywed from a socially prominent Boston family, Mrs. Josephine Shaw (Charles Russell) Lowell. After the war, Mrs. Lowell, whose husband was killed in battle, retired from public service but returned within a few years and devoted the rest of her life to a variety of activities including civil service reform and women's suffrage. In 1873 she became a member of the New York State Charities Aid Association and in 1867 the first female member of the New York State Board of Charities. Though a great deal of her philanthropic work was to be with the private charities, she was an enthusiastic supporter of improved public facilities for the insane, the feeble-minded and the dependent children.[43]

Reform philanthropy was by no means the exclusive province of the "idle" rich nor of women. Franklin Sanborn, the First Secretary of the Massachusetts State Board of Charities and a founder of the American Social Science Association as well as its offspring, the National Conference of Charities and Correction,[44] had a long and varied life as a teacher, a biographer, an editor of the anti-slavery *Boston Commonwealth,* a journalist for the *Springfield Republican*, and as a philanthropist whose special pleadings were for foster home care of juvenile delinquents, dependent children, and the insane.

A number of others had come to charity reform by way of the church. Charles Loring Brace, for nearly forty years the champion of foster home care for dependent children, started out as preacher to the prisoners of Blackwells Island and as a missionary worker among the poor at the Five Points Mission of New York City.[45] In Indiana the guiding light was the Congregational minister, Oscar McCulloch, the son of a drug salesman. As successor to Henry Ward Beecher, he turned his Plymouth Congregational Church into a center of social gospel activism. Though much of his charitable work was associated with the church, McCulloch was instrumental in establishing and refurbishing most of the welfare agencies of Indianapolis and in setting up the Indiana State Board of Charities as well as the local public Boards of Children's Guardians throughout the state. One of the most respected members of the National Conference of Charities and Correction, McCulloch became its president in 1891, the year in which he died.[46]

Frederick H. Wines, the First Secretary of the Illinois State Board of Charities and Corrections, a president of the NCOCC in 1883 and the Secretary of the National Prison Association from 1887 to 1890, had spent the first years of his career as a hospital chaplain during the Civil War and then as minister of the First Presbyterian Church in Springfield, Illinois. In addition to having stimulated a more enlightened public policy toward the insane, Wines also established an enviable reputation as a statistician and as a social welfare expert.[47]

His careful statistical analyses in *The Liquor Problem in its Legislative Aspects* and his work in preparing and supervising the statistics for the U.S. Census Bureau also testify to the strong scientific atmosphere that surrounded reform philanthropy. It not only attracted professional doctors like Samuel Gridley Howe and Richard C. Cabot of Massachusetts, it enlisted the support of many university-based social scientists such as Professors Franklin H. Giddings of Columbia, Francis Wayland and John J. McCook of Yale, Simon Patten of Pennsylvania, and Charles R. Henderson of the University of Chicago.

In many cases, the "scientific" studies were actually poorly conducted surveys, and the "scientific approach often required little more than an intelligent exchange of opinion or led to little more than an exercise in classifying data. Nonetheless, the belief that problems of poverty and dependency could and should be subjected to scientific analysis provided one of the several sources of agreement among the numerous disparate factions within the reform movement. Corollary to their notion that welfare programs could not in many cases pass the test of scientific scrutiny, the reformers felt that public welfare officials were too often chosen for political reasons rather than ability and honesty. In what proved to be the beginnings of professional social work, they were ensuring that the problems of the poor would continue to receive dedicated and expert attention. And in a very real sense, as the experts, they were carving out a sphere of interest.

On substantive issues reformers agreed that the public's obligation, particularly to the disabled poor, had been allowed to wither on the local vines. Although they were not in harmony over tactics, they approved the general strategy of overhauling the public's method of classifying its charges. In brief, they hoped to continue reforms begun in the 1830's and the 1840's, that is, to sift out of the almshouse all but the aged infirm, placing the homeless child in an orphanage or foster home, the blind and deaf in institutions designed to handle these problems, the insane in asylums, the habitual tramps in a workhouse, and the criminals in prisons. The reformers claimed that proper classification would enable the inmates to benefit from a more highly specialized treatment – whether in the form of medical attention, correction, or punishment – and that it would save the innocent from the corrupting influences of the guilty, the young from the depressing atmosphere of cheerless old age, and the guilty from the delusion that they were going to be pampered. In addition, it was hoped that the new procedures would foster more sympathetic and enlightened attitudes toward those whose reputations were undeservedly tarnished by having to associate with criminals and idiots.

NOTES

[1] John R. Craf, *Economic Development of the United States,* (New York: 1952), p. 379; A. H. Hansen, "Factors Affecting the Trend of Real Wages", *American Economic Review,* March, 1925, p. 39.

[2] New Jersey, Bureau of Statistics of Labor and Industries, *Report,* 1890, p. 361.

[3] *Ibid.,* pp. 366, 361, 387, 407.

[4] Robert W. Kelso, *Poverty,* (New York: 1929), p. 48.

[5] New Jersey, Bureau of Statistics, *Report,* 1890, pp. 363-364.

[6] Russell H. Conwell, *Acres of Diamonds,* 1890, p. 19.

[7] William Graham Sumner, *The Forgotten Man and Other Essays,* (New Haven: 1918), p. 480.

[8] New York State, *Proceedings of State Convention of Superintendents of the Poor,* (1890), p. 23.

[9] United States Commission of Labor, *Twenty-First Annual Report,* (Washington: 1906), pp. 15ff.

[10] Feder, *Unemployment Relief,* pp. 42, 52; David Schneider and Albert Deutsch, *The History of Public Welfare in New York State 1867-1940,* (Chicago: 1941), pp. 38-40.

[11] Massacusetts Bureau of Labor Statistics, *Tenth Annual Report, January 1879,* (Boston: 1879), pp. 100-116.

[12] U.S. Bureau of the Census, *Historical Statistics of the United States, Colonial Times to 1957* (Washington, D.C.: 1960), p. 741.

[13] U.S. Department of the Interior, *Report of the Secretary of the Interior,* I, (Washington, D.C.: 1887), p. 48.

[14] Bremner, *American Philanthropy,* pp. 76-89.

[15] Home for Old Men and Aged Couples (New York City), *Annual Report* (1885), p. 5.

[16] N.Y. State *SCSP Proceedings* (1876), pp. 31-33; *ibid.* (1892), pp. 28-30, 108-109; New York Board of State Commissioners of Public Charity, *Report* (1869), pp. 119-124; Boston, *Overseers of the Poor, Report* (1872), p. 37; *ibid.* (1874-75), pp. 46-48.

[17] National Conference of Charities and Correction, *Fourth Annual Report,* 1877, p. 94.

[18] John Lewis Gillin, *Poverty and Dependency* (New York: 1922), p. 154.

[19] Feder, *Unemployment Relief,* pp. 67-70.

[20] Massachusetts, Bureau of Labor Statistics, *Fourteenth Annual Report,* (1893), p. 32. (appendix).

[21] Alice Shafer, Mary Keefer, and Sophonisba P. Breckenridge, *The Indiana Poor Law,* (Chicago: 1936), pp. 53-54; National Conference of Charities and Correction (NCOCC), *Sixth Annual Report,* (1879), pp. 202-204; Feder, *Unemployment Relief,*

pp. 46-50; Robert W. Kelso, *Poverty* (New York: 1929), pp. 239-243; Bruce and Eickhoff, "Michigan Poor Law", pp. 34-38.

[22] Michigan, Board of State Commissioners for the General Supervision of Charitable, Penal, Pauper and Reformatory Institutions, *Fourth Annual Report, 1877-78* (Lansing, Michigan: 1879), p. 23.

[23] New York State, *Proceedings SCSP* XXII (1892), p. 35.

[24] *Ibid.*, p. 25.

[25] Franklin B. Sanborn, "The Years' Work in Administration and Legislation," National Conference of Charities and Correction, *Sixth Annual Report* (1879), p. 25.

[26] Michigan, Board of State Commissioners, *Fourth Annual Report*, 1877-78 (1879), p. 24.

[27] Jeffrey Brackett, *The Transportation Problem in American Social Work* (New York: 1936), pp. 7-8; Amos G. Warner, *American Charities*, pp. 114-115.

[28] American Economic Association, *Proceedings*, VIII, (1893), pp. 114-121.

[29] Charles R. Henderson, *Industrial Insurance in the United States*, (Chicago: 1908), p. 158.

[30] *Ibid.*, pp. 112-127; B.H. Meyer, "Fraternal Beneficiary Societies in the United States", *The American Journal of Sociology*, pp. 655-656.

[31] Henderson, *Industrial Insurance*, p. 63-65.

[32] U.S. Commissioner of Labor, *Twenty-Third Annual Report: Workmen's Insurance and Benefit Funds in the United States*, (Washington: 1909), pp. Chap. I; Murray Webb Latimer, *Trade Union Pension Systems*, (New York: 1932), Chap. II.

[33] *Ibid.*; Henderson, *Industrial Insurance*, pp. 190-211; I.M. Rubinow, *Social Insurance*, (New York: 1913), p. 287.

[34] Elizur Wright, "Life Insurance for the Poor", *Journal of Social Science* No. 8 (1876), p. 148; Meyer, "Fraternal Beneficiary Societies," *op. cit.*, pp. 660-661.

[35] *Lend a Hand*, VIII (1892), p. 292.

[36] Frank J. Bruno, *Trends in Social Work 1874-1956*, (New York: 1957), pp. 31-43; Schneider and Deutch, *History of Public Welfare*, Chap. I and II; James Lieby, *Charity and Correction in New Jersey*, (New Brunswick: 1967), pp. 156-164.

[37] Frank Dekker Watson, *The Charity Organization Movement in the United States, A Study in American Philanthropy* (New York, 1922).

[38] Robert D. Woods, *The Neighborhood in Nation Building*   (Boston, 1923), p 25.

[39] Julia Lathrop, "What the Settlement Work Stands For," NCOSS, *Proceedings*, Vo. XXIII (1896), p. 110.

[40] See directory of national agencies, *Encyclopedia of Social Work*, 15th issue (New York, 1965), pp. 911-1013.

[41] Bruno, *Trends*, pp. 4-7.

[42] *Encyclopedia of Social Work* (1965), pp. 679-680.

[43] *Ibid.*, p. 466; William Rhinelander Stewart, *The Philanthropic Work of Josephine Shaw Lowell* (New York, 1911), pp. 1-48.

[44] Bruno, *Trends*, pp. 10-12; Pumphrey and Pumphrey, *Heritage*, pp. 212-213; *Encyclopedia of Social Work*, pp. 671-672.

[45] Bruno, *Trends*, pp. 102-103; *Encyclopedia of Social Work* (1965), pp. 467-468.

[46] Edith Abbott, *Some American Pioneers in Social Welfare* (Chicago, 1937), pp. 128-139.

[47] *Encyclopedia of Social Work* (1965), p. 841.

CHAPTER II
CHARITY REFORM AND
SOCIAL REFORM: 1870 – 1893

There is an aspect of reform philanthropy which raises a critical question concerning its contributions to the reinterpretation of self-reliance. On the one hand, it seems clear that in trying to remind the community of its proper obligations to the poor, reformers were revitalizing the idea of collective responsibility. On the other hand, that they were operating largely within systems of charity, with all of its implications of recipient inferiority, certainly placed some limit on the extent to which they were willing to absolve the individual of personal fault. Particularly with regard to the able-bodied poor, most charity reformers regarded relief, even with a variety of safeguards, as inherently dangerous to self-reliance. If, as some historians have argued with particular reference to the conservative and powerful charity organization wing of reform, they were virtually social Darwinian in outlook, then their efforts would have to be considered the last tribute paid to the old virtues rather than the herald of new ones.

In a sense it was both. For even when we focus upon the charity organization movement, we not only find the seed of progressive thought, but we find it expressed in a manner that provides us with a classic example of American dualism in welfare. To settle exclusively on the charity reformer's obvious attachment to individual responsibility is to divorce them from all the other events swirling around them – the rampant individualism, the rise of new private welfare systems, and new consolidations of power – and the impact of these on their role and in fostering a different set of concerns. In effect, by gathering expertise in welfare, they were attempting to maintain control in a field that was once theirs almost exclusively by virtue of their class. And whatever the arrogance in this self-proclaimed role as keeper of the community's conscience, the perceptions that flowed from it – and from the struggle to maintain it – gave them a heightened sense of the threats posed to society by chaotic individualism as well as by certain of the contemporary attempts to order that chaos.

* * * * *

Not all charity reformers shared the Charity Organization Society's position on public relief and pauperism. It was on this question that Franklin

Sanborn, a founder of the National Conference and an eloquent spokesman for the expansion of public welfare, found himself parting company with many of his colleagues. He felt and persistently argued that public outdoor relief, if judicidously administered, was proper and in the long run a more efficient and humane method of dealing with adults who needed temporary relief. To force a family into the almshouse, argued Sanborn, was to strike at the very foundation of society. Neither the family or society would be improved. Outdoor relief to the able-bodied had been abused, he conceded, but the abuse could be corrected and was itself the result of a strong desire to "prevent breaking up of families, the corruption of the young and the unspeakable distress of the old and virtuous" who otherwise would be thrown into "association with the dregs of mankind in what was ironically termed a charitable institution."[1]

Sanborn was, however, the leader of a minority. Although his ideas ultimately gained a more favorable hearing, the early expansionist phase of the Conference had not only invited a diversity of social welfare opinion but was shifting the balance of power from the public to the private practitioners.[2]

Many of the latter, as well as some of the former who subscribed to the principles of the charity organization movement strongly disputed this contention and urged that the government, except insofar as it administered discipline or punishment, should turn the able-bodied dependents over to the private charities. In part, the reformist objection to public relief to the able-bodied stemmed from the miasma of scandal surrounding the relief offices. The implication of the New York City Department of Charities and Correction with the Tweed Ring in 1875 was merely one of the more notorious incidents in what the reformers believed a widespread and almost inevitable state of affairs.[3] But the issue of political corruption, bad in itself, merely compounded the more serious error of trying to ameliorate a situation by methods that were bound to perpetuate it.

Seth Low, Mayor of Brooklyn, described what had happened when the "general demoralization which set in after the war placed a corrupt man in charge of the poor funds." First preference, claimed Low, went to families with voters and particularly those who were known to be friends of the politicians.

> Large numbers of the population were taught to rely on the county help, and sought it for no other reason than that the county gave it. One woman received help under nine different names. Many sold what they received. Men came from the country every autumn to live at the expense of the city during the winter, because the city was offering a premium to come there and live in idleness.[4]

Even under the best of conditions public relief remained open to the fundamental criticism that it could so easily be misconstrued as a right. "The great defect in a state or city charity," declared the New York State Charities Aid Association, "is that it must necessarily be more or less impersonal in its character and general in its relief, so that those who use it grow in time to feel that they have the right to its aid and thus they become a burden upon society and we are brought face to face with 'pauperization.'"[5] One critic solemnly warned his readers that it was from the ranks of the able-bodied paupers "taught by Public Out-door Relief to live upon the earnings of others and that the State owes them a living," that the army of criminals are enlisted.[6]

According to these reformers, many of the private charities were believed to be almost as disastrous as public charity because of their extravagance in dispensing money, food, and clothing, and because of their failure to keep a careful check upon professional beggars. But private charity posed no inherent problem. The abuses, they argued, could be reformed, and the dangers to the recipients' self-reliance removed. It was largely toward this end that charity organization effort was directed. It was to correct, as one of its devotees remarked, the abuses of the "tenderhearted sweet-voiced criminals."[7] Edward Everett Hale, whose journal, Lend A Hand, espoused the principles of charity organization, put the matter more delicately and perhaps a bit more accurately when he claimed they were "giving form to the chaotic charitable sentiments sometimes floating in the minds of women."[8]

In the name of "New Charity" or "Scientific Philanthropy" they encouraged the keeping of careful case records in order that more solid investigation be made into the causes and cures of pauperism. They established a central record system in order to avoid duplication of effort, to save money and to reduce the pauper's opportunities for making the rounds. They insisted that relief, "a necessary evil," be dispensed with the utmost caution: that trained personnel make a thorough investigation into the client's need and moral character; that the applicant should prove a willingness to work, preferably at some unpleasant task such as stone crushing or wood chopping; and that the remuneration be well enough below the prevailing wage rates so as to discourage the applicant's further reliance upon charity. Some of the societies supplied a "friendly visitor," who would make periodic checks upon the recipients and supervise them in the ways of thrift, cleanliness or general moral uplift.[9]

The charity reformers were, in effect, among the most articulate in defending self-help, the staunchest in upholding the Puritan ethic of thrift and hard work. Work was at once a therapy for the idiots and the aged in the almshouses, a punishment for the criminals in prison, and a corrective measure for habitual tramps in the workhouse.[10] Not all the reformers shared the optimism of Charles D.B. Mills who felt that providing a man with work would confer upon him "the ecstasy of joy and delight."[11] "In fact, a number of the reformers seem to have had a deep suspicion that man was naturally inclined toward laziness. It is the truly extraordinary individual, commented Josephine Shaw Lowell, "who *works for a living* when it is not necessary, when the living is supplied from some source without any conditions which are dishonorable or irksome."[12] Another reformer went so far as to remove even these qualifications, boasting, or rather bemoaning the fact that with a cord of wood he could pauperize any family in Boston.

But whatever man's natural inclinations, the willingness to work was regarded as an essential obligation of life. No group could match the reformer's scorn for the man who would not work. Tramps, for example, presented an evil "almost beyond endurance." One relief official described them as "morbid growths, unsightly excrescences covered with filth and vermin, flourishing and fattening upon the community, a never yet described and indescribable mass of moral as well as physical pollution. . . . "[13] The "work test," that is, the test of a man's willingness to work or "to be a man" became the most widely used instrument for ferreting out the worthy from the unworthy. In the words of Reverend Gurteen, founder of the first city-wide COS, in Buffalo, it was "the most perfect system yet devised."[14] At times the enthusiasm for the worktest reached rather drastic proportions. One of the New York Superintendents of the Poor seriously proposed a scheme whereby tramps would be placed in a building so constructed that in the flooding of it with water, the tramp would be forced to bail or drown.[15]

The charity organization movement had an impressive albeit somewhat chequered career. By 1892, there were societies in fifty-two cities and more than six thousand workers, many of whom were "friendly visitors."[16] In 1880, three years after its inception, the movement had won official recognition from the National Conference of Charities and Correction which accorded charity organization a permanent section on its annual program. Though a minority voice at the Conferences for several years, the charity organizations had begun to dominate the National Conference by the early 1890's.[17]   In the larger easternmost cities of America the charity organization societies achieved an "overlordship" among the private charities and in New York, Buffalo and Philadelphia, they waged a reasonably successful campaign against public outdoor relief. It was in the large eastern cities, too, that societies furnished the most capable leadership.[18] In Boston, there was Robert Treat Paine, an eminent laywer and civic leader, and for nearly thirty years president of the Boston Associated Charities; and Zilpha D. Smith, who as Secretary of the Boston society, gave the organization a professional tone. Out of the Baltimore society came John Glenn, noted for his training courses in philanthropy, and his even more famous pupil, Amos G. Warner. Warner, who served as secretary of the Baltimore COS while he was a graduate student at John Hopkins, put together the classic *American Charities*, the first comprehensive survey and analysis of the contemporary philanthropic policies and concepts. In New York, Mrs. Josephine Shaw Lowell, who, along with Louisa Lee Schuyler, founded the New York society, became the movement's spiritual leader and was prominent in turning it into a foundation for professional social work.

Eastern societies and leaders did not entirely overshadow their western colleagues. Indianapolis could boast both Reverend Oscar McCulloch and the charity organization society he founded that became a hub of the city's welfare activities. Yet as the charity organization movement worked its way westward or into the smaller communities of the East where the problem of dependency was milder and handled more informally, the branches of the societies frequently were short-lived or were forced to compromise their principles nearly to the point of disqualifying themselves as part of the "New Charity." By 1892 thirteen of the charity organizations had collapsed and more than half of the remaining fifty-two had become relief giving agencies.[19]

Nowhere did the COS enjoy widespread popularity. Hostilities issued from a number of sources and for a variety of reasons. Labor and socialist groups pounced upon the New Charity as a misdirected effort to cope with grave social ills. The socialist *New York Standard* called it a "patch upon an ulcerous civilization,"[20] and urged that the snoopers not be invited into the homes of the workingmen. One charity reformer reflecting on the fortunes of the movement remarked: "It is a singular mark of the general and deep impression upon the public mind concerning the imposture and worthlessness of applications for relief that registration and investigation should be regarded as a sort of detective and repressive system. This feature of charity organization is to the popular and superficial mind the most obnoxious of our work."[21] Much of the criticism, however, came from the private charities that felt the COS to be an intrusion into their own bailiwick and from newspapers whose sponsorship or advertisement of the bundle drives and soup kitchens made them a major target of the COS. These critics concentrated on the "cruelty" of the reform. Money that should have gone to the poor, they argued, went instead to pay the costs of hired personnel and a lumbering, impersonal bureaucracy. Stories were told of widows who died while waiting out the red tape of the COS or of those unfortunate enough to have lived through the humiliating investigations only to receive too much advice and too little money.[22]

In keeping with these early criticisms, it has become commonplace to identify the scientific philanthropy with ultraconservatism. Yet the reformist temper cannot so easily be characterized. Even the historians who have linked the charity organizationists up with the social Darwinists have acknowledged another quite different current in charity reform, though it has generally been dismissed as a minor contradictory theme.[23] One critic recently referred to the reformers' "ambiguity of hovering between an archaic individualism and a possibly radical collectivism."[24] Although the author regarded this as an unhealthy characteristic which "the social work profession has never been able to rid itself of,"[25] the duality is quite possibly the source of a great deal of confusion surrounding charity reform in particular and American ideas in general.

The precise nature of this dualism is not easy to pin down. More than likely it can to some degree be explained away by remembering that charity reform was endorsed by a variety of individuals, none of whom shared precisely the same affinity for charity organization doctrines. In addition, scientific charity was born and came to maturity during a period of critical transformation in American society. Within the first fifteen years of the movement, philanthropists were confronted by three depressions; the charity reformers, no less than any other segment of society, were deeply affected by these events. One would expect that in comparing attitudes in 1877 with those in 1897 there would be some sharp contrasts. Yet even with these qualifications considered, the dualism appears to be so integral a part of reformist thought and at such an early point in the movement's history that it cannot be brushed aside.

Far from paying exclusive attention to the weakening of individualism in American society, the charity reformers seemed even more upset by the threats to social cohesion. This is not difficult to appreciate considering that so many of the charity organizationists, particularly in the first decade or so, assumed the manners if not the economic beliefs of the English aristocracy. And these patricians brought to the COS movement the same sense of social obligation that impelled them to fill the unpaid posts in public welfare offices. One may object to their *noblesse oblige* as a kind of futile and reactionary counterforce to the lusty industrialism of the day, but it was no more compatible with rugged individualism than with the corruption so frequently associated with late nineteenth-century capitalism.

Perhaps even more telling is the fact that charity organization principles were often applauded by many segments of the intellectual community whose progressivism has rarely been questioned. Actually it would be difficult to make very neat distinctions between the doctrines and personnel of New Charity and those belonging to the liberal movements within the church and academic professions. Charity organizationists were inspired by the same forces that drove their fellow social workers into the settlement house movement, or men of religion into the social gospel, or the social scientists into a reformist contemplation of the organic society. Leaders in the charity organization movement, notably Edward Everett Hale, Charles R. Henderson, Robert Treat Paine, John R. Commons, Reverend Oscar McCulloch, Josiah Strong, Richard Ely, Simon Patten, Amos G. Warner, and Josephine Shaw Lowell, roamed comfortably through the meetings of the National Conference of Charities and Correction, the American Economic Association, the American Social Science Association, the Evangelical Alliances, and sundry other groups.[26]

They might differ over specific causes and cures, but united by their professional and scientific interests in welfare, their class, their religion, and their anglo-saxon background, all were sensitive to the disintegration of American society and to the indifference, selfishness, and irresponsibility that paraded under the banner of charity and freedom and progress. While willing to acknowledge the cultural advantages and the excitement of large urban areas, charity reformers found them, nonetheless, centers of degradation; crowded perhaps, but in reality massed isolation where a cry for help might never be heard, let alone heeded. Much as large scale industrial organizations removed the employer from direct contact with his employee, urbanization was believed to be destroying the sense of community and neighborliness, once a hallmark of American urban life.

Even where urban-industrial life did not completely atomize, there developed in the processes of preventing it other more potent impediments to the social community. Many reformers were made uneasy by the presence of the foreigner and were especially disturbed, as was Josiah Strong, by the ethnic segregations in the cities — by "a little Ireland here, a little Germany there, and a little Italy yonder."[27]

Above all was the specter of class conflict, made all the more possible with the organization of labor and capital. And life in the large city accentuated the effects of the most fundamental source of disharmony: extremes of wealth and poverty. Apart from whatever economic deprivation this meant for the poor, the growing disparity in wealth had sharpened class lines to such an extent, according to these social critics, that rich and poor hardly knew each other and what was worse, scarcely took pains to reach any understanding. One observer noted that in all the large cities of the east, with the possible exception of Philadelphia, rich and poor neighborhoods were growing more and more segregated. "Until the population of a town reaches ten or twenty thousand", wrote Hale, "some of the important details in this matter take care of themselves,"[28] but in more populous areas social distinctions become sharper and the absence of contact leads to indifference.

The poor, then, while believed to be in danger of losing their self-reliance, were also pitied for having lost touch with the rest of the community and to some extent, accused of severing the bonds that are supposed to unite all classes in a well-ordered society. But for the most part, they were considered chiefly as the victims of social disintegration. The rich — and particularly the unthinking rich philanthropists — shared an even greater blame for widening the social breach since they were, by virtue of the power and education in a better position to control the situation. In the most obvious ways, the reformers complained, the well-to-do had removed themselves from the life of the poor. "In the first place," intoned an irate pastor, "look at the location of our churches. Just as soon as a district becomes known as a poor district, the churches move out. They follow the line of wealth and culture. . . . " And even where the rich and poor still worshipped in the same church, he continued, they are confronted by the pew system, "the most monstrous barrier that has ever been erected between the churches and the common people."[29]

From the reformers' point of view, conventional alms-giving, rather than bringing the rich and poor closer together, merely drove them further apart. Charity organizationists may have harped upon the theme that unwise charity undermined the individual's struggle for economic independence, but they usually did so in conjunction with an attack upon the donor's irresponsibility and indifference toward the loneliness, isolation, and friendlessness that accompanied the life of poverty. To the charge that scientific and business-like charity replaced the warm and informal procedures of traditional philanthropy with a network of heartless and impersonal bureaucracies, the charity organizationists responded that the New Charity was far more involved with the poor than was old charity. The much maligned phrase of charity organization, "the poor need a friend, not alms," had, for all its innocence, and patronage, the ring of a sincere desire for restoring social relationships. "It was not hard for the old charity to give bread and coal. But the New Charity," declared one of its proponents, "gives hand, heart, brain, gives nights of sleepless thoughts, gives in imitation of the Divine, gives its own self."[30] Neither the casual donors of small sums nor the wealthy philanthropists, argued the reformers, had any desire to get to know the poor. "Christians have not loved their neighbors," complained John R. Commons, "they have hired someone else to love them."[31] The New Charity, claimed its proponents, sought to restore individuals to self-reliance while the old charity was content to tide them over from crisis to crisis or bribe them into quiescence. "Let the rich toss pennies to the poor," declared Robert Paine, "as the boys toss nuts to monkeys or bones to dogs; to gratify a passing whim and see the sport."[32] In the same vein, another reformer denounced the annual Christmas dinner at Madison Square Garden "where two thousand 'poor' children were crowded together to receive their Christmas gifts wholesale, while the 'rich' children and their parents looked on from the boxes, paying twenty dollars for the boxes and one dollar apiece for the show."[33]

Although principally an attack upon the sins of over-indulgence, the reformist fire could be turned with equal force upon the social Darwinist injunction against any "artificial" support of the less fortunate members of society. The New Charity owed a heavy debt to science and business but it remained essentially a philanthropy and as such could not brook the failure to "lend a hand" any more than it could tolerate the buying off of the poor or the smothering of their incentive through extravagant almsgiving.

It was one thing to withhold aid for fear of permitting the unfit to weaken the stock of the race; it was quite another to withhold aid in the hope of making them strong. That a campaign against indiscriminate charity could be misunderstood as a crusade against all charity, was not missed by many of the reformers or those sympathetic to the cause. "Servants in the work of charity," warned Robert Mervin, "are required to proceed with care and caution in their daily minglings with the poor, and to be watchful that they do not cultivate within themselves a coldness of nature that wrongs worthy applicants for attention."[34] Starvation should not be permitted, declared Edward Hale, "simply that we may teach a needed lesson."[35]

Rowland Hazard, a retired manufacturer and prolific essayist on business morality, in reviewing William Graham Sumner's *What the Social Classes Owe to Each Other*, praised him for correctly pointing to the evils of indiscriminate charity, but vehemently objected to the absence of any ethical considerations in Sumner's scientific framework. And Hazard bristled at Sumner's belief that after due respect to politeness every man should mind his own business. "If the question discussed were 'What can one social class *demand* of another?' the answer given by Professor Sumner would be entirely correct. Nothing can be demanded." But, Hazard reminded, "Goodness, morality, religion impose obligations."[36]

At the second meeting of the American Economic Association, Henry C.

Adams who had recently been fired from Cornell for having espoused collective bargaining in the midst of a railroad strike, explored the question of charity with the tools of economic analysis. Quoting in part from Spencer's *Man versus the State*, Adams agreed that, "'The intrusion of family ethics into the ethics of the state' by which philanthropy becomes compulsory and misfortune establishes a claim, is illogical to say the least, and will probably result in harm."[37] But after establishing his credentials as an opponent of sentimental charity, Adams went on to say that it was wrong to speak "of a presumption in favor of individual initiative or of state control as though these stood like contestants opposed to each other . . . the true principle must recognize society as a unit, subject only to the laws of its own development."[38]

It was not the science nor the organicism in Spencer to which reformers objected. Rather, it was the unwillingness of the Spencerians to include in their analyses a presumption that society was in essence an organic entity in which the misfortunes of one affected the fortunes of all. "Let the minister clothe in Christian eloquence the results of science," advised John Commons, "He should begin with the organic nature of society, showing that it is based properly on Christian ethics."[39]

Oscar Craig, a prominent offical of the New York State Board of Charities, argued that to attack humanitarian reform on evolutionary grounds was to misread Darwinian natural selection and Spencerian survival of the fittest. Altruism, according to Craig, was the "last outcome of evolution . . . which executing the Divine degree, selects those civilized peoples as the fittest to survive who obey among themselves the Christian law of Kindness."[40] Thus, in presenting what really amounted to a general critique of American society — its corruption, its temptations to the weak, its materialism, and its lack of social cohesion — the charity reformers indicted both the very rich and the dependent poor, the extreme individualists and the organized special interests. They were not suggesting that the poor be left to struggle by themselves, nor were they suggesting that the sole criterion for assistance be in its incentive for self-support. They were trying to create an atmosphere in which self-reliance would thrive but not at the expense of the equally important virtues that brought individuals in society closer together. If the reformers could endlessly chant the liturgy of hard work, thrift, and self-reliance, they were equally fond of friendship, brotherhood, neighborliness, mutual obligation, and the organic society. "*Together*, which is the central word of Christianity", proclaimed Hale, "is the central word of a commonwealth or republic."[41]

If there existed some contradiction in their insistence upon greater individualism and at the same time greater collectivism, the charity reformers were no more troubled by this than they were troubled by the marriage of science and philanthropy. On the contrary, what has appeared to critics as ambivalence or unresolved contradiction was regarded by the charity reformers as a necessary and vital characteristic of their philosophy or philanthropy.

The unique contribution of Christianity, declared Washington Gladden in his sermon to the Twentieth National Conference of Charities and Correction, lay in its having made human beings "at once more independent and more interdependent, more self-reliant and more sympathetic, more individual and more social."[42] Gladden, a leading figure in the social gospel movement and a founder of the American Economic Association, claimed that the "perfect law of charity" issued from contradictions that were generously sprinkled throughout the New Testament. In particular, he cited as the text of his sermon: "Bear ye another's burden and so fulfill the law of Christ . . . For every man shall bear his own burden." These commands, he said, have always troubled the "logic mongering dogmatists" but "when we begin to grasp their import," we would "find in these antitheses . . . one of the most luminous of all laws of thought." Gladden sought the solution to this puzzle in the classic doctrine that "unity consists in opposition" and he likened the pair of opposites to the two sides of an arch "that form a perfect unity," each opposing the other and by its opposition supporting the other.[43]

In somewhat similar fashion, Francis G. Peabody, professor of Christian Morals at Harvard and like Gladden a prominent social gospeler, played upon the theme in a sermon delivered at the Twenty-Third National Conference of Charities and Correction. Peabody, however, refused to concede any contradiction in the "twofold teaching of individual and the social order." Indeed, the "very essence of the Christian doctrine of society," lay in this dualism. Yes, Christ was an individualist. "There never was so absolute an emphasis laid upon the imperishable and incalculable value of each human soul." Yet we cannot say that Christ was not a socialist, he maintained. "It is impossible to read his Gospel without perceiving how throughout his ministry there always hovered before his mind the dream of a perfected and united human society in which the brotherhood of man was at last to be fulfilled." But, insisted Peabody, there was no contradiction. The individual is not precious for its own sake but only "for their sakes." The starting point is individual, the end is social — the "common good, the social welfare." The Christian paradox, maintained Peabody, "is just what reveals the larger truth, and the philosophy of the individualist and the socialist are one. The single life finds its significance in the service of the whole, and the whole finds its security in the integrity of each single life.[44]

To most of those who fully subscribed to the "twofold teaching of the individual and the social order," neither socialism nor conservative social Darwinism would have been reasonable political alternatives. Yet the fair ground between two extremes was vast, and the doctrine by no means ruled out adherence to a basically conservative social economic welfare policy. The concept of brotherhood, for example, did not in itself seriously undermine the presumption that the dependent was personally responsible for his plight. One may have felt obliged to help the dependent, for example, to protect society or because Christian duty required that the strong shall help those who through some inner weakness or character deficiency could not help themselves. Many of the charity reformers interpreted their activities as a type of stewardship, "reaching down" to help the failures. Even when most solicitous about the feelings of the poor, they betrayed their attitudes of superiority. Reverend James McCosh, giving some hints to the friendly visitor, said, poor people "must be approached respectfully according to the command, 'Honor all men.' Above all, they hate 'condescension' as it makes them feel their inferiority."[45]

Given the persistent belief of some of the Charity Reformers in the personal fault or weakness of the dependent, they would no doubt continue to prescribe that outside help to the poor be in the form of discipline, rehabilitation or charitable relief. Not even a commitment to some form of collective social action necessarily implied progressive social reform. Environmental analyses of poverty were by no means uncommon in charity literature, but many of them centered around such traditional concerns as a lack of moral instruction, evil associations, the temptations made by cheap and accessible liquor and indiscriminate charity. Attention to these types of environmental causes of dependency neither led to progressive social reform nor did much in the way of shifting blame away from the individual. On the contrary, it may have served merely to highlight individual depravity and weakness. The presumption here was that the "easy life" bred pauperism and the cure lay in the removal of temptations, a stringent environment, discipline and moral instruction.

However, alongside of the hard-nosed diagnosis of the causes and prescribed cures for dependency, charity reformers were invoking a vastly different set of assumptions about the nature of pauperism and poverty. Overshadowed as these often were by the traditional social psychology, they were nevertheless an integral part of charity reform thinking and more than likely predisposed the advocates of scientific philanthropy to move in the direction of modern social reform.

Essentially the individual-social ethic of charity reform ruled out the notion that an unmitigated struggle for economic independence necessarily toughened the individual's will and ability to survive the battle. The poor, claimed these reformers, surrendered in the life struggle not only because they were pampered by the gifts of the indiscriminate almsgiver, but also because they were deprived of the friendship, social contact, and moral support so necessary in the maintenance of self-reliance. When Washington Gladden asked rhetorically how the individual's burden could be borne by others and by himself at the same time, his answer was unequivocal. The "law of sympathy which Christianity has so strongly developed," he maintained was not really in conflict with the "law of self-help which it has so vigorously asserted." Indeed, each was the cause and the effect of the other. "Social interdependence," he asserted, was based upon individual independence and it was no less true that "the perfection of the individual is an outgrowth of social interdependence." "Never could you have found such sturdy growths of character," he insisted, "except in communities where the law of combination, the law of mutual help, the law of brotherly kindness was recognized as the Royal Law."[46]

Apart from whatever advice and moral instruction the genuine philanthropist might proffer the needy, he was believed to have performed a valuable service to the poor simply by establishing a relationship with them. To perform a truly charitable act — that is, to restore the individual's self-reliance — did not mean to give lavish handouts. It did not mean, remarked John R. Commons, that the rich should build a college or subscribe to a philanthropic organization. "It means," he said, "to go yourself, to get acquainted with your neighbors, to pick out some hard-worked mechanic, some slave of drink and love him."[47] And Edward Hale, in an even more effusive mood wrote that "love is the whole, and that what we need to abolish pauperism, to make home happy, to crush out sin, to bring light in the place of darkness, is always and forever more love and more."[48] In the most concrete of ways the reformers expressed the interdependence of social and individual needs: by sending thousands of "friendly visitors" into the homes of the poor.[49] As Dr. Wines summed up the case:

> Charity organization seeks to bring the rich and the poor together believing that the Lord is the maker of them both. It encourages individuals to seek out individuals and to supply their individual necessities, in the spirit of brotherhood. It believes that by such personal contact, hearts of the rich and poor will alike be made better, and that the gulf which separates social classes and which, with the increase of wealth, yawns wider and wider, can be partially bridged.[50]

In short, the charity reformers believed that individual regeneration of the poor would have to be built upon social regeneration, that their self-reliance would thrive only in a society that cherished the idea of bearing another's burdens. In more concrete terms, it was felt that the poor required some assurance that the effort to remain self-supporting would not end in futility, otherwise they might break under the strain. The hope of success was deemed as important as the fear of failure in motivating the impoverished. Love was as vital as discipline. In the opinion of Reverend Humphrey Gurteen, pauperism sprang not only from excessive monetary relief, but from the hard, dangerous and "gloomy life faced by the poor."[51]

If you bring Christians into contact with the poor, claimed Josiah Strong, "the social wrongs, the industrial abuses and nameless evils of the city, which now thrive in secret, would set the Christian blood to burning, and Christian nerve to tingling and Christian tongues to crying aloud until public sentiment was aroused. . . . "[52] While the call for love, brotherhood and social obligations was not dramatically translated into steady employment, decent wages and healthful working conditions, the individual-social ethic was being more liberally and more democratically interpreted throughout this period because the reformers observed at first-hand the "external" as well as the "internal" obstacles to self-support.

Actually, dependency was never a simple matter for the reformers. Underneath all the declarations that indiscriminate charity in a land of opportunity posed the most serious threat to self-reliance, there lay a curious uncertainty — otherwise how explain the intensive search for the causes of dependency undertaken by these self-conscious scientists of charity? There were events, for example, usually recognized as too severe even for the normally provident to overcome successfully: a long illness; a natural disaster such as flood, fire or storm that would have disrupted the most carefully laid plans for a rainy day; or a sudden death that snatched away the family's breadwinner. There were also admissions that basic social malfunctions unduly taxed the strong as well as the weak. The New York State Charities Aid Association, as early as 1875, tacitly recognized the problem of unemployment by removing that section of its by-laws proclaiming this "a country where work can always be obtained."[53] As crudely designed as the charity organization tabulations were, they demonstrated that only in a small minority of cases was the poverty of the charity applicant caused chiefly by "misconduct." The data gathered by the Buffalo COS for the years 1878 to 1887 revealed that out of more than 6,000 cases, 1,140 or 18.9% were categorized under the heading of "causes indicating misconduct," while 81% were attributed mainly to "misfortune." When other charity organizations were asked to make similar breakdowns, the results were similar. For the year 1892, for example, "misconduct" cases in the Baltimore society were 21.5%; in New York, they were 22.6%; in Boston, 31.4%, and Cincinnati, 30.1%. The bulk of the remainder were classified as problems due principally to misfortune, including neglect and abandonment of the breadwinner, sickness, accident, poorly paid employment, insanity, old age, physical defect, and lack of employment. Interestingly enough, lack of employment, poorly paid employment, accident, illness, and old age, taken together represented for each of the reporting societies well over half of the cases labelled as misfortunes.[54] The charity organizationists continued to discover that a large percentage of their applicants were asking for relief because they could not find work. By the end of the period (1893), Charles Kellogg's calculations showed that fully a third fell into this category.[55]

Although charity reformers were willing to admit that in some cases men sought relief through no fault of their own, they seemed to have believed that in the majority of cases — even of those who suffered misfortunes — the individual was in some way to blame for his plight. Where he fell victim to the ordinary hazards of life or even in cases of "involuntary idleness," he was expected to remain self-supporting. Many of the "worthy" poor were said to have failed in these situations because of their own ignorance or improvidence. It is true, as Amos Warner was forced to conclude in 1892, that most of the information collected by the reformers failed to clarify the thinking on the causes of dependency, leaving the analyses where they were twenty years before — with an emphasis on the individual's moral and mental weakness. Warner noted that part of the stagnant quality of their science lay with the imprecise and mechanical concepts of causality with which the investigators approached their materials. They constructed overlapping categories that made little allowance for the interplay between remote and immediate factors or among several contemporaneous conditions that conspired to produce dependency. This often resulted in selecting a personality trait as the most obvious and immediate "cause."[56] But the point remains that even though the charity reformers talked of pauperism as a "self-inflicted mortification," they generally left room for adverse environmental conditions and since they were inclined to treat each case individually, they recognized different degrees of personal responsibility. And even though many applicants for relief were considered inferior and may have been held largely or fully accountable for their inability to succeed in the life struggle, one may seriously question whether in fact this outlook either impeded full-scale investigations of social conditions or placed great restraints on social reform.[57] With much the same ease that they preached that bearing another's burden would help the individual to bear his own, the charity reformers moved into these investigations in the name of improving character. In their scientific endeavor to find out why an individual was so thriftless or lazy or so utterly degraded as to feel no shame in pauperism, they returned as did their predecessors in the 1840's and 1850's again and again to the environment.

Though it may strike the mid-twentieth-century mind as curious, the increased attention paid to heredity in the post-Civil War years seems actually to have reinforced the interest in environment. When in 1875 Richard Dugdale, an executive committee member of the New York Prison Association, published his study of the Jukes,[58] he created an immediate clucking of approval among those who already suspected that bad blood ran through the veins of the criminal and pauper elements. In his book, Dugdale exposed three generations of a family whose reliance upon public relief had become a thoroughly ingrained way of life. According to the author, it was a classic case of hereditary pauperism. And according to the Massachusetts State Board of Charities, Dugdale had demonstrated "more forcibly than ever before," the importance of heredity in the production of pauperism.[59] The concept of heredity, however, did not in this period have quite the clarity that it was to achieve at a later date nor was it so sharply contrasted to the environment. A quite common belief held, for example, that hereditary characteristics could be acquired. In fact, it was on this score that the Jukes family presented such a crushing indictment against indiscriminate charity, since constant injections of public relief supposedly enhanced the natural propensity to be dependent. In his treatise, Dugdale stressed not only the intimate connection between heredity and environment, but concluded that except in cases of idiocy, insanity, and disease, "environment is the ultimate controlling factor in determining careers, placing heredity itself as an organized result of invariable environment."[60] L.P. Alden, who considered his environmentalist position as moderate by comparison with Dugdale's "extreme" environmentalism and Spencer's extreme position on heredity, believed that the hereditary legacy — something on the order of an innate predisposition — could be curbed by proper environment. Like Dugdale and many others during this period he put great stress on the curative or preventive powers of a healthy environment on children. Even the overlay of generations of bad habits could be arrested if caught in time, and there always remained the likelihood that a child "would resemble remoter, and perhaps virtuous ancestors."[61]

The most revealing portions of Dugdale's study, however, dealt with pauperism as a physical weakness (as opposed to criminality which was a sign of strength and misdirected moral inclinations). Hereditary pauperism, "the sociological aspect of physical degeneration," issued from a physically weak constitution or a disease inherited from the parents. "In this light," wrote Dugdale, "the whole question is opened up whether indolence which the dogmatic aphorism says 'is the root of all evil' is not after all a mark of undervitalization and an effect which acts only as a secondary cause."[62] As in the case of intemperance, which Dugdale similarly regarded as the result of physical exhaustion, his evidence clearly pointed to an environment of "well ordered sanitary, hygienic and educational measures."[63] And the Massachusetts State Board of Charities concluded, as did Dugdale, that the inherited propensities toward ignorance, idleness, intemperance could be "very much alleviated if not checked in their operation, by hygienic means...."[64] Significantly, most of the recommendations of the Board were in the nature of improved sanitation and tenement house reform.[65]

The National Conference of Charities and Correction heard any number of papers on the connection between pauperism and poor sanitation. A Dr. Luther Diller from Pennsylvania spoke of the "deteriorated condition of character" that could be "transmitted entire" or cultivated with or without heredity through "houselessness, unhealthy sanitary conditions and bad associations."[66] Reverend Oscar McCulloch of the Indianapolis Associated Charities, speaking before the same audience, in 1880, described a scientific experiment in which rabbits, whose warrens were not cleaned for a long period, were found to kill their young or to become quarrelsome because the "organism of the animal was injured and rendered miserable by dirt...."[67]

Although the relationship between a physically unhealthy environment and moral weakness were frequently mentioned, other forms of discomfort were also cited as having a bearing on the personality. Dr. Diller, for example, pointed to business misfortunes, domestic afflictions and accidental injuries.[68] McCulloch described the "descent into pauperism" as beginning with the discouragement that resulted from difficulty in finding a job. Men pour into the cities, he said, and they are forced to live in hovels and soon seek entertainment in the saloons where they meet evil associations. "Thus many a hard-working man and honest woman has broken under the social pressure."[69]

Franklin Sanborn, at the Sixth Conference of Charities and Correction in 1879, claimed that the reduction in tramping was partly the result of the stringent tramp laws but "more by reason of the revival of industry."[70]

There was, in addition, considerable interest in the psychic value of leisure time – not of "enforced idleness" which merely cut down income and created anxieties – but noon rest periods and short vacations. "It is impossible to estimate the direct and indirect advantages," wrote one enthusiastic supporter of leisure time, "resulting from such a blessed change in atmosphere and surroundings. Many women on the verge of utterly breaking down, saved by these two weeks of rest have returned to the city with renewed strength for work."[71] John R. Commons pictured the life of the poor as a "dreary burden of work, work, work, with no relief in sight."[72]

It was because of these insights that the charity reformers, whose work is normally associated only with the rather conservative task of individual regeneration, were also often in the vanguard of environmental reform. Many of the charity organization societies were in fact founded with a commitment to seek the welfare of the poor through "social and sanitary reforms." These did not, of course, necessarily involve governmental action, but even the limited interventions issued from a belief that something more than personal shortcoming was at work, that the corrective lay in community action, and that it be directed toward easing the burden of life. Thus the charity organization societies early encouraged and actively engaged in setting up nursery schools, municipal playgrounds, creches, provident loan associations, and penny savings banks. As early as 1883 the Buffalo Charity Organization Society reported that the permanent improvement of the poor could not be realized unless their housing be improved. Its founder, Reverend Humphery Gurteen, had been campaigning for better housing for several years, and by 1891 Buffalo enacted its first city ordinance regulating tenement housing.[73] Tenement housing along with sanitation measures for the prevention of tuberculosis were the two most significant departures from laissez-faire undertaken by the early charity reformers. A number of the reformers, too, were willing to concede that brotherhood included the payment of decent wages and that the employer was obligated to provide his workers with good working conditions.

One of the more eloquent voices speaking in behalf of these social obligations was that of Mrs. Josephine Shaw Lowell. Mrs. Lowell might just as easily be remembered as the spokesman for individualism. Her stern reminders of the natural inclination toward laziness of all men, her arduous campaigning for the elimination of public outdoor relief to the able-bodied, and her ardent defense of the highly individualized casework method of charity organization, place her in the front ranks of those committed to one strand in the American tradition of individualism. Yet it was she who helped to found what was probably the first significant community action program in America — the Consumers League. The society was in effect both a political pressure group — with Mrs. Lowell wielding her influence before the state legislatures to buttress the factory legislation — and a women's labor union – with Mrs. Lowell engaging her time and money in the organization of strikes. As the League's first president, she articulated its objectives and philosophy, taking pains to place the responsibility for bad working conditions both on the "direct employers" and perhaps more importantly, on the "indirect employers" – the community as a whole, the consuming public. If the direct employers were prevented by competition from "following their own sense of duty," then it was up to whole purchasing public who "must be made to feel their responsibility, must be made to realize that it is for the supply of their wants that all business of the world is carried on, and that their demands, however unconsciously to themselves, are actually the cause of evils from which the working-men, women and children suffer."[74] Although ever reluctant to grant to the government any direct economic interference, her conception of private property was far removed from the rugged economic individualism implicit in either traditional laissez-faire or in the philosophy of Herbert Spencer. Ownership may be primary, she claimed, but not absolute. The modern industrial enterprise may permit the possessor of capital and brain power to claim a first lien on the wealth produced but fundamentally the wealth is owned by all who helped produce it. Under the principle of "diffused ownership" the question of dividing the wealth is not to be left exclusively to the capitalist who presumes to pay the laborer out of the capital invested; rather it is to be settled by all the producers out of what they all produced. The industrial enterprise was not to be compared to a private household where one man is master but to a state where each participant has a voice. It was, in short, a "complex spiritual organism, whose constituent parts are the vital functions of human beings."[75]

As early as 1890, none other than the editor of *Lend a Hand*, Edward E. Hale, began promoting what he called "universal life endowments". He suggested that money collected from the poll tax be used for pensioning the aged, who could accept the aid "without regarding themselves as paupers".[76] It was a simple plan and represented the more radical "non-contributory" idea rather than the contributory concept of the German insurance programs. It seems to have been inspired partly by the American Civil War pension, to which Hale made reference, and partly by Hale's very liberal interpretation of the organic society. Every honest worker, claimed Hale, had in fact made a contribution to society; "they have done a certain duty by the commonwealth, which the commonwealth is proud to recognize and wants to recognize it in any fit way." The commonwealth already recognizes this, remarked Hale, by keeping the aged in the almshouse. But, he asked, would it not be better and more humane to give "every such veteran" a pension?[77]

Again the focus on the environment did not immediately and directly change the attitude of all the reformers toward the individual pauper.

Whatever his past misery, his present degradation appeared before the relief offices. The "darker side" of charity organization, complained one sympathetic critic, was still too much in evidence; there were too many "questions asked by mysterious persons in heavy veils, questions that stir up a cloud of suspicion round some defenceless girl, who is fighting hard to keep her self-respect and her good name".[78]

In spite of their crusade for the restoration of self-reliance, however, charity reformers were softening this doctrine through the social ethic of their philanthropy and the observations of their science. That they were preoccupied with the "pauper" may have dictated their case method of restoring the individual's self-reliance, but it by no means ruled out a policy of progressive social reform. For by exploring the fundamental reasons for laziness, thriftlessness, and other moral defects, and by observing that in some cases the necessity to ask for charity may have struck even the morally strong, charity reformers were pushed in the direction of progressive social reform. Edward Everett Hale was probably not too far off the mark when he claimed that "almost every effort in the direction of better food, better ventilation, more country exercise, better physical conditions for toilers, has, for its avowed or unavowed object, the holding of men and women back from the temptation of the saloon."[79]

The real dilemma was whether to spend their energies in restoring those who had fallen or in preventing the masses from falling. Mrs. Lowell had, in the 1880's, already begun to wonder whether it might not be fruitful to devote more time to the social needs of the morally healthy worker.[80] Although even in Mrs. Lowell's case the prevention of pauperism was still uppermost, social reform was justified on the grounds that certain aids to the poor were not only proper but morally imperative.

It was quite common for the charity organizationists, citing the conclusions of the British Poor Commissioners Report of 1834, to argue that charity in effect subsidized the businessman and permitted him to pay lower than normal wages. This was another way of saying what was sometimes a difficult indictment and sometimes a sop to the poor — namely that even the well-to-do were willing to accept a handout. It was also another way of saying that unscientific charity supported a faulty social system and impeded social justice. The motto declaring "the true aim of charity is to end all charity" meant more than teaching the pauper habits of thrift. "Who does not know," asked Henry C. Adams in 1892, "that much of our so-called philanthropy tends to blunt the edge of our moral perception, and consequently, to perpetuate these conditions which seem to make philanthropy necessary?"[81]

NOTES

[1] Franklin Sanborn, "Indoor and Out-door Relief," NCCC, *Proceedings*, 17 (1890), pp. 78-79.

[2] Bruno, *Trends*, pp. 6-7.

[3] Schneider and Deutsch, *The History of Public Welfare in New York State*, p. 35; Seth Low, "Municipal Charities," *Lend A Hand* (1888), pp. 498-505.

[4] Seth Low, *Proceedings of NCCC* (1879), pp. 202-204.

[5] New York State Charities Aid Association, *Fourth Annual Report* (1876), p. 20.

[6] Alfred T. White, "Public Out-door Relief Practically Tested," *Lend A Hand*, I (1886), p. 336.

[7] Rev. H.L. Wayland, "A Scientific Basis of Charity," Evangelical Alliance, *Christianity Practically Applied* (1893), p. 452.

[8] *Lend A Hand*, I (1886), p. 99.

[9] Watson, *The Charity Organization Movement;* Humphrey S. Gurteen, *A Handbook of Charity Organization* (Buffalo, 1882).

[10] See for example: New York State, *Proceedings SCSP*, XVI (1886), pp. 62. 105.

[11] *Ibid.*, p. 10.

[12] Josephine Shaw Lowell, "The Economic and Moral Effects of Public Out-Door Relief," NCCC, *Proceedings* (1890), p. 82.

[13] New York State, *Proceedings*, SCSP.

[14] Humphrey S. Gurteen, *Handbook*, p. 31.

[15] New York State, *Proceedings*, SCSP, VI (1876), p. 56.

[16] Watson, *The Charity Organization Movement*, pp. 213-215; *Proceedings*, NCCC (1893), p. 67.

[17] Pumphrey and Pumphrey, *Heritage*, pp. 162-163; Bruno, *Trends*, p. 7.

[18] NCOCC, *Proceedings* (1893), p. 62; Watson, *The Charity Organization Movement*, pp. 184-188.

[19] Watson, *The Charity Organization Movement*, pp. 212-215.

[20] June 9, 1888.

[21] NCOCC, *Proceedings* (1893), p. 73.

[22] Watson, *The Charity Organization Movement*, pp. 222-225; Humphrey S. Gurteen, "Paper", *Authorized Report of the Proceedings of the Seventh Church Congress in the Protestant Episcopal Church*, (New York: 1881), pp. 79-80.

[23] Roy Lubove, *The Professional Altruist*, (Cambridge: 1965), pp. 7, 14-15.

[24] Marvin E. Gettleman, "Philanthropy and Radicalism," *Science and Society*, XXIX (Fall, 1965), p. 316.

[25] *Ibid.*, p. 316.

[26] Robert Hunter, "The Relation between Social Settlements and Charity Organizations", *Journal of Political Economy*, XI, (December, 1902), pp. 75-88; Charles Howard Hopkins, *The Rise of the Social Gospel in American Protestantism 1865-1915*, (New Haven: 1940), pp. 103-104; John G. Brooks, "The Social Question in the Light of the Social Organism", *Lend a Hand*, I, (1886), pp. 9-13.

[27] Josiah Strong, "The Needs of the City", *Evangelical Alliance, National Needs and Remedies*, (New York: 1890), p. 60.

[28] *Lend a Hand*, VI, (1891), p. 78.

[29] Arthur A. Pierson, "Estrangement of the Masses from the Church," *Evangelical Alliance, op. cit.*, pp. 117, 119.

[30] *Lend A Hand,* I (1886), p. 211.

[31] John R. Commons, "The Christian Minister and Sociology," *Lend A Hand,* VIII (1892), p. 124.

[32] Robert Treat Paine, Untitled Paper Read at Seventh Episcopal Congress (1881), p. 97.

[33] A. Blair Thaw, "Notes from New York," *Lend A Hand,* VIII (1892), p. 113.

[34] Robert N. Mervin, "Address of Welcome," New York State, *Proceedings SCSP,* XVI (1886), p. 10.

[35] *Lend A Hand,* I (1886), p. 211.

[36] Rowland Hazard, "What Social Classes Owe to Each Other," *Andover Review,* I (February, 1884), pp. 173-174.

[37] Henry C. Adams, "Relation of the State to Industrial Action," *American Economic Association,* I (1887), p. 472.

[38] *Ibid.,* p. 495.

[39] Commons, "The Christian Minister and Sociology," *Lend A Hand,* VIII (1892), p. 126.

[40] New York Board of State Commissioners of Public Charities, *Twenty-Sixth Annual Report* (1893), p. 23; see also, Woods Hutchinson, "Darwinism and Philanthropy," *The Charities Review,* VII (January, 1898), pp. 897-913.

[41] *Lend a Hand,* VI, (1891), p. 77.

[42] Washington Gladden, "The Perfect Law of Charity," NCCC, *Proceedings* (1893), p. 271.

[43] *Ibid.,* pp. 263, 265, 271.

[44] Francis G. Peabody, "Charity and Character," NCCC, *Proceedings* (1896), pp. 416-417.

[45] James McCosh, "Relation of the Church to the Capital and Labor Question," Evangelical Alliance 1887, *National Perils and Opportunities* (New York, 1887), p. 22.

[46] "The Perfect Law of Charity," *op. cit.,* pp. 271-272.

[47] Commons, "The Christian Minister and Sociology," *Lend A Hand,* VIII (1892), p. 121.

[48] *Lend A Hand,* VI (1891), p. 78.

[49] L.P. Rowland, "The Friendly Visitor," NCCC, *Proceedings,* XXIII (1896), p. 257; Gurteen, *Handbook of Charity Organization,* p.39.

[50] Frederick H. Wines, *Lend A Hand,* VIII (1892), p. 37.

[51] *Proceedings of the Seventh Church Congress* (1881), p. 83.

[52] Josiah Strong, "Needs of the City," Evangelical Alliance, *National Needs . . .*, pp. 65-66.

[53] New York State Charities Aid Association, *Third Annual Report* (1875), pp. 76-77; see also, *Fourth Annual Report* (1876), p. 54.

[54] Warner, *American Charities,* pp. 46-47.

[55] *Ibid.,* p. 45.

[56] Amos Warner, "Notes on the Statistical Determination of the Causes of Poverty," American Statistical Association, *Publications,* New Series I, No. 5 (1889), p. 183ff; *American Charities,* pp. 41-48.

[57] Bremner, *From the Depths,* pp. 70-71. Oddly the two examples that Bremner cites in this argument, Amos Warner and Robert Dugdale, least support his case. "Even *American Charities* (1894), by Amos Warner," writes Bremner (pp. 71-72),

"which incorporated the most recent findings of European and American research, treated poverty, no matter what the cause, as synonymous with 'degeneration.' " First, it should be pointed out that the term "degeneration" often had a biological as well as a moral connotation. In his article, "Some Experiments on Behalf of the Unemployed," *Quarterly Journal of Economics,* V (October, 1890), pp. 21-22; Warner refers to the unemployed as lacking in inventiveness, initiative and energy; he speaks of their bad habits and of the "physical degeneration." In another piece (quoted in Pumphrey and Pumphrey, *Heritage,* p. 251), Warner states that "the commonest cause of poverty that approaches pauperism is incapacity resulting in most chronic cases from sickness or other degenerate and degenerating conditions." But what is an even more important point, Warner himself was complaining that many charity workers were content to dwell upon the immediate character defects in the causes of pauperism. "Yet, if we search far enough," wrote Warner, "we find that the primary cause is environment." (Warner, "Notes on the . . . Causes of Poverty," *Publications ASA,* I, p. 201.) The bad habits of the unemployed, declared Warner, "are themselves often begotten of enforced idleness and other unfortunate conditions." ("Some Experiments . . . Unemployed," *QJE,* p. 22.) Interestingly enough, Amos Warner cites as one of his authorities none other than Robert Dugdale. A discussion of Dugdale follows below in the text.

58 Richard L. Dugdale, *The Jukes: A Study in Crime, Pauperism, Disease and Heredity* (New York, 1910).

59 Massachusetts Board of State Charities, *Fourteenth Annual Report* (1878), p. xviii.

60 Dugdale, *The Jukes,* p. 66.

61 Alden, "Can Vicious Tendencies . . . ," Michigan, Board of State Commissions, *Report,* pp. 716-721.

62 Dugdale, *The Jukes,* p. 38.

63 *Ibid.,* p. 40.

64 Massachusetts State Board of Charity, *Fourteenth Annual Report* (1879), p. xix.

65 *Ibid.,* pp. xx-xxxii.

66 Luther Diller, "Causes and Prevention of Pauperism," NCCC, *Seventh Annual Report* (1880), p. 246.

67 *Ibid.,* p. 124.

68 NCCC, *Seventh Annual Report,* p. 247.

69 *Ibid.,* p. 123.

70 Franklin B. Sanborn, "The Year's Work in Administration and Legislation," NCOCC, *Sixth Annual Report* (1879), p. 29.

71 *Lend A Hand,* I (1886), pp. 487-488.

72 Commons, "The Christian Minister," *LAH,* VIII (1892), p. 118.

73 Watson, *The Charity Organization Movement,* pp. 287-293; Gurteen, *Proceedings of the Seventh Church Congress* (1881), p. 76.

74 Excerpts from Josephine Shaw Lowell, *Consumer's Leagues,* quoted in Stewart, *The Philanthropic Work of Josephine Shaw Lowell,* pp. 337-338.

75 The quoted sections are not Mrs. Lowell's own words; they are from Mary Putnam Jacobi's "The Property Rights of Employees", which Mrs. Lowell included in the Consumers League Governing Board Report for 1895 because "they cannot be too often repeated". *Ibid.,* pp. 350-356; see also pp. 390-397.

[76] Edward E. Hale, "Universal Life Endowments", *Lend a Hand*, V,   (1890), p. 524

[77] *Ibid.*, p. 525.

[78] James O.S. Huntingdon, "Philanthropy – Its Success and Failure," in Jane Addams, et. al., *Philanthropy and Social Progress*, (New York: 1893), p. 134.

[79] *Lend a Hand*, I, No. 8, (1886), p. 481.

[80] Stewart, *Josephine Shaw Lowell*, p. 358.

[81] Jane Addams, et. al., *Philanthropy and Social Progress*, (New York: 1893), p. x.

CHAPTER III

CHARITY CHALLENGED 1893 – 1902

Long before the Depression, American society was in the process of redefining the doctrines of self-reliance. The eagerness for profit in the post-war industrial boom had ironically encouraged a cynical disregard for the old idea that by dint of the individual's own efforts he would meet with success. And Gilded Age philanthropy — whether motivated by guilt, sentimentality, or political considerations — seemed indifferent toward the old idea that subsidies and handouts were destructive of the moral fiber. In addition, the acceleration of industrial and urban growth after the Civil War had created a series of problems that could not be so clearly attributed to an individual's misconduct nor solved by the individual's efforts. Business Associationism, Unionism, and the expansion of welfare services were different ways of saying that individuals were helpless unless they combined in some way. Reform philanthropists, while taking a dim view of sentimental charity, were searching for a way to invigorate social responsibility without weakening individual responsibility. Thus, unlike its predecessor of 1872, the depression of 1893 came at a time when "rugged" individualism was already at bay; and it came, unlike the recession of 1885–86, with a severity that clearly exposed the weakness of more traditional ideas and practices.

Although the accretion of industrial problems would probably have generated an atmosphere receptive to social reform in the 1890's, there seems little reason to doubt that the economic depression of 1893 hastened a reinterpretation of self-reliance and created a more urgent climate for social change. On the surface, the depression appears to have led merely to a more frenzied and confused response to poverty. The years between 1893 and 1902 are notable for the variety of proposals dished up to satisfy the public's appetite for answers. However, amid all the conflicting diagnoses, prognostications, and cures offered in the last decade of the 19th century, certain basic trends are discernable.

For one thing, the average worker emerged from the depression with a cleaner bill of moral health. Although this newly won respect was a meagre reward for all his suffering, it not only stimulated a demand for greater collective responsibility, it was instrumental in changing the nature of the aids offered to the poor.

Whereas an earlier generation might have readily accepted an expansion of public and private charity, many in this generation questioned the propriety of charity and asked for social justice. Charity, of course, did not die in the 1890's; the demands for social justice were by no means fully honored. Nonetheless, feeble and inchoate as were the efforts to cope with the problems of insecurity, it seems clear that two different approaches to social security were being worked out.

By far the most popular proposals were "voluntary-collective" in nature. They were devoid of any connection with traditional welfare systems as well as any resemblance to the radical European social insurance idea. Government might have to play a marginal role, but voluntarism was expected to carry the program to success.

A tiny minority, however, was not satisfied. Of that small band of people who in the nineteenth century dared to question the feasibility of the "American System," a significantly large proportion were connected with welfare work. They are remembered most for their crusade against outdoor relief to the able-bodied, but, as previously suggested, might as well be remembered for their critique of a disintegrating American society. For their part, social justice would be found in a compulsory-collective welfare system.

* * * * *

At the very least, the depression put an end to much of the innocence about the nature of the American economy. There were, to be sure, plenty of voices that dismissed the crisis with a reference to massive immigration or to the unwillingness of laboring men to work for low wages. But the mood of the country dictated a more realistic appraisal of the situation. And though far from scientific, the numerous studies that measured unemployment generally confirmed its seriousness.[1] Indeed, Horace Wadlin, Commissioner of the Massachusetts Labor Bureau, urged other Labor Bureaus to initiate more accurate studies in order to dispel the "unnecessary apprehension" and the wild statements given such free vent during the crisis.[2]

Not all critics came to grips with the major flaws of an unregulated capitalism; many were inclined to reduce the unemployment problem to a maldistribution of labor between farm and city, or to the lack of properly trained workers. But the increased willingness to recognize the recurring presence of large scale "involuntary idleness" (or unemployment as it was now being called) marked a definite advance over pre-depression thinking. The *Massachusetts Board to Investigate the Subject of Unemployment* (MBISU) in conceding that its tardy report would be of little value for the current crisis, justified publication on the grounds that "there is no reason for believing that industrial or commercial crises will not return in the future."[3] If nothing else the "hard times" resulted in "the increase of public interest in the facts and figures of existing conditions of life, and of their probable causes."[4]

The depression by no means swept away considerations of personal fault, but it accelerated the tendency to regard this as a product of the larger social environment. J. J. McCook, one of the more respected authorities on the tramp "menace," noted the statistical correlation between vagrancy and periods of economic distress, and claimed that the tramp had often been a good worker until he got a taste of the "natural" life.[5] Or, as Stanton Coit expressed it, "The steps from enforced idleness down into loaferdom, drunkenness, vagrancy and crime are short and near together."[6] With increasing frequency similar arguments were made in reference to more general social maladjustments. Robert Treat Paine, in his condemnation of the "rotten slums," made an urgent plea for immediate municipal action to wipe out these "hot-beds which propagate low life; shattering the health of occupants and so promoting pauperism, loosening the morals and so promoting vice and crime."[7] If not with all the onerous connotations of the past, the concept of pauperism remained, then, as a reference to the kind of dependency requiring special reformative or rehabilitative treatment. Though he might be regarded as the end product of a rotten slum or be partially excused because social conditions admittedly made self-support difficult, the "pauper" remained a "defective" in the eyes of the community.

For another class of relief recipients, however, the depression did recast "personal responsibility" in a role of lesser importance as an immediate contributing factor in the production of dependency. And the greater reluctance to apply the term "pauper" or "defective" to all cases of dependency, more precisely and more significantly represents the newer trends in social welfare. The depression, in other words, wrought a much clearer separation between a relatively small group of dependents with special problems and a much larger group – indeed the more unfortunate of the healthy wage earners – in need of little or no character rehabilitation.

Having worked in close contact with the "pauper" element no doubt left its mark upon the attitudes of public and private relief officials. It may have inspired a sympathy and understanding for the poor as John R. Commons claimed it did for him. "I should not speak so strongly nor know so surely," wrote Commons, "the terrible power of capital over labor, through the denial of the right of employment, had not work in a charity organization society brought me into contact with individual cases."[8] On the other hand the experience may have strengthened whatever prejudices the charity workers brought to their jobs. And sympathy did not necessarily lead to respect. Several witnesses, including some affiliated with the charity reform movement, suspected that relief officials were prone to spin their theories of human nature from the damaged materials they dealt with. "I sometimes fear," declared L. Ginckel, "that in our advanced charity we may become hardened and calloused to apparent destitution and suffering; suspicious of everybody, sympathetic with nobody."[9] Simon Patten, the noted economist and a pioneer in the attempt to elevate the academic standing of social work, usually advised his students to spend some of their time away from the charity applicants in order to achieve a better perspective on social conditions.[10]

The unflattering view presented by the *MBISU* of the typical relief official would suggest that during the depression little or no change took place in his attitude. "They are so well accustomed," concluded the Board, "to deal with the degraded or particularly unfortunate class that they necessarily lose a certain sort of tact and generous discrimination which is needed in dealing with men and women, who under ordinary conditions, are steady wage earners."[11] Yet the Board, perhaps, was not in the best position to appreciate the "before" and "after." The winter of '93–'94 presented an excellent opportunity for the relief officials to rub elbows with a different breed of dependent, and it seems the experience did make a noticeable impact upon them. Overseers of the Poor in Massachusetts, for example, testified that most of the applicants came for the first time and hardly in a manner demonstrating an eagerness to plunder the public treasury.[12] A study made by Isaac Hourwich for the Chicago Relief and Aid Society, revealed that the average recipient endured about five months of unemployment before making an application for relief.[13] Shaw and Clausson, reporting on the emergency relief measures in Denver, concluded that "most men would prefer to earn their meals if they could but find the work."[14] In Erie County, New York, the supervisor was startled to find that so many of the unemployed were willing to give two weeks salary in return for a job.[15] Stanton Coit, generally more sympathetic to the poor, worried lest they carry their pride to extremes "for hunger undermines and destroys the will power and intelligence of a man more rapidly than support of charity; so that men are wrong to prefer starvation, as they do, to begging."[16] And Josephine Shaw Lowell, never overgenerous in her assessment of character, lent authority to many of these testimonials on behalf of the applicants' character by declaring their distress "was not due to moral or intellectual defects on their own part, but to economic causes over which they could have no control, and which were as much beyond their power to avert as if they had been natural calamities of fire, flood or storm."[17]

As was the custom in periods of economic stress, relief administrators dispensed their charity with a greater sensitivity to and respect for the recipients. In Massachusetts, where the receipt of public charity normally carried with it political disfranchisement, many cities administering work relief did not place the recipients on the official pauper rolls.[18] Even more so than in previous recessions, relief officials endeavored to transform the work relief from the usual unproductive make-work into more useful projects such as street cleaning and stone crushing. A number of cities throughout the country made greater headway in removing the stigmas of work relief by expanding public works project such as sewage or road building. Workers were still often hired on the basis of their poverty rather than their skills, but the usefulness of the work at least made the men feel less humiliated in accepting it.[19] Although the depression raised the specter of the tramp problem, the anxieties over this question often included sharper warnings to administer the tramp laws with greater discrimination in order to avoid mistreating the honest unemployed. Actually, there seemed to be a general relaxation of the tramp laws and settlement laws; and both private and public alms dispensers were less inclined to fret about the harmful effects of the dole.[20] Frederic Almy, the newly elected Secretary of the Buffalo COS, strongly disapproved of paying relief workers in supplies rather than money as "an unnecessary degradation."[21] And a number of the officials were beginning to think that the wages paid under these circumstances should be adequate.[22]

In spite of all the concessions to the mental and moral health of the relief applicants, not all charity workers agreed on the desirability of the newer methods in administration. Among charity organizationists the opposition to public outdoor relief remained firm; there were any number of objections to the expansion of public works projects; and the work test still found a great deal of support as the *sina qua non* of any type of relief to the able-bodied. In part, the resistance hardened because the depression struck at a time when the charity organization movement was in the process of developing a set of self-conscious professional standards. The customary scrutiny of the applicant, and the highly individualized treatment that preceded and followed the payments were, to the purists in the reform, the hallmark of their activities. They agreed that many of the applicants were honestly unemployed, but they asked how one could discern this without the proper investigation.[23] Mary Richmond, General Secretary of the Baltimore COS, lamented the laxity with which the poor laws were being enforced, and proclaimed she preferred strict application even at the risk of letting some children starve.[24]

Other reformers, however, justified their "mass" approach by pointing to the deluge of applicants, and preferring mistakes to widespread suffering. Robert Treat Paine, president of the Boston Associated Charities and a member of the Boston Emergency Relief Committee insisted that the problems of employing the unemployed and treating the pauper should be kept "absolutely distinct". It would not have been wise, he said, "to have obliged the laboring men and women out of work last winter to submit to the ordeal of the usual charity application."[25]

To a certain extent the disputes within the reform movement would ultimately, if somewhat imperfectly, be resolved without either side capitulating completely. The purists, on the way to establishing a concrete manifestation of their professionalism through the founding of the New York School of Philanthropy (1898), would also find their area of work confined increasingly to those who had fallen into the "abyss" of pauperism. The charity workers who sought a sharply different approach for the average healthy worker, therefore, also won a victory — perhaps a greater one than many of them really wanted. The insights gained as a result of the depression were, in effect, removing the dispute on to a much larger battlefield. Indeed, many of the reformers themselves had implied a rejection of all charity in their attempts to make their charitable relief more palatable. Reverend James Pullman, president of the Lynn, Massachusetts Associated Charities, explained the success of the city's special emergency relief committee by pointing to the fact that it "took away the atmosphere of charity."[26]

In spite of the glowing rhetoric and the mushroom growth of philanthropic foundations during the 1880's and 1890's, there existed, long before the depression, a strong undercurrent of pessimism about the efficacy of all charitable services. The reformist faith in prevention, particularly as it was manifested in the rush to "save the children," was in itself a deflection from the notion that adults were probably beyond the pale of reform. "In work for the aged, the sick, the defective — even for the unemployed," reflected Amos Warner, "one is conscious that for the individuals dealt with there is no possibility of any high measure of success. There is little else possible than to make the best of unfortunate circumstances to deal with palliatives, to brighten the individual lives and to prevent misfortune from spreading."[27] Yet even in their attempts to prevent the spreading of pauperism and misfortune they were also conscious of their failures. Though reformers might point with pride to their achievements with individual cases or speak hopefully of the prospects of any number of special projects, they were as often concerned about the overwhelming proportions of the problem. On the eve of the depression Robert Treat Paine asked pointedly if the general orientation of the reform movement had not led to a blind alley.

> Has not the new charity organization movement too long been content to aim a system to relieve or even uplift judiciously, by single cases without asking if there are not prolific causes permanently at work to create want, vice, crime, disease and death, and whether these causes may not be wholly or in a large degree eradicated? If such causes of pauperism exist, how vain to waste our time on single cases of relief, when society should rather aim at removing the prolific source of all the woe.[28]

The depression, of course, did little to make these tasks easier. When in 1894 many charity workers throughout the country were asked to evaluate their success in reducing pauperism, only a handful out of more than a hundred indicated satisfactory progress.[29]

The depression, in addition, exposed a peculiar weakness of private charity. If in the endeavor to reduce pauperism and improve character, scientific philanthropy had made only a small dent in the problem, the attempts of all types of private charity merely to relieve want, fell far short of the mark. In spite of all the breadlines, soup kitchens, makework, and other sundry projects, only a small fraction of the needy received adequate relief. Had it not been for the injections of tax money and the expansion of public works projects, the suffering would have been even greater. The private charities had greatly expanded their facilities but these were clearly insufficient to cope with an economic crisis. And equally serious doubts were now raised about the financial resources of private relief even for less troublesome times.[30]

But more than its inadequate financial resources or its relatively impotent attack upon the pauper problem, it was the inappropriateness of charity that hastened its demise. The idea of a gift that could not be demanded as a right, presumed that the recipient, because of his personal blame, was in no position to make demands. At the very best the donor presumed that even in cases where the recipient was not at fault – where he fell victim to "flood, fire or storm" – he could make no demands, since these contingencies could not be attributed to the injustices of one's fellow man. He was of course "worthy" – but worthy of a gift. In so far as these assumptions were applied to the mass of workers, the depression made the first of them untenable and the second, irrelevant. Dependency for the masses was neither a matter of personal weakness nor of forces beyond the control of man; it was the result of a social environment, perverted by man-made injustices.

Among those who worked directly with the poor, the settlement workers were probably most sensitive to the inappropriateness of charity and the most eager to dissociate themselves from it.[31] Many of them looked upon their work as an exercise in social democracy where the rich and poor could mingle and work with each other without being so self-conscious of their differences of status. "Hull House is not a charity," declared the historian, Henry Barrett Learned, and in a reference to one of the residents who sought information about the members, Learned claimed "she moves among the people in a social rather than in an official way; and she obtains the information she desires without prying or exercising any unusual tact."[32] In a discussion at the Twenty-Third National Conference of Charities and Correction, a Chicago settlement worker repudiated the whole philanthropic spirit. "It gives us the idea," she said, "that we are better than the other people, when we are really not half so good as a great many."[33] Robert Woods, head of Andover House in Boston, took pains to explain that the residents were not "visitors" in the professional sense. They were interested in the members as a group rather than as individuals and sought an identification with the life of the people in a natural and gradual way.[34] This type of identification was not always easy to establish, however. When the Maxwell Street Settlement House, in Chicago, first opened its doors, it had to extend an invitation to the police to control the riots raised by the neighborhood people who feared another attempt to save their souls. "There was great indignation generally," reported Jacob Abt, head of the House, "because it seemed to savor too much of 'charity.' "[35]

From the early days of the Reform movement the case workers in the COS and the group workers in the settlements often worked side-by-side. They shared experiences and discussed common problems.[36] The Chicago Relief and Aid Society even tried to create some sort of blend between the two groups. But here, as elsewhere, the relationship was one of uneasy cooperation. The charity organizationists often accused the settlement workers of promoting irresponsible activities. Their disclaimers of any connection with philanthropy were treated as the mouthings of errant offspring.[37] But when *Charities* took umbrage at Charles Henderson's comment that the settlement idea "has far wider and higher aims than those commonly associated with the COS," the magazine was scolding the founder of the Terre Haute branch.[38] And Edward Hale, in the pages of his *Lend A Hand,* accorded settlement work generous and favorable recognition as the truest expression of brotherhood.

At first, with what seemed to be a painful reluctance and then with a certain modish regularity, the COS stalwarts indulged in a series of critical self analyses on the "problems of charity."[39] "I know the sickening story of human weakness," wrote John G. Brooks, in 1894. He had not, he avowed, forgotten the "commonplace of self-help."[40] But he urged, in spite of these feelings and in spite of the "sinister fact" that current methods of dealing with the poor were coming under unfair attack, that his colleagues make a rapid adjustment to the demands for social justice. They had merit; and more important, commented Brooks, they would not pass away with the depression.[41] Men like Charles Henderson, Edward Hale, John R. Commons and Edward Devine joined the chorus. They were not about to disavow the value of charity; rather they conceded its limited application, and acknowledged that for the average wage earner it was at best a poor substitute for social justice. And their efforts on behalf of social justice did not constitute a rigorous plowing up of new ground, so much as an impressive revelation of what lay just beneath the surface.

No doubt they were coaxed a bit by the pressure of public opinion, just as they had been coaxed into a more relaxed administration of charity during the winter of '93–'94. "Some of us have grown so sensitive to the charge of hardness," complained Mary Richmond, "that though we know we are right, we fear to lead public opinion."[42] The Charity Organization Societies were certainly not unfamiliar with the problem of a hostile public, but prior to the depression their most vocal enemies were from the right – from the private charities who accused them of stinginess and from social darwinists who disapproved of any interference that would enable the "unfit" to survive. Now the torrents of abuse came principally from the left – from what Brooks referred to as an unbeatable combination of respectable intellectuals and labor unionists, who were generating a great deal of enthusiasm for socialism. "All this whether desirable or otherwise," warned Brooks, "is a world movement that grows apace with the extension of an educated democracy."[43]

The trade unionists had in fact gone out of their way to avoid charity. They demanded an expansion of public works rather than relief work and doles. They patronized the low cost restaurants rather than the free soup kitchens and breadlines. Union leaders urged the workers to hold out as long as possible and a few unions dispensed out-of-work benefits in order to spare them the necessity of taking charity. In Indianapolis, union leaders turned away from direct communication with the established charities, seeking instead cooperation with businessmen.[44] But in many cases union men were simply not invited to help administer the variety of programs established during the emergency. The workers in Boston, according to Robert Woods, "were disappointed and injured," when the mayor failed to call upon them for advice.[45] Some of the charity officials, regretting this oversight, suggested that their societies broaden their base so as to include a greater representation of the social structure.[46] But neither these suggestions nor other attempts[47] of the charity people to make their services more attractive curtailed the hostilities of the unions. Their criticism was bitter and unrelenting.

The workers, wrote one union leader, "look upon charity as something that must necessarily be for the care and comfort of the weak, disabled and unfortunate."[48] The calculated exclusion of the workers from the relief committees was in fact merely a confirmation of the aristocratic flavor of philanthropy. John Brooks observed that under any circumstances charity is disliked because the recipient is expected to feel grateful; even worse is the charity donated by the upper classes. "Here is the arch offense. The traditional charity carries with it a sense of distributing favors. It is a gift from success to failure, from superiority to apparent inferiority; from one who pities, to one who is an object of pity."[49]

In a sense the unions turned the arguments of the COS back upon all charity, wise or otherwise. Thus the failure of the charitable societies to provide adequate relief during the crisis was not to be corrected by increasing the doles. On the contrary, all charity was to be eliminated. It was pictured as a self-defeating palliative artificially supporting a faulty social structure, obviating the necessity of the employer to pay a living wage and indulging him in all the tendencies toward social irresponsibility. It is no remedy for basic social evils, declared Samuel Gompers, but "simply a patch upon the awful sore of the body economic of our time."[50] As if parroting the jeremiad of the charity organization society, union men warned against the erosion of character in the charity recipient. Receiving charity not only humiliated the individual but "unmans the character."[51] "Men who once accept charity," claimed Gompers, "unless their conditions materially change, are likely to become accustomed to depend on that charity, and make no great effort to work out of the rut."[52] But where the charity organizations stressed the deleterious effect upon the worker's desire to remain self-sufficient, the union men had something else in mind. Coupled with the notion that charity assuaged the guilt of the rich or dulled their sense of justice, was the fear that the receipt of charity would undermine the workers' opposition to an evil system. "They regard pecuniary relief extended to them as an opiate," said Rober Hunter of the laboring men. "The fatal draught, once imbibed, they say, degrades each newly made dependent to the level of a spaniel whining after a bone; he is no longer God's freeman, demanding justice."[53]

Those outside the labor movement got their licks in also. *Gunton's Magazine* cast a plague on the houses of both Old and New Charity:

"Indiscriminate charity is no better than discriminate charity," ran the editorial. Edward A. Ross, in the *American Journal of Sociology,* dismissed an exclusive reliance upon altruism as a weak basis for social control in the better society. Sympathy is a necessary social virtue, he declared, but in the modern complex society the compassionate spirit is eroded by inequalities. "It will check men when the evil deed is sure to fall upon a known individual, but not when it is lost in the vague mass called 'the public' ".[54] Several of those giving testimony to the *Massachusetts Board to Investigate the Subject of Unemployment* urged that the state must first recognize the "right of the workingman to employment."[55] The Board itself took a somewhat ambiguous position on the question of charity. It suggested that the current public and private relief officials should not handle the honest unemployed because of the stigmas attached to their programs.[56] "Under the present system the wayfarer is treated as if he were beneath respect, and it is not entirely remarkable if he soon becomes so."[57] He was to be given comfortable accommodations without the ordinary disciplinary features, "and he should be given these not as a charity, but" – and here the Board stopped short of invoking the principle of social justice – "as a favor for which he pays what he can."[58]

Along with the direct assaults upon the philanthropic activities of the period, the problems of the workman's poverty, insecurity and dependency were gradually being removed from the charity workers, and turned over to a host of public agencies dealing with the mass of essentially healthy poor. That factory inspectors, members of state bureaus of labor, and officials of the public employment offices rarely come in contact with the "pauper element" undoubtedly affected the work done by these officials. Their performance, of course, was far from perfect. Factory inspectors were rarely known for their diligence; and none of the agencies, with the exception of the Interstate Commerce Commission and perhaps the New York, Illinois, and Massachusetts Bureaus of Labor, presented much in the way of reliable statistical information. Many of the state bureaus, some of which were created prior to the depression, were still fighting for respectability and most of all for adequate funds.[59] One of the Commissioners of the North Carolina Bureau of Labor Statistics charged that his post was merely a sop to the Knights of Labor and he confessed that he had accomplished "virtually nothing."[60] As time passed, however, they were on more solid ground. The worst of the battles for funds were drawing to a close and a few of the labor bureaus, notably Kansas and Colorado, were able to take credit for having inspired or aided in the passage of important legislation. But whatever their specific accomplishments, the newer governmental bodies were both a symptom and a cause of the growing disenchantment with the charitable approach to dependency. Their roles moreover, were complementary to the more direct one being performed by the private non-charitable groups such as employers, unions, fraternal societies and private insurance companies, who were staking out their claim in the field of worker security.

"Is there then in the parlance of the day 'no future' for Charity?" asked one critic. "In the sense in which it is commonly understood," wrote J.K. Paulding, answering his own question, "let us hope none at all."[61] In truth, there was little "future" for charity. But neither the reevaluations of dependency nor the demands for social justice led to widespread consideration of the advanced social welfare plans currently in operation or under discussion in Europe. For the most part they were ignored or dismissed rather abruptly as being unacceptable in America. In 1885 an editor of *The Nation* wondered why so few Americans bothered to discuss the "extraordinary" accident and sickness insurance system recently passed in Germany. Then, leaving little room for discussion, *The Nation* closed the case against this "radically false" and alien piece of legislation. Sickness was not a calamity, the editorial declared. It was good fortune in that it served as a reminder and an incentive to prudence and thrift. The law was damned at one point for being a "vast extension of the poor law principle . . . that those who are not able to take care of themselves are to be taken care of by the public at large," and damned at another point because in practice the employer would pay out of his own pocket or take the money from the employee's wages or pass on the cost to the consumer. In such cases there would "be the result of one set of people being provided against illness and misfortune, not by the community at large but by another set of people — a result hardly consistent with those principles of economic 'justice' which are supposed to underlie the schemes of socialistic legislation."[62]

Americans by and large ignored the foreign system of insurance, but their new programs represented more than the idea of the individual voluntarily entering into cooperative savings plans. For the success of these actually required a considerable expansion of collective responsibility. In a somewhat restrained criticism of the European Insurance Systems and one influenced by the temper of the 1890's, Paul Monroe, a young sociologist, outlined "An American System of Labor Pensions and Insurance." It had to be founded he said, on "Anglo-Saxon character, self-help and individual initiative."[63] Americans had, he acknowledged, recently violated these principles through the Civil War Pension, the protective tariff, and the granting of public lands and subsidies; but these were all indirect and subtle violations. The principle of self-support remained fundamental, indeed a fetish, and any overt attack upon it would be intolerable "for many decades to come". The compulsory insurance system did not, in his opinion, necessarily destroy self-help in Germany; but in America, where self-help was so vital a part of the social fabric, "the immediate effect would be unquestionably a weakening of this principle to the detriment of society, an evil not entirely offset by the principal of solidarity".[64] However, contended Monroe, some form of financial assistance or voluntary "collective responsibility" would have to be included in any American system, since social conditions were partly to blame for individual suffering, and because a large portion of the work force simply could not make provision for unemployment, sickness, old age, and accidental injury. "Such saving upon the part of these classes, even if possible, would lower the whole standard of life, a standard now implying a minimum of social welfare."[65]

In one form or another it was largely in search of these additional economic resources to which the laboring man was entitled that the quest for social justice expressed itself. There was no consensus as to whether the employer or society as a whole was to pay the bill. To those who subscribed to the philosophy of the Consumers' League, the distinction was almost academic, since the consuming public was in effect an "indirect employer" and must be willing to pay higher prices for decent wages. In many cases, however, the responsibility was to fall more directly upon the employer in the form of profit sharing or a company welfare plan financed by the employer's contribution.[66] For organized labor, social justice meant a greater share of the wealth in the form of higher *actual* wages and not in "deferred" wages of the company welfare schemes. In a speech before a group of charity organizationists, Gompers spelled out in direct language what the laboring man demanded in the way of social justice. "More! More today, and more tomorrow; and then we shall want more and more ... Then I think you will find your eleemosynary occupations will be gone."[67] For the most part, the redistribution of wealth was to be made voluntarily, encouraged by religious admonitions, or by the pressure of consumer strikes, and union demands. Another gesture in this direction was made by the public through state legislation designed to augment the workers' income. Laws pertaining to child labor, deferred payment of wages, attachment of wages, and company stores, however febrile or poorly enforced, at least meant that society was beginning to pay lip service to the idea that workers were being unjustly deprived of an adequate living standard.

Social justice and "collective responsibility" also implied a host of programs designed to improve the opportunities for self-help by preventing or reducing the severity of the contingencies faced by the worker. In varying kinds and degrees, most of the measures called for governmental aid. They included sanitation controls, tenement house reform, factory inspection, and stronger employer liability laws, all of which, hopefully, would cut down illness and accidental injuries. Since unemployment was thought to be caused essentially by poor education and lack of a needed skill, solutions were sought in the extension of compulsory education and in the expansion of vocational training in school curricula. Public employment bureaus were heralded as a means of coping with the more immediate problem of matching an existing job with a willing and able but unemployed worker. And largely as a result of the post mortems on the great depression, a number of the advocates of social justice urged that the state intervene even more directly by creating jobs through the expansion of public works projects during times of exceptional stress.[68]

These programs, of course, did not exhaust the offerings of the period nor did any one of them win the loyalty of all the advocates of social justice, let alone the more conservative segment of the population. Social justice, though displacing charity as a proper cement for social relationship, paid the price of all widely popular ideals; it became the protective covering for a multitude of sins and blessings. Many of those associated with organized labor, for instance, were suspicious of the industrial education programs as a threat to the union apprenticeship system. They also regarded the public employment bureau as a potential strike breaking weapon. On the other hand, the unions heartily endorsed the expansion of public works. "We do not claim the world owes us a living", declared Gompers, "but society does an injustice in denying the opportunity to work. . ."[69]

Taken as a whole, these activities represented another modification of "self-reliance": the individual was recognized as having a legitimate claim upon society as a whole or upon his employer to provide the missing economic resources sufficient to cover the contingencies of life; and he could legitimately ask for governmental aid that would reduce the hazards of life. And taken together with the private benefit plans, these assistances constituted what may best be termed the American System. It was predicated on the assumptions that by raising the worker's income through mostly private pressures and by reducing his expenses through mostly government pressures, his economic position would be enhanced sufficiently to obviate the necessity of relying upon compulsory welfare programs of the European type. The worker would be able to protect himself and would be expected to display the sophistication and initiative necessary to avail himself of the various voluntary welfare programs.

That European experience with this approach offered little basis for optimism did not faze those who maintained a profound belief in the uniqueness of the American character and in the abundance of American opportunities. Nor had the experience here, which thus far had not significantly altered the actual security of the average worker, appear to dampen any enthusiam for the American system. For in spite of its many shortcomings, the progress in so short a time was encouraging.

Commercial life insurance offered little help to the poorer workers who could barely afford the sacrifices made for their burial benefits. Yet the uninterrupted expansion of industrial insurance in the 1890's showed how successfully the workers could be induced to participate in a private program. By 1900 there were 11 million policies in force.[70]

Similarly, fraternal insurance companies providing death and sickness benefits merely scratched the surface of need among the lower income groups. The most reliable estimates placed the wage earning membership at roughly 20% of the total. Moreover, many of the fraternals were run on unsound actuarial principles. Insufficient reserves and rates with little relation to mortality statistics plagued many a fraternal society and left its members with little or no security at all. Yet here too there were promising aspects. The National Fraternal Congress, which by 1900 represented 47 orders with an aggregate membership of 2.6 million, had instructed its members to adopt more scientific mortality tables, while another federation, the American Fraternal Congress, insisted upon sufficient reserves. And several of the states compelled the fraternals to conform to certain of the regulations required of the commercial companies. Like the commercial companies, the fraternal insurance movement prospered in the last decade of the century. By 1900, with coverage amounting to $6 billion, there were close to 600 societies, 60% of which had been founded since 1890. Membership had climbed from 3.7 million to 5.3 million.[71]

The welfare activity of the unions tells a similar story. Union workers represented so small a proportion of the total work force — and the better paid segment at that — that under the best of circumstances, the neediest would not have been affected. Moreover, the death benefit, found in 69 out of 80 national unions, was scarcely a sturdy enough foundation for genuine security. Only 16 of the national unions made provisions for temporary disabilities; 21 provided permanent disability benefits, and only two unions had operable superannuation funds. Even considering the numerous informal welfare features in the local unions, relatively few union men had anything approaching adequate protection. But again, the rate of growth in union benefit schemes inspired confidence. As many death, disability, and unemployment programs were inaugurated in the ten years since 1892 as in the previous three decades.[72]

And in a general way, what was true of the union programs held true for the employers establishment funds: only hundreds of thousands out of possible millions covered by one type of benefit or another, yet the number of establishment funds doubling during the decade.[73]

Chances are that the incentive to push ahead with the American system issued from something other than tradition-bound perceptions of its overall prospects for precluding the necessity of adopting an alien system. For the voluntary welfare programs had a value apart from – and sometimes in conflict with – their contributions to the system as a whole. And there is every reason to believe that underneath the eagerness to promote the voluntary programs, the desire to promote the special interests of the sponsoring organizations weighed as heavily as the concern for creating a comprehensive and adequate welfare system.

Fraternal insurance societies, no less than the commercial companies with an interest in profit, would have found their fraternalism and brotherhood – their raison d'etre – untenable without the insurance feature. Among the societies catering to ethnic and racial groups, mutual aid proved to be one of the most enduring and potent elements in filling the critical needs of outcast minorities for group pride, identity, leadership opportunities, political visibility, and adjustments to the larger society.

The same twin concerns were to be found in the welfare work fostered by the two groups whose conflicts with each other tend to overshadow their common strategies. Both the employers' and unions' welfare programs were humanitarian enterprises designed to satisfy the individual's need for security and at the same time practical measures intended to preserve and enhance the larger interests of the group. In a few early cases, company welfare was merely an inducement offered by enlightened employers who, long before the fashion of industrial psychology, realized the value of making the workers happy. Where an employer's welfare work was not forced upon the workmen, and where it was universally applied, no one questioned its virtue. Some may have scoffed, as did Gompers, that providing the work force with pure drinking water was lauded as a philanthropy but no one doubted that both employer and employee gained through some types of welfare. In most cases, however, the dual motives of employers' welfare could not achieve so happy a blend. They often amounted to an invasion of the worker's privacy or freedom and the philanthropic purposes were insignificant when compared with corporate self interest. In the words of the New York State Commissioner of Labor, employer philanthropies were "in reality an instrument for undermining the independence of the workmen."[74]

Charles Harrah, president of the Midvale Steel Company in Philadelphia, testified that he periodically preempted part of the worker's wage and gave some of it to the worker's mother and some of it to a savings bank. He sent the younger men to night school where they learned foreign languages and American history. He sometimes paid for their weddings and a two-week vacation and sometimes, he said, "we have to bury an Irishman and that takes about a week." Harrah took great pride in his benevolence and his fatherly instincts; yet he obviously had other things in mind. "I like to see old faces," he said, "and we like to make the men understand that they must stay with us."[75]

The Pullman Company's humanitarian enterprises, though on a more grandiose scale were likewise ill-concealed attempts to bind the worker to the company. Whatever the advantages to the worker in terms of pleasant low-cost housing and convenient services, the Pullman paternalism was designed to saddle him with debts and obligations that could be called in by the company when he became obstreperous.[76]

Of the relatively few workers who, in the late nineteenth century, got the benefit of an employer's insurance or pension system, the majority came under the compulsory accident insurance schemes promoted by the railroad corporations. Essentially accident insurance was a device by which the employer tried to escape liability from industrial accidents. In being forced to sign the so-called "contracting out" clause the worker agreed to waive his right to sue the employer, in return for the compensation received from the company's accident fund. Yet the contributions to that fund came almost entirely from the workers' paychecks. The company rarely paid for more than the cost of administration, which significantly remained under its control. Thus the worker was required either to surrender the rights to his own money, in the event he chose to sue the corporation, or surrender his right to sue the employer in the event he claimed the rights to compensation. "When men are compelled to pay their insurance," complained one labor leader, "it is their property no matter whether it be the company employing them or some private corporation selling the insurance and the fact that they accept the insurance for which they have paid should have no more bearing upon their right to collect from the company for damages received than the acceptance of groceries upon the same terms."[77]

Emory Johnson, who taught economics at the University of Pennsylvania and served on the United States Industrial Commission of 1899 as an expert in transporation felt that the railroads did not save very much by releasing themselves from liability, that the chief value to the company was "to identify its own and its employee's interests to the fullest possible extent in order thereby to cultivate a spirit of loyalty strong enough not only to prevent strikes but also to prompt men to give the highest grade of service of which they are capable."[78] Railroad representatives, however, were often more outspoken and frank in revealing their purposes. George B. Eilliot, a lawyer for the railroads, conceded when questioned, that to guarantee the recipients of the relief fund the right to sue would reduce the fund to a philanthropy and thereby lead to its dissolution by the company.[79] "What we want to do," declared another railroad spokesman, "is to avoid litigation, that is the whole object of the relief department . . . ."[80]

Whatever the primary goals of the employer were, the relief associations served incidentally to thwart the development of unions since the enforced contributions to the company fund diminished by so much that portion of the worker's wage that might have gone to union dues. E.F. O'Shea, the Grand Secretary and Treasurer of the Brotherhood of Railroad Brakemen, claimed that many of the men saw through the "ostensible purpose of 'caring for our dear employees,' "and understood "the real purpose . . . to undermine and ultimately destroy the brotherhood."[81]

Union men, however, were just as quick to capitalize upon the practical value of welfare work. Not that labor sentiment was unanimously in favor of union welfare measures, but those leaders who saw this as a proper function of the unions recognized welfare as a source of stability to the organization. Samuel Gompers, whose efforts on behalf of union welfare plans go back to his first years in the union movement, continued throughout the late nineteenth century to promote them in the interests of the worker as well as in the interests of the union. Well aware of the workers' fear of having to resort to the "grudging and meagre dole of charity" in periods of misfortune, he claimed that unions that had imposed the highest dues and gave the largest benefits had made the most progress in both America and Britain.[82] In 1900 in an editorial urging his men to "Establish Union Benefits," he declared that the needed further adaptation of the trade union must be in the direction of more fully safeguarding the workers against all the vicissitudes of industrial life in order that the war of the workers against social injustice may be more continuously maintained and that it may become more and more persistent and aggressive.[83]

Labor leaders in the railroad brotherhoods were perhaps the most enthusiastic about the merits of welfare, and with good reason, since the brotherhooods in some cases had evolved out of the voluntary benevolent associations formed to insure the railway employees against sickness, accident and a pauper burial. As in the case of the employers' benefit systems, the union welfare measures were not necessarily obligatory upon the worker but the tendency seemed to be for them to become compulsory once the union had reached a certain size and achieved a degree of strength. By the end of the century, for example, three of the four large brotherhoods had switched from a voluntary to a compulsory system of insurance, while two of the smaller brotherhoods changed from compulsory to voluntary systems. Professor Emory Johnson, who studied the employee's as well as the employer's welfare departments in the railroad industry, found that the former "have aided the brotherhoods in enlisting the interest of the railway employees, have given the members greater loyalty to their brotherhood and have strengthened those bonds of fraternal feeling which are so essential to the vigorous growth of labor organization."[84]

The evidence collected at the turn of the century by the United States Industrial Commission reveals that labor leaders were as candid as employers in discussing the purposes of the private welfare measures. Adolph Strasser, ex-president of the Cigarmakers International Union, claimed that a union benefit system introduced under his presidency was largely responsible for the growth of the union. "I do not know of any better way to build it up than high dues and benefits. It has been practically demonstrated all over the globe."[85] Henry White, General Secretary of the United Garment Workers of America, asserted that the benefit feature of his union was instrumental in preventing a dissolution of the membership during the great depression.[86] On the basis of testimony received at these hearings, the Commission concluded that despite many of the weaknesses in the benefit systems, they were of significant value to the union; and while the management of the funds was often detrimental to the individuals, it was a strength to the organization. "The increase in loyalty and of permanence is perhaps the chief gain which the union as an organization derives from the insurance system. . . it furnishes an additional means of discipline."[87]

Given the extent to which private welfare programs had already come under the auspices of groups that prior to the late nineteenth century had played only a marginal role in welfare, and the increasing degree, therefore, to which welfare was made to serve a variety of powerful parochial interests, it should come as less of a surprise that the viability of the American system should have been seriously questioned at the point of its greatest promise, and that of the few Americans who even considered European models, many were welfare specialists still gravely concerned about the pauperizing effects of out-door relief to the poor. Apart from the socialist press, the most sympathetic interest in the foreign experiments was to be found in magazines such as *Outlook* and *Gunton's Magazine,* in the various journals of social science, in the reports of federal and state departments of labor, and, significantly, in the publications of the charity reform movement, *Charities* and *Lend a Hand.* Some of this interest was bundled in apology and elaborate qualification. Richmond Mayo-Smith, who had just attended an international conference on workingmen's insurance, reported in *Charities Review* that sooner or later the United States would have to move in the same direction but that for the present could only take a "scientific interest" in what was happening in Europe. "The state insurance of workingmen," wrote Mayo-Smith, "seems incompatible with the spirit of American institutions and especially difficult to reconcile with our system of federal and state governments."[88] John G. Brooks, who under the auspices of the Department of Labor became the first American to make a detailed inquiry into the German insurance plan, was rather more sympathetic to the idea of accident insurance, though likewise cautious about its immediate practicability. On the basis of statistical evidence in Germany, Brooks, who was still wringing his hands over the "sickening story of human weakness", told an audience of charity organizers that the worker "must have a higher wage or . . . he must have some sort of insurance, some protection that would be adequate to these extra risks."[89] But when he discussed the problem of unemployment, he preferred a program of compulsory saving to one of compulsory insurance. Though the specific plan he offered would have amounted to four dollars a year — an admittedly inadequate sum — he not only argued that compulsory individual savings was more practical in the absence of good statistics and labor exchanges, but that under compulsory saving "no extra burden is thrown upon those who continue to work".[90]

Others were more specific but somewhat less hesitant in their rejection of the prevailing methods of dealing with insecurity and dependency. One critic, reminding her readers that Amos Warner urged charity workers to push for more modern forms of Employers' Liability, presented a brief but trenchant plea of her own. Mary Oppenheimer, an inspector for the New York State Board of Charities, argued that in light of the appalling annual rate of industrial accidents, which she estimated to include 15,000 deaths, and in view of the failure of all current methods dealing with injuries, the best solution would be workmen's compensation. The burden, she said, should be shared by the consumer as a cost of production rather than borne solely by the worker whose loss in money and moral fibre results in chronic pauperism.[91]

Edward Devine, Grand Secretary of the New York Charity Organization Society, a founder of the New York School of Social Work, and editor of *Charities and the Commons* (later known as *Survey*), was also an early enthusiastic supporter of social insurance. So, too, was Charles R. Henderson, professor of sociology and founder of the Terre Haute COS.[92]

Not all of those who flirted with the idea of social insurance had been actively involved in the charity reform movement but virtually all were prototypes of the "progressive reformer"; people of comfortable economic circumstances, working in some professional or quasi-professional capacity for a university, a magazine, a civic service society, or the government. The author of the first American book on social insurance, for example, was William F. Willoughby, a graduate of Johns Hopkins, and in 1898, when his *Workingmen's Insurance* was published, an "Expert" for the Department of Labor.

In a review of William Willoughby's *Workingmen's Insurance*, Charles R. Henderson wrote:

> When we consider the anxiety, the terror with which the average thoughtful wage earner regards the probabilities of accident, sickness and infirmity of age, and when we take into account the grave social unrest which springs from the solicitude about the future we may well give a large place in our social studies to the modern inventions for distributing the burdens of provision for the emergencies of the workman's life.[93]

Actually, Willoughby challenged the voluntary-collective ideal only as it was applied to the problem of accidental injuries. Sickness, old age and unemployment insurance could not be defended on the grounds of necessity, workability or desirability. Workmen's accident compensation, however, could be justified on all three counts. Indeed, if anything, the seriousness of the American condition presented a more pressing need than did the European. In addition, workmen's compensation would neither be as costly as old age insurance nor require the complicated administrative machinery of an unemployment insurance plan. But most interesting was Willoughby's distinction between the legitimacy of workmen's compensation and the impropriety of other forms of social insurance. Sickness and old age, he reasoned, were the results of life, not labor, and insurance against these therefore "cannot be urged as a right." In justifying workmen's compensation he argued that all accidents sprang from the industrial situation for which the employer should be held responsible. Workmen's compensation, in other words, was merely an extension of the employer's liability so as to cover not only negligence cases but also accidents that sprang from the inherent danger of an occupation created by the businessman. Against these dangers, the workingman had a claim of "natural justice."[94] Given this claim of "natural" justice and the futility of the current American approaches, Willoughby defended what all critics of the American system defended: an "enormous extension" of governmental power to preserve the individual's security and prevent him from having to depend on charity.

Willoughby was correct in saying that America was still in the "primitive" stage of this new trend. "The most depressing feature of the situation," he declared, "lies in the fact that the very principles involved in the gradual evolution from limited liability of employers to that of compulsory indemnification . . . are as yet not even comprehended in the United States."[95] Yet much had changed in the years between the great depression and the first administration of Teddy Roosevelt. Many more people were willing to give the wage earner a clean bill of moral health, whatever his poverty, insecurity or dependency. And given this diagnosis, it was far more common to prescribe some form of social justice rather than some type of philanthropy. Moreover, within a few years, the prescription for social justice would begin to take concrete form.

NOTES

[1] Feder, *Unemployment Relief,* pp. 71-88.

[2] National Association of Officials of Bureaus of Labor Statistics, *Eleventh Annual Report* (1895), p. 51.

[3] Massachusetts, *Report of the Massachusetts Board to Investigate the Subject of the Unemployed, Part I* (Boston, 1895), p. xiii.

[4] *Lend a Hand,* XII (1894), p. 324.

[5] J.J. McCook, "The Tramp Problem," NCOCC, *Twenty-second Annual Report,* pp. 288-295.

[6] Stanton Coit, "The Necessity of State Aid to the Unemployed," *Forum* XVII (May 1894), p. 276.

[7] Robert Treat Paine, "Pauperism in Great Cities," *Lend A Hand,* XII, (1894), p. 200.

[8] *Charities* II (December 3, 1898), p. 1.

[9] Lewis Ginckel, "Outdoor Relief in Ohio," *The Charities Review,* VII (November 1897), p. 760.

[10] Paul Kellog to Edward Devine, December 10, 1912, CSS, COS, MSS.

[11] Mass., *Report MBISU,* Part V. p. xiv.

[12] *Ibid.,* Part I, pp. 151-158.

[13] United States Industrial Commission, *Reports,* XIV, (1900), pp. 165-166.

[14] *Lend a Hand,* XII (1894), p. 131.

[15] New York, *Proceedings SCSP* XXIV (1894), pp. 163-164.

[16] Coit, State Aid to the Unemployed," *op. cit.,* p. 276.

[17] Josephine S. Lowell, "Methods of Relief for the Unemployed," *Forum,* XVI (February 1894), p. 659.

[18] Mass., *Report MBISU* Part I, p. lviii.

[19] Feder, *Unemployment Relief,* p. 169; *Charities Review,* IV (January 1895), pp. 119-124.

[20] Warner, *Charities,* p. 83; John Cummings, "Poor Laws in Massachusetts and New York, American Economic Association, *Proceedings,* X (1895), p. 542; H.A. Mills, "The Relief and Care of Dependents," I, *American Journal of Sociology,* III (November 1897), p. 387.

[21] Frederic Almy, "The Problem of Charity from Another Point of View," *The Charity Review*, IV (February 1895), p. 171.

[22] Feder, *op. cit.*, pp. 179-180.

[23] Feder, *Unemployment Relief*, pp. 88, 131, 143-146.

[24] Mary E. Richmond, "Married Vagabond," NCCC *Proceedings*, 1895, pp. 518-519.

[25] Mass., *Report MBISU*, Part I, p. 34.

[26] Mass., *Report MBISU*, Part I, p. 53; see also Part I, p. 24.

[27] Warner, *Charities*, p. 203.

[28] Quoted in Watson, *Charity Organization*, pp. 502-503.

[29] H. C. Taylor. "A Plea for Better Methods in Charity Work," New York State, *Proceedings SCSP*, XXII (1894), pp. 47-67.

[30] Mass., *Report MBISU*, Part I, pp. 27-28; Feder, Unemployment Relief, p. 175.

[31] Robert Woods and Albert J. Kennedy, *The Settlement Horizon* (New York, 1922), pp. 174-175; James Reynolds, "The Settlement and Municipal Reform," NCCC *Proceedings*, 1896, pp. 138-142; Graham Taylor, "The Social Settlement and the Labor Movement," *op. cit.*, pp. 106-110.

[32] Henry Barret Learned, "Hull House," *Lend A Hand*, X (1893), pp. 329, 331.

[33] NCCC, *Proceedings*, 1896, p. 462.

[34] Robert A. Woods, "Extracts from a Report on Andover House," *Lend A Hand*, XI, XI (1893), pp. 184-185.

[35] NCCC, *Proceedings*, 1896, p. 463.

[36]. Mary E. McDonnell, "The Settlement and Organized Charity," NCCC, *Proceedings*, 1896, pp. 123-127; Allen F. Davis, *Spearheads for Reform: The Social Settlements and the Progressive Movement 1890-1914*, (New York: 1967) pp. 17-22.

[37] Charities, I (April 1898), pp. 1-2; A.O. Wright, "The New Philanthropy," NCCC, *Proceedings*, 1896, p. 11.

[38] "Social Settlements," Charities, II (March 11, 1899), p. 2.

[39] Watson, Charity Organizations, pp. 276-280; Almy, "The Problem of Charity . . .," *op. cit.*, pp. 174 ff.; John G. Brooks, "The Future Problem of Charity," *Annals of the American Academy of Political and Social Science*, V (1894), pp. 1-27; Roderick Stebbins, "Some Social Problems of a Country Town," *Lend A Hand*, X (1893), p. 96.

[40] Brooks, ". . . Problem of Charity," *op. cit.*, p. 14.

[41] Brooks, ". . . Problem of Charity," op. cit., pp. 10-16.

[42] Richmond, "Married Vagabond," *op. cit., p. 518*.

[43] Brooks, ". . . Problem of Charity," *op. cit.*, p. 13.

[44] Feder, Unemployment Relief, pp. 94-97, 119; Mass., *Report MBISU* Part V, p. 28; Mary Oppenheimer, "Employers Liability," *The Charities Review*, VI (June 1897), p. 328.

[45] Mass., *Report MBISU*, Part V, p. 6.

[46] *Ibid.*, pp. 4-6.

[47] See for example: Josephine Shaw Lowell, "The Evils of Investigation and Relief," *Charities*, I (1898), esp. p. 10.

[48] J.D. Flanigan, "Benevolent Features of Trade Unions," NCCC, *Proceedings*, 1896, p. 155.

[49] Brooks, ". . . Problem of Charity," *op. cit.*, p. 15; see also J.K. Paulding, "Democracy and Charity," *The Charities Review,* IV (April 1895), pp. 287-288.

[50] Samuel Gompers, "On the attitude of Labor Toward Organized Charity," *American Federationist,* VI (June 1899), p. 81.

[51] *American Federationist,* I (March 1894), p. 11.

[52] Samuel Gompers, "Organized Charity," *op. cit.,* p. 81.

[53] "Outdoor Relief in the West," *The Charities Review* VII (October 1897), p. 688.

[54] Edward A. Ross, "Social Control," *American Journal of Sociology,* VI (1896), p. 526.

[55] *Report, MBISU,* Part III, p. 110; Part I, pp. 4-6, 24.

[56] *Report, MBISU,* Part V, p. x.

[57] *Report, MBISU,* Part II, p. xii.

[58] *Ibid.,* p. xii.

[59] Bremner, *From the Depths,* pp. 72-74.

[60] National Association of Officials of Bureau of Labor Statistics, *Tenth Annual Report* (1894), p. 114.

[61] J.K. Paulding, "Democracy and Charity", *op. cit.,* p. 284.

[62] *The Nation,* February 26, 1885, pp. 174-175.

[63] Paul Monroe, "An American System of Labor Pensions and Insurance," *American Journal of Sociology,* II (January 1897), p. 503.

[64] Paul Monroe, "An American System of Labor Pensions and Insurance", *American Journal of Sociology,* II, (January, 1897), p. 505.

[65] *Ibid.,* pp. 503, 505-513.

[66] *Ibid.,* pp. 505-513.

[67] Samuel Gompers, ". . . Organized Charity", *op. cit.,* p. 82.

[68] Sidney Fine, *Laissez Faire and the General Welfare State,* (Ann Arbor: 1956) pp. 352-369.

[69] American Federation of Labor, *Report of Proceedings,* VIII, (1893), p. 35; United States Industrial Commission, *Reports,* VII, (1901), p. 372.

[70] Henderson, *Industrial Insurance,* p. 158.

[71] *Ibid.,* pp. 113-115; Meyer, "Fraternal Beneficiary Societies", *op. cit.,* pp. 655-656; Walter S. Nichols, "Fraternal Insurance in the United States: Its Origin, Development, Character, and Existing Status", *The Annals of the American Academy of Political and Social Science,* vol. 70, (March, 1917), pp. 119-122.

[72] *U.S. Twenty-Third Report of the Commissioner of Labor,* (1909), pp. 36-51.

[73] *Ibid.,* pp. 128-129; Murray Webb Latimer, *Industrial Pension Systems,* (New York: 1932), Chap. II.

[74] New York, Bureau of Labor Statistics, *Seventeenth Annual Report,* (1900), p. 1158.

[75] USIC, *Report,* Vol. XIV, p. 351.

[76] Almont Lindsey, *The Pullman Strike* (Chicago, 1942), *PASSIM.*

[77] *Railway Conductor* (March, 1897), p. 180.

[78] Emory Johnson, "Railway Departments for the Relief and Insurance of Employers," 1895, extracts sent in letter from E.E. Clark, Order of Railway Conductors, October 1, 1904, NYPL, NCF MSS #111.

[79] U.S. Congress, House, *Hearings on Bill HR 17036,* 1908, p. 97.

[80] *Ibid.,* p. 93.

[81] U.S. Commissioner of Labor, *Fifth Annual Report* (1889), p. 39.

[82] "Establish Union Benefits," *American Federationist*, VII (January, 1900), pp. 10-11.

[83] *Ibid.*

[84] Emory R. Johnson, "Brotherhood Relief and Insurance of Railway Employees," U.S. Department of Labor, III, No. 17 (July, 1898), p. 589.

[85] USIC, *Report,* Vol. VIII, p. 257.

[86] *Ibid.*, p. 183.

[87] *Ibid.*, 1902, Vol. XIX, "Final Report", p. 829.

[88] Richmond Mayo-Smith, "Workingmen's Insurance", *Charities Review*, I, (December, 1891), p. 50.

[89] John G. Brooks, "A New Hope for Charity", *Lend a Hand*, XII, (1894), p. 8.

[90] John G. Brooks, "Insurance of the Unemployed", *Quarterly Journal of Economics,* X, (April, 1896), p. 348.

[91] Mary Oppenheimer, "Employer's Liability," *The Charities Review,* VI (June 1897), pp. 326-331.

[92] *American Journal of Sociology,* IV (March 1899), p. 696.

[93] *American Journal of Sociology,* IV (March 1899), p. 696.

[94] William F. Willoughby, *Workingmen's Insurance,* (New York, 1898), pp. 327-328, 361-362.

[95] *Ibid.*, p. 329.

CHAPTER IV

SOCIAL SECURITY AS A
PROGRESSIVE MOVEMENT

Shortly before the reformist fever broke out, Richard Ely complained that if America, with her federal-state system of government, were to make as many strides as the English, they would have to have fifty Earls of Shaftsbury. If neither in quantity nor in quality the Progressive Era spawned the kind of leadership that Ely had in mind, the reforms of the period were impressive, engaging the time and money of an extraordinary number of people.

Among the more notable achievements of the Progressive Era were those in the field of social welfare. To a considerable extent, they were foreshadowed in the late nineteenth century; they were the expansion of programs already begun, and they were the extensions of a logic that found the individual's independent efforts no match for low wages, unemployment, and hazardous working conditions.

Self-reliance remained in the vocabulary of the progressives, but even more than their predecessors, they resorted to collective measures to restore the individual to independence. In keeping with the distinctions brought into focus by the depression of 1893, the Progressive generation recognized two kinds of able-bodied poor. For those who had fallen into the abyss of pauperism, philanthropy remained the principle form of relief. The progressives still regarded these recipients as having some defect that had to be corrected, but they modernized and professionalized their philanthropy.

The more significant development, however, had to do with the efforts to aid the healthy worker and, as was the case in the 1890's, the trend was in the direction of promoting programs of social justice. In the beginning of the Progressive period, the most visible activities were those on behalf of strengthening the voluntary-collective programs that had won the day in the 1890's.

However, in spite of outward gains in the American system, it came under increasing attack. Voluntary collectivism was by no means forsaken during the Progressive period, but the skeptics of the 1890's steadily increased their ranks, became organized, and convinced their fellow

Americans that at least in two areas the American system did not work.

What can explain even the limited success of the social security movement when the voluntary-collective system offered so much promise? For one thing, the workers' problems of insecurity were outstripping most of the attempts to solve them, while at the same time the society perceived the plight of the worker even more sharply. But equally important, society perceived the individual's unmet needs as threatening to its own welfare. Historically, of course, this had always been the case. Since colonial times, the public welfare system had come to the aid of the poor partly out of altruism and partly out of a desire to preserve social order. But beginning with the post-Civil War industrial problems, the fear of widespread pauperism and class hostilities added a new sense of urgency to the traditional concern for the well-being of society. Few of these fears were allayed by the Progressive period; indeed, they were compounded by an outlook which took great interest in conservation of human as well as of natural resources. And the social wastes of the American system were not only draining the national strength, but they were discounting the national prestige. Ironically, in a period of heightened nationalism an American system was nudged aside and a foreign system called upon to breathe new life into social welfare and to rescue the national honor.

* * * * *

There were a large number of relief recipients who were untouched by the changes of the Progressive period. Many of the government reports on state institutions read like those first grim investigations of a much earlier day. More than a fourth of the states had as yet no central administrative board. And roughly the same number retained constitutional authority to deprive the charity recipient of his civil rights.[1] By and large, though, the dependent hit upon better days.

Welfare work was increasingly thought of as the work of professionals. The training of charity workers, a relatively modest and informal undertaking in the 1890's reached a new phase in the Progressive period. Numerous colleges were offering courses designed to prepare the undergraduate for a career in "social work." More important, nearly a score of professional schools of social work were in operation by 1917. Although the professionalization of welfare work was not an unmixed blessing for the poor, there were undoubted benefits in administration and practice that accrued from the special attention paid to enhancing the skill and knowledge base of the welfare worker. At the very least there was bound to be some tonic effect from the fact that the relief applicant came to the "expert" as a client rather than to Lady Bountiful as a beggar.[2]

Character rehabilitation remained the principal goal of the social worker, yet he went about his tasks without the fears that plagued his predecessors. For one thing the investigations were as much a "social diagnosis" as they were a search for individual misbehavior.[3] And the doctrine holding that an inadequate dose of relief offered the best cure for continued dependency was being rapidly replaced by the theory that insecurity merely bred insecurity. Edward Devine may have scoffed at the notion that relief societies should make up the difference between the workers' actual wage and the "fair living wage," but he admitted that this "naive" view was preferable to the older, excessive safeguards that neither improved the character nor met the immediate economic needs of the applicant.[4] Some charity workers even went so far as to reconsider the merits of public outdoor relief to the able-bodied.

Charles Henderson, somewhat in advance of many of his colleagues, publicly made his qualified peace with outdoor relief in 1904. "So long as one holds to the principle of individualization," wrote Henderson, "he will concede that outdoor relief with well qualified helpers and visitors, gives the greater assurance of careful investigation and continued surveillance of the environment of dependents, and of their rapid return to normal economic conditions."[5] The more subtle safeguards were also crumbling so that relief recipients were spared many of the indignities usually associated with charity. As early as 1903, for example, Homer Folks instructed the orderlies and internes of the New York City hospitals that patients were not to be addressed in "terms of reproach such as are calculated to remind them that they are dependent upon the city...."[6] And in the ensuing ten years the Bureau of the Census reported that of all the changes that had taken place, among the most important was the new attitude that an "inability to support oneself does not necessarily involve any disgrace." Thus the term "pauper" was giving way to the more general and less connotative "poor," "indigent," and "dependent"; the "pauper asylum" and "poorhouse" were passing out of use and in their place were "infirmaries," "hospitals" and "homes for the aged." State "charity" became state "aid."[7]

Yet the degree to which the Progressive period set new standards in social welfare is not to be measured solely by the refinements in charitable services. As in the recent past, it was in the nature of this reform that charity should have been wrapped in a less degrading package and at the same time become more unappealing — so much so, that public pressure to find substitutes were far greater than demands for improving it.

This is not to say that either charity or social justice was defined with such precision that each of its fields of operation was clearly staked out. Nor can it be said that every case of need clearly presented itself as requiring one or the other forms of relief. There were, for example, certain types of dependents, notably the dependent mothers, who became pawns in a jurisdictional dispute between the advocates of private charity and the advocates of social justice. Even where clear-cut theoretical distinctions existed they were often blurred in practice. For in the absence of more appropriate aid, charity was dispensed to people admittedly victims of some social injustice. And some of the noncharitable relief was associated with charity because the charity organization societies were called upon to administer it. Moreover many social workers, including those caseworkers most closely connected with charity, did not consider fundamental social reform as antagonistic to their own work.[8] On the contrary, they were more than ever convinced of the relationship between reform and individual rehabilitation and as a result they were to be found in abundance in the civic groups that proliferated prior to the First World War. Indeed the National Conference of Charities and Correction, despite its misleading name, was in the forefront of the battle for social justice.[9]

Nonetheless, desires for social justice and social reform flourished at the expense of charity; all the hostilities that had come to the surface during the 1890's were still very much in evidence. When Samuel Gompers addressed the National Women's Trade Union League in 1905 he got his heartiest response from a declaration that their organization was "not a work of charity! It is not a work of endowing someone with a gratuity. It is instituted so that the girls and the women may be placed in a position where they may be helped to help themselves. (Vigorous applause) What the workingmen want, is less charity and more rights (Applause)."[10] By 1908 the wings of the charity angel had been so clipped that *Charities and Commons* was forced to sacrifice its name on the altar of public relations and change the name of the journal to the *Survey*. "The name 'Charities' " conceded its editor, "has been found to have distinct disadvantages, particularly in reaching new audiences. Whatever its rightful significance, the average person receiving a sample copy or a letter with the name 'Charities' at the top distrusts it as an appeal for funds or as an organ of a distinctly relief giving organization."[11] And evidently those too closely identified with organized charity were impaired somewhat in their effectiveness as advocates of social justice. At one point Charles Henderson warned that the American Association for Labor Legislation, rather than some charitable organization, should manage a certain project. "It should *not* be directed by the charity people; I am one of them and they are of the best, but if the movement gets the tag of 'Charity' in the U.S. it is hurt."[12]

The increasing distaste for charity not only helps to explain the upsurge in efforts to find socially just programs of worker security, but where the distaste was particularly strong, it accounts in part for the popularity of certain programs over others. The search for social justice continued in two main directions, and as in the past, the voluntarily collective programs, operating independently of the tainted welfare systems, continued to attract most of the attention, at least until about 1908.

In many cases, though certainly not in all, these measures were encouraged by people who still had faith in the American system and who saw them as an alternative to the more radical governmental pension and insurance programs enjoying a vogue in Europe. These sentiments found wide approval among the members of the National Civic Federation, an organization created in 1900 to establish a harmony between the interests of organized labor and organized capital.

The response to the issue of old age dependency, for example, discussed rather extensively at the ninth annual meeting (1908) was typical. Darwin Kingsley, president of the New York Life Insurance Company, declared that the worker could make no direct claim upon the government but that he should demand by contract with his employer some type of insurance as a "right." This was slower than the German and English methods, conceded Kingsley, but it was more American: "A system which teaches these people how to protect themselves against this menace, is more in harmony with the genius of our institutions, than a system which coerces them into action or a system which finally places the burden of their support and care upon general society."[13] Judging from the response here and elsewhere, many workers would have preferred to demand a much higher wage as a right and in turn divert some of their wage in their union benefit systems.[14]

However, still another version of the voluntary collective approach was offered by Louis Brandeis, the "people's attorney." Brandeis who had represented the policy holders of Equitable Life in the investigations of that company in 1906, and who had more recently presented his famous brief in the Muller v. Oregon case, was now proposing a system of low cost insurance. His own investigations in Boston and those of the Armstrong Committee in New York had given him sufficient evidence to make public and dramatic cause against the bigness and exploitationist policies of the private insurance companies.

He found them not only guilty of shady financial manipulations but of making their profits at the expense of the small insurer who was pressured into buying a policy he could not afford to maintain. In too many cases the worker was forced to cancel his insurance, having lost the initial investment;

and since many of the insurance contracts provided for no claim until after several payments had been made, policies frequently lapsed even before the holder was actually insured. Moreover, advertising costs, house-to-house solicitations and collections, along with the profits absorbed nearly two thirds of the money spent on insurance. Under his Massachusetts Plan, the savings banks were empowered to write out small and safe insurance policies. Profits were kept within reason, abuses arising out of lapsed policies were avoided and solicitation was left to unpaid agents, namely, unions and employers.[15] Although the plan had placed the state in the position of promoting quasi-public enterprises that would compete with the private insurance companies, the Brandeis measure was considerably more moderate than both the state owned and operated voluntary insurance and the European systems of social insurance and public pensions. Brandeis who had not yet endorsed social insurance considered his measure as the last step before state insurance. He agreed that the success of the savings bank plan depended upon wages high enough to allow for saving, but he also argued that, "If the wage permits it, and the workingman does not apply that proportion to it, he is simply shifting upon the community the burden that should be borne by himself."[16]

Except for the private insurance interests represented at the meeting, the Brandeis plan won a generally favorable response. Haley Fiske, vice president of the Metropolitan Life defended his company: "If you gentlemen will just look at it for a moment; please tell me what interest on earth the Metropolitan Life has that is not in the interest of the workingman. We cannot make any profits. We have shown we would not if we could. We have nothing in the world at heart but their interests. . . . "[17] Marcus M. Marks, founder of the National Clothiers Association, said he would have preferred a postal savings bank system because the "gambling element is entirely absent." There was, according to Marks, "no easier, safer, or more independent provision for old age, sickness or the ever-threatening 'rainy day' than the gradual accumulation of savings." But his principal objection lay in the fact that many areas in the South and West of the nation had few banking institutions upon which to graft the plan.[18] Andrew Carnegie gave the plan his strong endorsement, hailing it as the American way. With an eye to the recently passed British Old Age Pension, he declared that "we are in that happy position that we can postpone that question and give our attention to things of great and immediate importance. I do not think it necessary for government to take up the subject."[19]

On the whole the events of the day would seem to have gone far in fulfilling the hope that America need not follow in Europe's path. For one thing, the progressive drive to "abolish poverty" was accompanied by a steady increase in the rate of wages. And what is just as important, the "living wage" was now commonly understood to include provision for more than bare subsistence, or even more than "physical efficiency." It should allow for some pleasures and recreation, declared one of the more prominent students of wage earner's budgets, and "for sickness, short periods of unemployment, and some provision for the future in the form of savings, insurance or membership in benefit societies."[20] Along with the upward trend in wages, laws regulating hours of work, and factory conditions and even something as remote as the Pure Food and Drug Act gave promise of making the worker less susceptible to industrial illness and accidental injury. Through legislation, court interpretation and sympathetic juries the employer liability laws were not only acting as a pressure on the safety codes but affording the injured worker a better chance of recovering in cases of employer's negligence. State child labor laws, compulsory education codes, improved facilities for industrial education and the creation of public employment bureaus presented an ostensibly impressive array of weapons against adult unemployment. And finally, the popularity of the voluntary collective schemes in which the early reformers placed so much faith, should have given pause to anyone who doubted the viability of the American system. When the National Civic Federation first established a separate department to promote employer welfare programs, businessmen responded coolly.[21] But within a few years several hundred of the employers in the organization played some role in the department. The business community did not always translate talk into action and in many cases "welfare," as Gompers sardonically noted, meant putting pure water in the drinking fountains; nonetheless, there were significant gains in the number of employer benefit systems. Pension plans, for example, rose from 12 in 1900 to 36 in 1905, and to 66 in 1910. Of the 461 "establishment funds" of all types uncovered by the Commissioner of Labor in 1908, 181 had been inaugurated since 1901. The Commissioner's report also revealed gains in the number of union benefit systems. In 1900, 229,000 union members were covered for at least one type of disability. By 1910, 622,000 were so covered.[22]

Whatever substance there was to the theory that the American system could have been reformed sufficiently to avoid the quasi-socialism of the European schemes, the early Progressive social reforms offered at least a reasonable basis for confirmation. From the beginning of the period, however, a number of social critics were unconvinced. They were not necessarily hostile to these early activities; but many looked upon them more or less as companion pieces to or pilot projects for a more formidable reconstruction of society.

One sign of skepticism in the American system was the interest in the European movements in social insurance. It was not until shortly before the turn of the century that Americans paid much attention to the European experiments in social security. Then, as if to compensate for the neglect of the past, articles and books and discussions on the European system flourished as virtually every mention of social security — whether in the counsels of civic groups, labor and business organizations, or in the newspapers and popular journals — included references to foreign systems. An increasing number of Americans, unsatisfied by second-hand reports, journeyed across the Atlantic in order to investigate for themselves. One such traveller returned as if under the spell of a genuine revelation. "Everything," wrote Lee Frankel of the AALL, itself an offshoot of the International Association of Labor Legislation, "is beyond my expectations and the possibilities of adapting European methods to the United States seems to me to be unlimited."[23] In the span of a few years American participation in the periodic international congresses on social insurance grew from a kind of silent observation by a few individuals to a more official representation involving the expenditure of public funds. By 1908 a drive to make the United States the host nation had already begun and would shortly receive the endorsement of President Taft. However, even before this plan got underway, Americans had the benefit of direct personal confrontations with men who made the transatlantic trip from Europe. Groups as disparate as the National Women's Trade Union League and the National Association of Manufacturers entertained foreign dignitaries and experts who testified on behalf of their respective social security programs. The latter organization even got a small but probably unexpected dose of the German satisfaction with their social welfare system from Count Johan Heinrich von Bernstorff, the German ambassador. Having come before the manufacturers to speak on the widely admired progress of the German economy, he told them what he had said to other audiences in the country: that "the German social legislation had had a great and beneficial influence on the standard of life of the German workmen."[24] Within a year, the NAM was sending two of its own men to investigate the highly touted success of the German insurance program.

The doubters, scattered and isolated in the late nineteenth century, had come together for the first time in December, 1901, when the National Conference of Charities and Correction set up a special committee to investigate the subject of social insurance and to report three years hence. Shortly thereafter, the American Social Science Association devoted one section of its meeting to a discussion of the same topic. In the same year, 1902, the Maryland legislature passed a limited workmen's compensation act, declared unconstitutional by an inferior court six months later. But the movement continued to flourish. No sooner had the NCCC committee issued its reports than several states, notably Illinois, Wisconsin and Massachusettes, were setting the stage for their own public inquiries into the problem. Within the American Federation of Labor advocates of a national pension were growing more numerous and stirring up more heated and extended debates on the subject. In 1905, a resolution to put the AF of L on record as favoring a national pension failed by a few votes; two years later it passed.

Clearly there was emerging a newer conception of the government's role toward the worker whose insecurity could not be attributed to his own inner weaknesses.[25] Of those who feared that the direct governmental intervention would sap the individual of his self-reliance, Henry Seager asked if this "outweighs the loss in self-respect, the injury to manhood, womanhood and childhood which results from allowing thousands of families to feel the bitter pressure of destitution? Such a view seems to me to make 'liberty' not a reasonable object of desire but an irrational fetish."[26] The state, wrote F.W. Lewis, "should not invoke compulsion for trivial reasons; but when large interests are involved concerning the welfare of its inhabitants and a desired end can be accomplished only through compulsion, it ought not to hesitate."[27]

A willingness to discuss or investigate the issue of compulsory social security did not always indicate approval of any particular form let alone the principle of compulsory social security. The 1910 Massachusetts Commission on Old Age, for example, despaired at the thought of a non-contributory pension plan: "If such a scheme be defensible or excusable then the whole economic and social system is a failure. The adoption of such a policy would be a confession of its breakdown."[28] A contributory system, on the other hand, even though "unthinkable" and "distasteful" to Americans in 1910 was certainly a future possibility and could be construed as "enforcement upon the individual of the obligation of self support."[29] Some form of old age insurance may, in 1910, have been unthinkable and only a future possibility, but the enactment of other forms of social insurance was imminent, according to the Commission. John Kirby, president of the National Association of Manufacturers applauded the efforts of its Industrial Insurance Committee to study the problem but catching the mood in 1910 issued a grave warning against any hasty action. "The spirit of the times," he declared, "is tending toward visionary conceptions of life and duty, and ... the atmosphere is charged with the murmurings of discontent upon which the agitator fattens and political demagogue thrives."[30]

Had Kirby wished to elaborate on his assessment he need only have pointed to the rapidity with which the social security movement had mounted sufficient pressure for legislation, for it was in 1910 that New York State passed the first in a series of state workmen's compensation acts. By 1911 the first of the widow's pension laws went into operation, and soon after, the agitation for a comprehensive attack on all forms of worker insecurity would begin in earnest. Thus what had appeared less than a decade before as an unnecessary and a dangerous and a visionary digression from the accepted American path was by 1910 fast becoming a fact of American life.

In part, no doubt, the willingness to examine European methods stemmed from the more obvious failures of the American system and from the realization that industrialism was the leaven for a multitude of social ills that infected otherwise diverse nations in a similar fashion. Whatever reservations remained about the degree of adaptation possible, the Europeans at least offered a rational alternative as well as a laboratory in which the feasibility of the experiment could be safely and intensively studied. Since the government had just discredited the concept of personal negligence in its own employee compensation act, declared George Bartlett in 1908, "it will be obvious that a careful examination of what has been done in the countries of the Old World will materially assist our endeavors to meet the situation in our own country as far as our systems and conditions may make it possible for us to adopt their general ideas and to profit by their experiences.... "[31]

In a sense, the more "conservative" progressive wish to preserve the status quo was in itself the more visionary approach. As the nation's economy grew more complex and mechanized, the worker discovered its mixed blessings in ever more acute form. On the whole, the risks of accidental injury, industrial illness, unemployment and old age dependency were outstripping the efforts to ameliorate or prevent these contingencies. All workers were potential sufferers, of course, but the older the worker the more likely was he to succumb and the more likely was he to find his dislocation permanent rather than temporary. Dependency in old age was often merely the logical conclusion of labors cut short prematurely by industrial accident or illness, or of a lifetime of poorly paid and unsteady labor. Had it not been for the Civil War pensions, which provided aid for two-thirds of the aged native white population in the Northern states the problem of aged dependency would have been far more serious. As it was the Civil War pensions did not necessarily fall into the hands of the neediest and they could not be given to the post Civil War immigrants. Moreover the pension had about reached its peak; its days were numbered at a time when the hazards to the individual were greater and when the proportion of the aged population was steadily increasing, accounting for 3.5% of the total in 1880 and 4.3% in 1910.[32]

Ironically, nothing in the American system could match the effectiveness of this half-century old American practice. For in spite of all the fanfare over the voluntary-collective programs, they still amounted to little more than an inadequate hodge-podge. Neither in terms of quantity, quality nor kinds of coverage did they approach anything like a comprehensive solution. Employer pension programs, for example, the most popular of the employer welfare measures were established in companies that had a total work force of 450,000 and not all the men were covered. By 1910 approximately 9,000 men were receiving pensions from employers.[33] The organized worker fared somewhat better from his union but even had every trade union developed a complete and adequate system of benefits, their ranks made up only 10% of the work force. And union men, much as the unorganized worker buying private insurance or joining a fraternal society, still had relatively little protection except that against a pauper burial.[34]

To have insisted upon waiting for what Henderson called the capitalist utopia was not only to have underestimated the difficulty in reducing all the hazards of industry — or for that matter the hazards of life — nor simply to have overestimated the power of workers to demand and the willingness of employers to grant wages that would cover these hazards. It was, in addition, to have misjudged the American worker's eagerness to take advantage of the opportunities for self-protection. Even if a strong case could have been made in defense of the notion that American workers were more jealous of their self-reliance than European workers, the difference was hardly great enough to make the voluntary system successful. Whether out of ignorance or the desire to satisfy current needs, the average worker did not automatically convert his "extra" cash into some form of savings or insurance. The advocates of compulsory social security were not the only ones to realize this.[35] The private insurance companies in response to the Massachusetts Savings Bank Insurance Plan, defended their costs of solicitation and advertising as necessary. "Getting life insurance, like 'getting religion,'" wrote the *Insurance Post*:

> "has never been achieved to any appreciable extent by hanging out a sign or distribution of printed exhortations in the one case, nor by the passing around of Bibles and printed tracts in the other case . . . . Nobody need lose any sleep over the dream of the Boston theorist, for the dream has about one chance in a million of ever coming true."[36]

Although the odds were a bit steep the Brandeis theory worked out in practice about as well as similar experiments in Europe. By 1912, five years after its inception, there were fewer than *7,000* policies in force in the state of Massachusetts.[37]

That the social security movement thrived in spite of the plethora of private and public efforts intended by some to stifle it need not entirely be explained by the objective weaknesses of these efforts. For the growing dissatisfaction with them was, to a considerable extent, the result of having examined them with improved techniques. Virtually every refinement in the scientific investigations of the period uncovered heretofore unrealized evils and with the help of a press eager to report them in a sensational way, the problem seemed to be getting more serious than the facts would warrant. By the same token, social reformers were apt to puncture some of the inflated appraisals of economic progress attributed to an essentially laissez-faire government. However much real wages may have risen, for example, the newer concepts of poverty would tend to belittle these gains. For one thing, poverty was increasingly recognized as a condition relative to prevailing standards.[38] Thus a comparison with wage levels of an earlier and a less prosperous generation did not so easily permit the luxury of self-congratulation. Moreover the tendency to express poverty in concrete money terms enabled the investigator to express the extent of the condition in a specific quantitative way. Although the rash of studies revealed that a "fair living wage" would vary with the investigator as well as from place to place and from time to time, a rather graphic presentation of the problem could be made with a reference to the numbers of families falling below the "poverty line."

Indeed, the performance of the American system generally — and the alternatives — were being judged by a new set of standards. The Progressive Era, after all, was not static; the reformist impulses fed upon themselves unleashing new energies and expectations, and quelling old fears. On the one hand, social security became a more palatable solution because of the recent and "legitimate" incursions by the government into areas previously left to the devices of "natural law." In its cautious way the Massachusetts Commission on Old Age took note of a phenomenon known, during the Progressive Era, as the "entering wedge." Compulsory insurance, stated the Commission, "might be defended as a needful measure of further State interference for the protection of society against the burden of old age pauperism, precisely as compulsory education and compulsory sanitation have been instituted to protect society against ignorance and disease."[39] The remark, however, points to another way in which the reform spirit stimulated the social security movement. The threat to society posed by the "burden of pauperism" happened to be an historic concern of those who addressed themselves to the problem of worker insecurity; nonetheless, it suggests the broader, if not the more liberal, view in which the Progressive Era interpreted the problem. This is not to say that the social critics were uninterested in the suffering of individual workers; rather, that their impatience with the conservative reforms was partly a product of having perceived worker insecurity as more than an individual problem.

The penchant for science and efficiency, apparent in the statistical inquiries into poverty, accidental injuries, industrial illness; and productive of such disparate developments as the "Wisconsin Idea," "Conservationism," and "Scientific Management," played an important and direct role in the social security movement. Its advocates, great adherents of the efficiency ethic, pointed to the *social* waste – to the unfulfilled productive capacity and the man-hours wasted as a result of injuries, illness, and unemployment. They were struck by the dissipation of energy and the disinclination to put forth one's best efforts because of the anxieties and insecurities in the life of the average wage earner. Significantly the motto of the American Association for Labor Legislation, the pioneer organization in the movement, was "The Conservation of Human Resources." In a speech entitled, "The Conservation of Vision," and read before the Society of Illuminating Engineers, Dr. Ellice Alger defined the social problem in rather stark mathematical strokes:

> There is a growing tendency in modern times to consider the individual a mere unit in a great industrial organization. If he dies in childhood he has cost his parents and society a definite average sum which death has deprived him of the opportunity to repay. Every such death is a total loss. . . . If he creates more than he consumes he is an asset; if he consumes more then he creates he is an actual liability, since society no longer allows him to perish miserably of neglect but collectively assumes the responsibility of his support and care. Society, therefore, has a direct interest in the health of each of its units, because ill health not only increases cost but lessens productivity.[40]

An even more potent force was to be found in the nationalism that often lay beneath the concern for social waste. It was becoming a commonplace to project statistics into sets of nationwide figures and to refer to the social costs as "national liabilities" or the social welfare as a "national asset." It was in this vein that Irving Fisher preached the gospel of "National Vitality," and William Hard declared that every accident "hurts the country as well as the individual."[41]

In part the heightened sense of the national interests issued from a desire to repair the disharmonies within the nation: to seal ever more tightly the divisions of the Civil War, to prevent the national interest from being neglected on the alter of competing private interests, and to prevent the national character and national loyalty from being weakened by hordes of immigrants.

It may appear that the nationalistic temper of the country would have fostered a climate unfavorable to the adoption of domestic legislation so identified as an alien system.[42] For native Americans to have expressed deep concern over the pollution of Americanism by the presence of unassimilated foreigners and then to have urged acceptance of foreign-inspired legislation would seem a rather unlikely stance. Or, to have identified the national interests with a vigorous conformity to and defense of the status quo would likewise appear to be incompatible with a critique of the American System of welfare. Certainly by the end of the progressive period, this type of nationalism worked to the detriment of the social security movement. But for several years before, a less cranky nationalism prevailed and at least in so far as it affected the incentives of welfare reformers, functioned as a spur to the social security movement.

Among welfare reformers, the attitude toward the immigrants during the early 1900's had remained as mixed as in the late nineteenth century though somewhat more sympathetic. The connection between heavy immigration and pauperism continued to worry Edward Devine, for one, and the changing composition of that immigration, now heavily weighted in favor of Southeastern Europeans, caused grave concern over the preservation of our heritage in the minds of John R. Commons, E.A. Ross and Robert Hunter. On the other hand, some of the more devastating attacks upon the immigrants' alleged responsibility for a host of economic ills could be found in Kate Holladay Claghorn's "Immigration in its relation to Pauperism" and in Isaac Hourwich's *Immigration and Labor (1912)*, a detailed critique of the 1911 U.S. Immigration Commision Report. And some of the more appreciative observations of the immigrants' plight and potential contributions to American culture emanated from the settlement houses as well as from various studies sponsored by the Russell Sage Foundation.[43]

As in the past the debates over the immigration question were far more heated and divisive when dealing with legislation regulating the flow of immigration than when focused upon policies affecting the immigrant population already here. Even a strong commitment to immigration restriction did not necessarily lead to a conservative position on the domestic question. Had the economic situation of the immigrant somehow been isolated from the question of his assimilation, he may not have received as much sympathetic attention from restrictionists. But the more the immigrant communities were studied the easier it was to see how intimately connected were the issues of poverty and assimilation. And in the desire to hasten the process of assimilation, a goal all reformers supported, they had little trouble in recognizing the value of social and economic reforms.

Very simply they had discovered that the legal and social discriminations denying the immigrant of the rights to a fair trial and those depriving him of property, or the right to hold certain jobs, merely created a disrespect for the country's institutions. Until we cleared up this "disgrace of American Jurisprudence" declared one critic in what she called the "gentle art of alienating the alien", little headway could be made toward Americanization.[44] In addition to the pervasive injustices of the legal system reformers contended that an oppressive economic system could be expected to engender little love for the country. They pointed out that no sooner had the immigrants set foot on American soil they were fleeced and cheated by agents promising cheap lodgings and good jobs and then sent out to poorly paid work that squeezed every last bit of energy out of them. The Massachusetts Bureau of Immigration declared that no amount of propaganda hurled at the immigrant could succeed unless based upon "just treatment for one and for all", and in particular reference to the economic stranglehold of foreman over foreign workers, concluded that "The elimination of this type of exploitation will do much to convince the foreign worker that he can find in America an opportunity for fair play."[45]

Welfare reformers were also quick to pick up on one of the side-effects of the immigrants' disenchantment with America which disturbed both liberals and conservatives. As a result of the failure to give assistance and correct abuses, the immigrant was forced into the hands of the machine politicians or what was worse into relying upon the host of immigrant institutions which in turn merely delayed or prevented assimilation. The threat posed by immigrant associationism was a key element in the unwillingness to leave the tasks of Americanization in the hands of private groups. While the native voluntary institutions – the YMCA's, charity organizations, settlements and trade unions were enlisted in the effort, the emphasis appeared to be on public institutions – the school system, the courts, the Bureau of Immigration. Experience convinced Lillian Wald and many others that "in the interests of the state itself the future citizen should be made to feel that protection and fair treatment are accorded by the state."[46]

Frances Kellor, a founder of the North American Civic League, who skillfully combined her pleadings for social insurance reform with her crusade for Americanization warned her audiences to "face the indisputable fact that almost without exception every foreign born male adjut is a member of some racial organization which takes precedence in his mind over every other form of association, of which he is a part, and in which he is recognized as a member of worth and standing."[47]

An even more emphatic statement was made by Teddy Roosevelt, equally skillful in meshing welfare reform with Americanization. In a plea urging the removal of conditions that led to social and industrial unrest, he declared:

> The American people should itself do these things for the immigrants. If we leave the immigrant to be helped by representatives of foreign governments, by foreign societies, by a press and institutions conducted in a foreign language and in the interest of foreign governments, and if we permit the immigrants to exist as alien groups, each group sundered from the rest of the citizens of the country, we shall store up for ourselves bitter trouble in the future.[48]

In view of the fears aroused by the efforts of immigrants to seek out "their own" for comfort and safety in a strange land, the immigrant mutual aid societies, so central a feature of this phenomenon, played an important and rather fascinating role in progressive welfare history. Under other circumstances the prevalence of these societies might have been used by champions of the American System as evidence of its strength and potential. Although contemporary information pertaining to the immigrant fraternals left much to be desired, it left no doubt as to the popularity of them among the immigrants.

As highly fractionalized by religious, philosophical, and geographical ties as they were, the membership reported at various times during the period was truly impressive. The Carniolian Slovenian Catholic Union had a membership of 17,000 and had paid out $1.3 millions in benefits. The Slovenian National Benefit Society reported 18,000 members and benefits of over a million dollars; and the Slovenian Workingmen's Benefit Association by 1918: 7,300 senior members, 4,500 junior members and a million dollars paid out in benefits.[49] And these were only three of the Slovenian societies. The Serbs and Croats had their own organizations, — as did the Magyars, Roumanians, Lithuanians, Bohemians, Slovaks and Czechs. Membership in the principal Czech organizations was over 150,000 in 1918.[50] The Massachusetts Immigration Commission in 1914 found these self-help organizations in every community with clusters of immigrants. In every city and town with a colony of Greeks there were two Greek fraternal organizations seven of which estimated their membership at 1000 or more. In Springfield, a town with fewer than 3000 Italians in 1910, there were a dozen Italian societies, one reporting a membership of 400.[51] And across the country, in Chicago, there were 110 Italian mutual aid societies.[52] Not to be outdone, the million and a

half Jews in New York City could boast of more than 1000 mutual aid
societies containing 100,000 members, as well as 12 Fraternal Orders
(including the famous Workmen's Circle) comprising 982 lodges and 162,000
individuals who paid more than $2 million in dues. Nationwide the 12 Orders
represented more than 2700 lodges and 454,000 members.[53]

No less an authority than Isaac Rubinow declared in 1913 that "outside
of the immigrant groups, Negroes represent the only class of population
where the habit of mutual insurance through voluntary association has
developed to the highest degree in the United States."[54]

Yet the example of these societies was rarely summoned to gain support
for the American system. Indeed there appears to have been an almost
suspicious lack of interest in the details of these organizations. Of the
forty-one volumes published by the United States Immigration Commission
in 1911 only a portion of one unusually slim volume purports to treat the
immigrants' aid societies, but there is no mention of mutual aid. Throughout
the rest of the work there are only scattered references to the subject, one of
which oddly enough noted that among the immigrants of the Pacific coast
and Rocky Mountain areas "The most conspicuous feature perhaps is the
extent to which these various races have organized benevolent societies for
the care of those who met misfortune."[55]

The mutual aid organizations were destined to suffer the same fate as
other signs of healthy immigrant behavior which were either ignored or
twisted into conformity with a negative stereotype, or the negative aspects of
which were blown out of all proportion to the positive features. Like the
Blacks who were accused of being docile and savage or called "uppity" when
independent, the immigrants caused a considerable amount of ambivalence,
illogic, and confusion in the mind of the native American. Their
extraordinary and successful efforts at saving despite low wages were
considered a sign of their greed rather than thrift; their readiness in following
the demands of the labor market was a mark of their unsettled nature rather
than mobility. For their willingness to take the grubbiest jobs and live in the
most vile slums they were charged with having lowered the American
standard of living rather than applauded for having courageously endured the
struggle for survival. When they sent money back home to their families in
the old country this mature act of responsibility was cancelled out by the
concern for the drain of American gold.

In the case of the mutual aid and benevolent societies, the
Immigration Commissions' comment pretty much sums up the feeling. The
immigrants were applauded for being thrifty and for not having to fall
upon charity as much as the Irish and "native races". But the commission

also noted that the mutual aid societies were frequently "indicative of the fact that the race is far from Americanized" and that "they frequently retard the process of assimilation."[56]

In short, their service to the American System was nullified, and they proved to be by virtue of their suspected potential for fostering disloyalty, a good reason for having insurance come under the auspices of the State. By no means were all social welfare reformers as worried as Teddy Roosevelt by these organizations. Quite a number regarded them as essential in the assimilation process particularly in its early phases, for they not only made "for the immigrant the first difficult contacts with American life," but translated "to him new political and social ideals" and insured "that what is best in his old world traditions is not neutralized by the new influence."[57] But even Jane Addams, who more than anyone was responsible for spreading the message of the immigrants' contributions and ability to assimilate, regretted the opportunities missed by the failure to enact state insurance.

> Almost every Sunday in the Italian Quarter in which I live various mutual benefit societies march with fife and drum and with a brave showing of banners, celebrating their achievement in having surrounded themselves by at least a thin wall of protection against disaster, upon having set up their mutual good will against the day of misfortune. These parades have all the emblems of patriotism; indeed, the associations present the primitive core of patriotism, brothers standing by each other against hostile forces from without. I assure you that no Fourth of July celebration, no rejoicing over the birth of an heir to the Italian throne, equals in heartiness and sincerity these simple celebrations. Again one longs to pour into the government of their adopted country all this affection and zeal, this real patriotism. A system of State insurance would be a very simple device and secure a large return.[58]

A related and equally important national need affecting the insurance movement arose from America's new relationship to the rest of the world. It was not simply a question of the requirements of power nor of the prestige that accrues from power — though these were certainly major considerations — for there seemed to be other standards to meet; and these were measured not solely in terms of the citizens' health and efficiency, which would enhance the nation's military might, but also in terms of those intangible assets that enrich the national character. The strength of a government, declared a Colorado Commissioner of Labor, "does not consist in the strength of its standing army, but in the sense of happiness and security against want which it inspires in every citizen within its jurisdiction."[59] The social welfare measures enacted in Europe, wrote another observer, "seem to have assumed for government a new moral obligation. Have these other countries beaten us by a decade to a now old and settled New Nationalism?"[60]

The question was asked repeatedly and more often than not answered in the affirmative, and with great despair. The American eyes cast upon Europe were not merely those of the scientist or logician testing for practicability or validity. They were the eyes of a nation in the throes of a critical self-examination. If nineteenth-century Americans could take legitimate pride in their uniqueness and in their leadership as an enlightened and progressive people and indeed look upon one as the corollary of the other — the Progressive generation questioned the virtue of the one and savored the other only as a reminiscence. Germany's example of discarding the negligence theory has been followed by so many other nations, declared Launcelot Packer, "until we, in spite of our vaunted leadership of the Old World, stand practically alone in maintaining that absolute method."[61]

"It was an outrage," roared Teddy Roosevelt in a special message to Congress in 1908. "It is a reproach to us as a nation that in both Federal and State legislation we have afforded less protection to public and private employees than any other industrial country in the world."[62] When the Employer's Liability Bill of 1908 was debated on the House floor one congressman urged its passage even though it was weak and satisfied no faction. It would mean, he said, "that this great government is not lagging too far behind the other great nations of the earth."[63]

For the most part our failure to keep abreast of Europe was regarded as a mark of our inhumanity or even our barbarism. This was implicit in the sentiment — and expressed in a phrase so commonly articulated that it cannot be ignored — that "every other civilized nation" took better care of its people than the United States. It was this point that Roosevelt made over and over again in his special messages to Congress. Perhaps the unkindest cut of all came from the suggestion that "even" Turkey or Bulgaria or China had more humane social welfare measures than the United States.

There were other concerns too. Some critics felt that our retarded development of social welfare policies indicated a retarded scientific spirit. "Shall we always ... 'stand by the roadside and see the procession go by?'" asked Charles McCarthy. "Shall we always hear the returning traveller's tale of the improvements throughout the entire world with a provincial and smug spirit and be foolish enough to believe that we can learn nothing, while right in our midst are problems which have confronted every nation at some time in its history?"[64] And according to Florence Kelley, the state of American affairs amounted to a confession that our creative talents had run out. "Our inventive genius," she declared, "I think we have never before declared so bankrupt."[65] Graham Taylor summed up our industrial management as a "shame to American democracy."[66]

In some cases perhaps the anxieties over the national self-image had little to do with what Americans feared others thought of them. But in most instances, world public opinion rather clearly was involved. Industrial insurance was needed to keep us on a par with the leading civilized nations of the world, argued Frank Fetter. "It is needed to justify us in the eyes of the world."[67] A concern for world public opinion, moreover, was not confined to any class or segment of society. "It is a fact," wrote Gompers, "that our country is regarded abroad with scorn and contempt when men of any class are discussing the matter of employers' liability in connection with industrial accidents.... The foreigners say that in no other way does our 'plutocracy' so signally exhibit its heartlessness, its greed, and its power to prevent the making of laws that benefit the people."[68] G.N. Wakeley, Secretary of the Expressmen's Aid Society, in a letter purportedly representative of the public response to a Bureau of Labor inquiry, wrote that even though pensions to private employees may be a long way off, at least a first step should be taken in granting civil servants old age benefits because "to be turned out without a cent like an old horse upon a barren common by an inhuman master, does not look good to the outside world."[69]

It would be difficult to assess the degree to which this question of national prestige affected the average American. Presumably the appeal was made in the hope that it would strike a responsive chord among a widespread audience. The editor of the *International Moulders' Journal* for one undoubtedly felt that a few invidious comparisons between the United States and the rest of the world would help the cause. "It is astonishing to the average individual," wrote John P. Frey to John B. Andrews of the American Association for Labor Legislation, "to discover that in the field of labor legislation our country lags far behind the other civilized nations of the earth, and nothing can tend to bring out these facts as much as the work which is being done by the association."[70] Whatever its effect, the proponents of social security were taking an aspect of that issue which had heretofore been one of the principal marks against it — namely, its alien origin — and meeting it head-on as one of the chief psychological weapons in favor of the new measures. In much the same way that Progressive nationalism in the areas of foreign affairs had forsaken traditional American isolation in favor of a more active participation in international power politics; so in domestic affairs it replaced the panygeric to our unique way of life with a plea to fall in line with the rest of the civilized world.

Actually the customary tendency to stress the distinctiveness of American life and the American character had always suffered from a somewhat myopic interpretation of the facts. In the field of social welfare, especially, American ideals and practices, although unique, were nonetheless largely adaptations of European and, particularly, English models. The earliest and most fundamental of the social welfare structures — the Poor Law system — was inherited from the English. Even many of the later modifications followed trends of the former mother country. It is true that the American laws lacked the integrity that comes from a centralized administration; the United States had nothing comparable to the English Poor Law Commission. Yet judging by the endless American references to the findings of its 1834 report, the English Commission served informally as an American commission as well. Many of its findings were still being cited as gospel some forty years later when Americans inaugurated their charity organization movement, another English import. And it was not long after the birth of this movement that Stanton Coit, inspired by his experience at Toynbee Hall, transplanted the settlement house idea. Americans not only copied but retained through correspondence and periodic visiting strong connections with their English counterparts.

As was the case with many of our legal principles the basic law of Employer's Liability and its modifications through the courts and legislatures were essentially borrowed from the English. This was true of a mid-nineteenth-century decision that significantly altered the liability to the advantage of the employer and it was true of subsequent reforms that slowly reversed the trend in favor of the injured worker.

Moreover the formal economic principles that lent theoretical support to the social welfare practices were, likewise, the creations of the European intellectual community. The English school held sway until challenged in the 1880's, when with the return of "these young men from Germany," the American Economic Association prepared to do battle with laissez-faire. Henry C. Adams, who was all in favor of removing the "crust" that had formed on the doctrines of Adam Smith, nevertheless found it distressing and ironic that the proponents of German historicism seemed to have little appreciation for the unique development of the American nation. "Is it not absurd," he asked, "for American economists to array themselves in opposing schools as advocates of what is English or what is German?"[71]

The discussions here as elsewhere toward the end of the nineteenth century suggest that Americans were shedding their parochialism, or at least not allowing the celebration of American uniqueness to get in the way of their receptivity to frankly alien ideas. Even Henry C. Adams paid tribute to the lessons of the German school. "I am not," he said, "arguing for obstinence but for independence."[72]

Although it was not until just before the turn of the century — more than fifteen years after Germany inaugurated her social insurance program — that Americans began taking serious and sympathetic notice of the European experiments, the delay cannot be attributed entirely to a rigid stance on American uniqueness. For the discernibly sharp rise of American interest in social insurance roughly corresponds to the agitation in England for old age pensions, sparked largely by General Booth's studies on the London and Liverpool slums, and to passage of the first English compensation act in 1897. In 1898, Edward Devine went so far as to issue a mild rebuke to the London COS for standing too rigidly against the tide of English opinion that wanted to thwart individual provision against accidents, sickness and old age. "We need not," Devine declared, "too readily accept the exact point of view of our more experienced and perhaps wiser cousins [the London COS] across the sea. They are possibly over conservative. New departures are perhaps too difficult with them. Possibly experiment is not estimated highly enough."[73]

As the American movement took on a life of its own, about 1902, the subsequent revisions and expansions of the English laws continued to make an equally great if not greater impact in the United States. "The passage in 1906 of the English Workmen's Compensation Act," according to Frederick L. Hoffman, "has crystallized American opinion, more perhaps than any other measure and in some of the most important states the question of Employer's Liability is under serious discussion."[74]

This is not to say that Germany had no influence on the American social security movement. Many of its supporters had at least a deep admiration for Germany as the world's leading social reform country. It was a time, as the editor of *Everybody's Magazine* wrote, to "take your hat off to Germany. . . ."[75] A number of social insurance advocates went so far as to express a preference for the German system. Indeed the English-German polarization that began among social scientists in the 1880's continued well into the Progressive Era, affecting the debates on the social security question as well as other reform measures. Some who took sides were highly selective in their preference for the German system, praising parts of it while suspecting the whole.[76] As compared with the English workmen's compensation and old age pensions, for example, the German program made much more use of employee contributions. But many of the most ardent advocates of social insurance, like Charles McCarthy, Charles R. Henderson and William Hard, looked upon the German system as the model because it was efficient, comprehensive and above all scientific. And their efforts to incorporate as many of the German principles as possible into the American social welfare measures cannot be discounted.[77] Yet, however influential these men were and however much they drew inspiration from Germany, had it not been for England, their influence as well as Germany's may not have gotten much beyond the academic circles.

In a sense the English venture brought to the movement a kind of respectability that the German experiment could never offer, since the association of social security with Germany in particular was probably more damaging than the identification with Europe in general. Encouraged by the interest being taken in the subject in 1909, Charles Henderson remarked that "a few years ago all suggestions were hushed by the sneering epithets, 'socialism,' 'sentimentalism,' 'paternalism,' and a hint that one was corrupted by German 'absolutism.'"[78] Even after the identification bore little relevance to the facts, the hint was still being dropped. In 1910 one member of the NAM saw fit to quote a warning of Secretary of Commerce, Charles Nagel that "we should not be unmindful of the fact that other countries have approached the question from the state of absolute government, whereas we have advanced from the other position."[79]

"In England itself, that stronghold of individualism," Willoughby early took note, "the compensation of injured workingmen by their employers is obligatory."[80] As an editorial in the Boston *Transcript* suggested several years later, the English social legislation is all the "more astounding in the fact that it should have been undertaken by the staidest of all governments. . . . May it not be that the time has come for us, after all, to frame slightly larger conceptions of government than we have been holding?"[81]

The United States Industrial Commission very early sensed the pull of the English legislation when in 1901 it declared that although German paternalism was "entirely foreign to American theories of government," their insurance program deserved some mention in the commission's report "particularly as there is already English legislation tending in the same direction, and it is possible that the movement may extend to this country."[82] Many of those who preferred the German form of social insurance also were quick to point out the progress in England. William Hard, for example, defended the first English Compensation Act with a sarcasm that would have been misplaced had it been applied to a comparable piece of German legislation. "This hideous assault on property," he declared, "was accomplished in the parliament of 1897 by a trio of political adventurers, consisting of that unbridled visionary, Joseph Chamberlain, that ruthless revolutionist, Arthur Balfour, and that red-handed proletarian, the Marquis of Salisbury."[83] Miles Dawson, using a similar technique before an audience of businessmen tried to break down their resistance against the compulsory aspects of the German workmen's compensation act by showing that the English themselves were no longer convinced that compulsion was alien to the Anglo-Saxon spirit. "They are adopting compulsion in Great Britain as an accepted national proposition. It is today one of the vital parts of the program of the existing administration that they shall introduce compulsion in the insurance against sickness and invalidity and in the isurance against unemployment."[84]

For all of Germany's acknowledged leadership in the area of social welfare and for all the accolades showered upon her alledgedly superior system, she had the stiffest competition from England when it came to actual implementation of the compensation laws in America. The American states had, as in the past, copied the British. P. Tecumseh Sherman, explaining the reasons for adapting the English laws, expressed a common sentiment of the day: the continental laws may be better in some respects, he conceded, but "we think that the English laws as a basis, furnish the easiest path by which we in America can run the proper stage of compensating workmen for accidents."[85] This was also the path taken by the Wainwright Commission of New York in preparing for that state the first piece of modern social security legislation. By and large, the state compensation acts that followed were, as one observer noted, something between the English laws of 1897 and 1906.[86]

England, thus, provided the model as well as the initial seal of approval for compulsory-collective security programs. She provided something else: an incentive in addition to those stimulated by the failures of the American system. It was not so much Germany the "radical" and "absolutist" nation that gave many Americans a feeling of inferiority. Running through most of the comments on our need to follow Europe was the suggestion that if "conservative," "staid," "individual" England could do it, we better had also.

No sooner had the English compensation movement borne its first fruits than the pressures in America to keep pace were widely felt. It was not, for example, so much our susceptibility to the English influence that troubled the New York labor commissioner in 1899; rather it was the time lag. The 1880 English liability law, wrote John McMackin, was liberal for its day but no longer satisfactory in England. Yet, he complained, "even today the American workingmen are prone to take it as a model for proposed legislation."[87] A decade later, Charles Henderson threw up his hands for similar reasons. The English Compensation Act is being urged upon the United States, he said, "because it is English. But," he declared, "the British Act is itself a pioneer experiment; and heretofore, as in the case of the poor laws and employer's liability laws we have imitated England only after that nation has abandoned an untenable position."[88]

NOTES

[1] Abbot, *Public Assistance,* pp. 125-128, 220.

[2] Bruno, *Trends,* pp. 133-134; Lubove, *Professional Altruist,* pp. 23, 35.

[3] Feder, *Relief of Unemployment,* pp. 191-192; Mary E. Richmond, *Social Diagnosis* (New York, 1917), pp. 38-50.

[4] Edward Devine, "Social Forces," *Charities and Commons,* XIX (1907), pp. 1083-1084.

[5] Charles R. Henderson, *Modern Methods of Charity* (New York, 1904), pp. 16-17.

[6] CUSS, Homer Folks MSS Scrapbook Clipping from Brooklyn *Daily Eagle* dated January 19, 1903.

[7] U.S. Bureau of the Census, *Summary of State Laws Relating to the Dependent Classes* (G.P.O. 1913), p. 5.

[8] Kathleen Woodroofe, *From Charity to Social Work* (London, 1962), Chap. V.

[9] Bruno, *Trends in Social Work,* pp. 220-229. Also see: Julian Mack, "Social Progress," NCOCC. *Thirty-Ninth Annual Report* (1912), pp. 1-11; Davis, *Spearheads for Reform,* Chap. 10.

[10] LC National Women's Trade Union League, MSS, Vol. I, March 1905.

[11] AALL MSS, 12-R, Arthur Kellog to John R. Commons, December 23, 1908.

[12] AALL MSS, 12 R. Charles Henderson to John R. Commons, August 17, 1908.

[13] Darwin P. Kingsley, *Life Insurance and the Moral Obligation of the Employer,* National Civic Federation (1909) p. 5.

[14] *American Federationist,* XVII, 1910, p. 596; NCOCC, *Thirty-Second Annual Report* (1905), p. 580.

[15] Alpheus Thomas Mason, *The Brandeis Way* (Princeton, 1938), Chapters IV and V see esp. pp. 84-98, 139.

[16] Louis D. Brandeis, "Massachusetts Savings Bank Annuity Plan," National Civic Federation, *Ninth Annual Meeting* (1908), p. 81.

[17] Haley Fiske, "Industrial Insurance by Private Companies," *Ibid.,* pp. 100-101.

[18] Marcus M. Marks, "Postal Savings Banks," National Civic Federation, *Ninth Annual Meeting* (1908), p. 88.

[19] National Civic Federation, *Ninth Annual Meeting* (1908), pp. 204-206.

[20] Louise Bolard More, *Wage Earners Budgets* (New York, 1907), p. 269; see also Bremner, *From the Depths*, p. 153.

[21] Marguerite Green, *The National Civic Federation and the American Labor Movement, 1900-1925* (Washington, 1956), p. 267ff.

[22] Murray Webb Latimer, *Industrial Pension Systems* (New York, 1932), p. 26; U.S. Commissioner of Labor, *Twenty-Third Annual Report*, pp. 36-39, 387-388; Murray Webb Latimer, *Trade Union Pension Systems* (New York, 1932), pp. 128-129.

[23] Lee Frankel to Charles Henderson, CPY, August 9, 1908, ILR, AALL MSS.

[24] NAM, *Proceedings of the Fourteenth Annual Convention* (1909), p. 234.

[25] Charles R. Henderson, "Workingman's Accident Insurance," *Charities and Commons*, XVII (1907), p. 825.

[26] Henry Seager, "Outline of a Program of Social Reform," *Charities and Commons*, XVII (1907), p. 832; see also: Adna F. Weber, "Public Policy in Relation to Industrial Accidents," *Journal of Social Science*, XL (1902), p. 40.

[27] Frank W. Lewis, *State Insurance* (Boston and New York, 1909), pp. 55-56.

[28] Massachusetts, *Report of the Commission on Old Age Pensions, Annuities and Insurance* (Boston, 1910), p. 310.

[29] *Ibid.*, p. 313.

[30] NAM, *Proceedings of the Fifteenth Annual Convention* (1910), p. 85.

[31] U.S. *Congressional Record*, 60th Cong., 1st Sess., XLII (1908), appendix, p. 334.

[32] Rubinow, *Social Insurance*, pp. 305, 405-406.

[33] Latimer, *Industrial Pension Systems*, pp. 470-471, 161.

[34] Latimer, *Trade Union Pension Systems*, pp. 128-129; see also: Charles R. Henderson, *Industrial Insurance in the United States*, 2nd Ed. (Chicago, 1909); Rubinow, *Social Insurance*, pp. 43-45, 292-293.

[35] Seager, *Social Insurance*, p. 119.

[36] Quoted in: Mason, *Brandeis*, p. 135.

[37] *Ibid.*, p. 53.

[38] More, *Wage Earners Budgets*, p. vii; Paul Douglas, *Real Wages in the United States 1890-1926* (Boston: 1930), Chap. XIII, exp. pp. 230-232.

[39] Massachusetts, *Report, Commission on Old Age Pensions* (1910), p. 314.

[40] Ellice M. Alger, *The Conservation of Vision*, December 14, 1911.

[41] Irving Fisher, *National Vitality* (Washington, 1910); William Hard, "Pensions of Peace," *Everybody's Magazine*, XIX (October, 1908), p. 530.

[42] See for example Lubove, *Struggle for Social Security*, pp. 23-24, 4-8.

[43] See for example Edward Devine, "Immigration as a Relief Problem", *Charities*, vol. XII, (February 9, 1904), pp. 129-133; Robert Hunter, "Immigration – The Annihilation of our Native Stock", *Commons*, vol. XI, (1904); Kate Holloday Claghorn, "Immigration in its Relation to Pauperism", *Annals of the American Academy of Political and Social Science*, vol. 24, (1904), pp. 187-205; for an excellent analysis of welfare reformers and the immigration question see especially John Higham, *Strangers in the Land: Patterns of American Nativism*, (New Brunswick, N.J.: 1955); and Davis, *Spearheads for Reform*, Chap. 5.

[44] Elizabeth Read, "The Gentle Art of Alienating the Alien", *Immigrants in America Review*, vol. I, (1915), pp. 70-79.

[45] Quoted in Philip Davis and Bertha Schwartz, *Immigration and Americanization*, (Boston: 1920), p. 481.

[46] Lillian Wald, *The House on Henry Street,* (New York: 1915), p. 292.

[47] Frances Kellor, "Americanization", in Davis, *Immigration,* p. 627. The issue is frequently discussed in *Immigrants in America Review,* see especially editorials, Vol. I (1915), No. 1, p. 4 in same; also Raymond Cale, "The City's Responsibility to the Immigrant" in same., pp. 36-41.

[48] Theodore Roosevelt, "Americanism" in Davis, *Immigration,* p. 655.

[49] Robert E. Park and Herbert Miller, *Old World Traits Transplanted,* (New York: 1921), pp. 128-130.

[50] Thomas Capek, *The Czechs in America,* (New York: 1920), Chap. 18, pp. 263-264.

[51] *Report,* 1914, pp. 203-207.

[52] Park and Miller, *Old World Traits,* p. 128.

[53] Leo Wolfson, "Jewish Fraternal Organizations", *Jewish Communal Register,* (New York: 1917), pp. 865-867; Frank F. Rosenblatt, "Mutual Aid Organizations", *JCR,* pp. 732-735.

[54] Rubinow, *Social Insurance,* p. 283.

[55] U.S. *Abstracts of the Reports of the Immigration Commission,* Senate Document 747, (Washington: 1911), p. 650.

[56] *Ibid.,* p. 650.

[57] *Immigrants in America Review,* Vol. I, (1915), p. 54.

[58] Jane Addams, *New Ideals of Peace,* (New York: 1911), pp. 90-91; see also Henderson, *Industrial Insurance,* p. 83.

[59] National Association of Officials of Bureaus of Labor Statistics, *Seventeenth Annual Report,* (1901), p. 99.

[60] Quoted in: McCarthy, *Wisconsin Idea,* p. 298.

[61] Launcelot Packer, "Accidents of Industry," National Civic Federation, *Ninth Annual Report* (1908), p. 143; see also NAM, *Proceedings of the Fifteenth Annual Convention* (1910), pp. 187-189.

[62] U.S. Congressional Record, 60th Cong., 1st Sess, XLII (1908), p. 3853.

[63] *Ibid.,* p. 6415.

[64] McCarthy, *The Wisconsin Idea,* pp. 296-297.

[65] NCCC, *Thirty-Second Annual Report* (1905), p. 578.

[66] *Ibid.,* p. 579.

[67] Frank Fetter, "The Need of Industrial Insurance," NCCC, *Thirty-Third Annual Report* (1906), p. 470.

[68] *American Federationist,* XVII (March, 1910), p. 220.

[69] G.N. Wakeley to Robert M. Durham, February 22, 1909, LC, RG 257, Ethelbert Stewart MSS, Bx. 32.

[70] John P. Frey to John B. Andrews, February 22, 1910, ILR, AALL MSS.

[71] ADAMS, "Relation of the State," *AEA,* I (1885-86), p. 493.

[72] *Ibid.*

[73] Edward Devine, "A Trip to England," *Charities* I (November, 1898), p. 4.

[74] Frederick L. Hoffman, "Fatal Accidents in Coal Mines of North America," *The Engineering and Mining Journal* (December 25, 1909).

[75] *Everybody's Magazine* (1912), p. 180.

[76] Henry L. Rosenfeld, "Cooperation and Compensation vs. Compulsion and Compromise in Employer's Liability," NAM, *Proceedings of the Fifteenth Annual Convention* (1910), p. 174.

77 Charles McCarthy, *The Wisconsin Idea* (1912), p. 10; William Hard, "Pensioners of Peace," *Everybody's Magazine,* XIX (October, 1908), p. 527; see for example, "Symposium [on the German System]," *Survey,* XXVIII (May 4, 1912), pp. 232-249.

78 Charles Henderson, "Logic of Social Insurance," *Annals of the American Academy of Political and Social Science,* XXXIII (March, 1909), p. 2.

79 NAM, *Proceedings of the Fifteenth Annual Convention* (1910), p. 209.

80 Willoughby, *Workingmen's Insurance,* p. 333.

81 Quoted in McCarthy, *Wisconsin Idea,* p. 297.

82 United States Industrial Commission, *Report... on the Relations and Conditions of Capital and Labor,* VI (1901), p. 229.

83 William Hard, "Pensioners of Peace," *Everybody's Magazine,* XIX (October, 1908), p. 531.

84 NAM, *Proceedings of the Fifteenth Annual Convention* (1910), p. 199.

85 NYPL MSS, MCF, "Workmen's Compensation," C25, "Compensation Committee Minutes," May 25, 1910.

86 New York, Commission Appointed under Chapter 518 of the Laws of 1909 to Inquire into the Question of Employers' Liability and other Matters, *Report to the Legislature of the State of New York,* First Report (March 19,1910), Albany, 1910, p. 50.

87 New York, Bureau of Labor Statistics, *Seventeenth Annual Report* (1899), Albany, 1900, p. 652.

88 Charles Henderson, "Logic of Social Insurance," *Annals of the American Academy of Political and Social Science,* XXXIII (March, 1909), p. 2.

CHAPTER V

WORKMEN'S COMPENSATION AND INDUSTRIAL ACCIDENTS, 1902 – 1911

There is little in pre-Progressive history suggesting that the injured worker would receive priority in the early twentieth-century social security movement. Unemployment far more than industrial accidents had been the central problem because of the numbers affected and because of its potential as a threat to the individual's self-reliance as well as to society's stability. When it was common to consider unemployment as a self-induced problem the idle worker received more abuse than any other indigent, and during the 1890's, when it became somewhat more fashionable to regard unemployment as a dysfunction in the economy, the problem triggered a set of responses that were instrumental in giving birth to the social security movement.

Even judging by the attention the question of accidental injuries received in the first formal investigations of social insurance between 1902 and 1905, there is little hint that workmen's compensation would be the first of the social security measures enacted. It is not simply that the social security movement began rather amorphously with discussions that concentrated on abstract principles of social justice or on the question of workingmen's insurance in general. That was to be expected. But even where there was some discernable focus on a specific area, insurance or pensions for the aged received far more consideration than workmen's compensation.

But if the injured worker played only a secondary role in calling attention to the problem of insecurity and received less attention than the aged in the first stage of the social security movement, his case was the one most capable of solution. And in spite of a rather slow start, by 1908 it was clear that he would be the first to benefit from a modern social security program. Insofar as it lent itself to a solution through social security, the problem of industrial accidents had several practical advantages over the problems of old age and unemployment. Perhaps the critical difference lay in the fact that the injured worker traditionally had a remedy in the law of Employer's Liability. Thus, workmen's compensation, in contrast to other forms of social security, represented a redefinition or expansion of certain limited rights the worker already had. Although in practice Employer's Liability generally served to protect the interests of the employer against complaints of his negligence, the worker was able to press and expand his claims throughout the late nineteenth and early twentieth centuries. It was not so much the minimal gains of the worker that bore on the question, however; rather it was the extent to which the liability system created new problems without solving old ones and in the process laid bare the flaws in the American system.

By 1910, only two years after the concerted drive for workmen's compensation had begun, a modern social security law was on the books in New York State. This first piece of workmen's compensation legislation was soon declared illegal by the New York Court of Appeals, but that proved to be only a temporary setback to the movement.

* * * * *

National agitation for workmen's compensation had begun inauspiciously enough as part of an exploration of the whole subject of social security. At the American Sociological Conference of 1902, many of the later proponents of the measure approached compensation with a good deal of caution. Samuel Gompers remained noncommittal but hinted at opposition to it. More than likely many at the convention realized as did J.R. Burnet, a representative of the New York Bar, that no widespread demand existed for workmen's compensation, that the question was still essentially academic. And Carroll Wright got the distinct impression that few of the participants really understood the question.[1]

Discussion and agitation continued, nonetheless. If the ill-fated Maryland Workmen's Compensation Act (1902) found no one to appeal the decision of the inferior court neither this nor any other of the setbacks dampened the growing national enthusiasm for the compensation idea. A Massachusetts commission in 1904 urged passage of a law based on the British Act but the recommendations fell upon deaf ears. And for several years, beginning in 1904, the Massachusetts legislature considered and rejected a workmen's compensation bill. The National Conference of Charities and Correction, having created an investigating committee in 1902, debated the merits of industrial insurance at the 1905 and 1906 annual meetings. Here, as in the social science convention the treatment of the subject included all forms of workingmen's insurance and the conference spent most of its time on the question of aged dependency. One of the participants suggested that since old age security was in the far distant future it might be better to devote more consideration to the pressing problem of accidental injury. Accident insurance did have several enthusiastic boosters at these meetings, among whom were Charles Henderson, Florence Kelley, Professor Frank Fetter, Secretary of the American Economic Association, and the Rt. Rev. Samuel Fallows. Yet neither the conference nor the special investigating committee could agree on anything more than that the states should begin to encourage the formation of the voluntary-collective type of industrial insurance. Reverend Samuel Smith, President of the NCOCC announced that the mobility of labor and the size of the unemployment problem render "the whole scheme of workingmen's insurance as totally impossible."[2] Even John Brooks, strongly affirming the soundness of the principle, nevertheless apologized for having to draw the same conclusion he had reached years before when he prepared the Labor Department report on the German system: that America would have to wait another ten years before embarking upon the experiment. The principal stumbling block, Brooks contended, was the sad state of the American civil service which could wreck any industrial insurance program within a year. A more immediate barrier, however, was the federal-state system of the American government. The time was not yet ripe for federal agitation, and he asked, "is there immediate hope of inducing a single state to try it?"[3]

Illinois offered some promise. In 1905 the state legislature unanimously passed a resolution calling for an industrial insurance commission. "There can be no apprehension more keen," declared the resolution, "than the constant clinging dread that when misfortune strikes there will be lacking the means necessary for ordinary maintenance." The commission members were all carefully chosen, and in 1907, when they made their report to the governor, they applauded the completeness of the German insurance system; they took note of the fact that all the great nations of the world had adopted some form of social insurance; and they assured the governor that the United States would not "long remain morally in the rear." But the commissioners offered as their recommendation merely a bill that would authorize the employers and employees to establish a mutual compensation plan which would then remove the employer from the liability laws.[4]

From time to time, individual businessmen, particularly those in the railroad industry, tried to shift attention away from liability and towards the compensation principle.[5] Yet, the most powerful voices among the business community remained virtually silent on the issue. On one of those rare occasions that the National Association of Manufacturers recognized the dangers of factory life, the reference was a thinly veiled attack upon the unions. C.W. Post, head of Postum Cereal Co., thus urged employers to inspect their plant and equipment scrupulously so as to eliminate all possibility of an accident due to their negligence. "Then make a contract with each employee," continued Post, "so carefully drawn that you will be protected from injustice ... and when accidents happen not from the faults of another make it impossible for a crafty designing person to extract money from anyone not owing that money and not responsible for such injury." Post characterized the union efforts to liberalize the liability laws as a tendency to "baby" the workers. "If a woodworker saws off his finger," declared Post, "he wants the employer to pay for it."[6]

Actually organized labor showed scarcely any more enthusiasm for compensation. Indeed, until 1906, when the liability law was debated in Congress, even this question received no more than routine treatment in the *American Federationist,* and in the annual meetings of the American Federation of Labor. Significantly though, by 1907, Gompers' suspicion of the compensation principle seemed to be fading. In the midst of what he regarded as an encouraging but still fruitless awakening to the yearly slaughter and maiming in the American factory, he bemoaned the timidity of the Illinois Commission and took favorable note of the 1906 English Compensation Act.[7]

Equally significant, so much of the ferment over worker insecurity was beginning to converge on the problem of accidental injuries. The passage in 1906 of the rather liberal Federal Employer's Liability Act and the stirring messages by Roosevelt in favor of extending the measure, were both portentous events. *Charities and Commons*, though suggesting that Roosevelt might very well be "the most potent force" in the land, could not tell whether his activities were the sign of a new social program or "merely the high water mark before a period of inaction and reaction."[8]

The Compensation movement was, despite some skepticism, entering a new phase;[9] and the American Association for Labor Legislation and the National Civic Federation were both in the process of harnessing and directing the new energies. As a replacement for the liability laws the compensation principle would remain something of a mystery. "These topics are so confused in the minds of many of us, " wrote an official of the AALL to Henderson in 1908, "that it would be a splendid thing if you could write five or six hundred words explaining the common use of the term."[10] H.R. Fuller, spokesman for the railroad brotherhoods expressed a fear that Congress might rush into compensation legislation even before the workers understood what compensation was all about.[11] Clearly, though, the die was cast by 1908. The agitation for it, according to one eminent economist, was "smoldering" and "likely to be fanned into a flame at any time."[12]

Although industrial accidents neither posed the greatest single threat to social order nor accounted for the largest single number of dependent persons, the problem of the injured worker understandably received priority in the social security movement. The injured worker suffered not only financial loss and mental anguish, but physical pain, disability and in many cases, death. The circumstances surrounding the accident were of a violent and inherently dramatic nature. And if the public could possibly remain indifferent to the constant exploitation of these tragedies by the press, there were always the crippled reminders in every industrial area. Moreover, by any standard, the number of accidental injuries was appalling. There were more deaths each year on the railroads alone than in the Spanish American War. In 1910 more than 3,300 railroad employees were killed in accidents arising out of the operation or movement of trains. Another 95,000 were wounded in the same way.

Estimates of most industrial accidents were inaccurate but as more inquiries were made, the guesses were constantly revised upwards. By 1910, the most conservative figures put the annual number of injured at 500,000 and the number of deaths at about 25,000. Moreover, the problem of accidental injuries was easily defined. While even experts pondered whether the term unemployment applied to the man who refused to work for substandard wages, or one fired because of incompetence or one willy-nilly seeking work, no such difficulty existed in reference to the accidental injury. It could be recognized with relative ease and though the statistics were faulty their rates were potentially predictable.

Until now the injured worker had not been as prominently discussed a figure as the aged dependent, yet neither could the former's cries for help be silenced by the steady stream of money that flowed into the pockets of the latter in the form of a Civil War pension. On the other hand, the injured worker, through the employers' liability laws, did have a limited though expandable remedy.

Essentially, the liability law placed an obligation on the employer when his personal negligence caused injury to one of his employees. Until the turn of the century most employers had a battery of defenses which even in pre-industrial days made proof of personal negligence a difficult task at best. If, for example, the injured employee shared slight blame for the accident, his "contributory negligence" completely absolved the employer. Or, if the worker having knowledge of the peril of his work remained on the job, he could not recover damages. In this case, the courts declared the worker to have "assumed the risk" on the theory that he was free to seek less dangerous employment. In the 1840's American courts adopting a recent English modification further weakened the position of the worker. Prior to this change, the principle of "Respondent superiore" charged the employer with responsibility for injuries to servants resulting from the negligence of another worker or fellow servant. Thus in what seems to be an almost perverse concession to the changing nature of business enterprise, the courts through the new "fellow servant" doctrine released the employer from responsibility for the negligent acts of his underlings at the very time he was turning over to them more authority in directing his operations.

As the mechanization of American industry advanced, these defenses tended to nullify the protective element of the law. Complicated machinery run by men working a ten or twelve-hour day increased the likelihood of the employee contributing to the negligence. Large-scale operations reduced the possibility of a worker ever becoming fully familiar with the dangers of his employment or the faults of his fellow servants. In a small shop with few pieces of equipment the worker might easily have been aware of improperly functioning machinery or of conditions that could set off an explosion. In large factories this knowledge would require a daily inspection tour. By officially notifying the employer of the hazards of his work, the employee risked being fired, and with the ever-present threat of poor job markets, the freedom to seek other employment presented him with a hollow alternative. Thus the worker often found himself the victim of men against whose negligence he found no practical remedy.[13]

Efforts to liberalize the employers' liability met with moderate success. Following Georgia's lead in 1855 a number of states modified or eliminated the fellow servant doctrine. By 1900, seven states had eliminated this defense in all or most of the cases involving an accident on the railroads. Nine state legislatures restricted the definition of "fellow servant" so as to exclude foremen and other workers in a position of authority. And six states applied this "vice principle" doctrine more broadly, covering mining and, in a few cases, all industries in the state. In addition, twelve state legislatures curtailed the "contracting out" clauses, a device whereby the employer sought to release himself from legal liability by forcing the worker to accept the company's relief association as an alternative.[14]

Although the state courts often reversed the legislatures or gave their modifications the least liberal interpretation, the worker continued to profit by legislative changes in the early years of the twentieth century. Several states adopted the principle of "comparative negligence" enabling the injured worker either to recover partial damages or to claim full damages in the event his own negligence was slight. Workers also had less to fear from their having assumed the risk of their trade. Notably in those states with safety codes, violations of them by the employer usually established a *prima facie* case of negligence against him and precluded his using "assumption of risk" as a defense. Though somewhat limited in its power to regulate these matters, the federal government played a part in this movement, too. In 1893, Congress declared that interstate commerce violators of the Automatic Coupling Bill would lose certain defenses. A few years later federal law broadly but apparently rather vaguely limited "contracting out" in interstate operations. It was not until 1906, however, that Congress passed legislation significant enough to set standards for the states.

Resistance to these reforms proved strongest, naturally enough, among employers of labor and particularly among railroad operators against whom most of the modifications were directed. The economic motive, of course, was strong and grew stronger. Accidents were increasing; the liberalization of the laws invited more court cases; and insurance costs were being adjusted accordingly. Employers, however, also argued that it was unwise to tamper with the "wisdom of the ages." One senator who championed their cause in the Congressional battles of 1893, declared that the "assumption of risk" principle was "the product of a long series of years, of many decisions, of the philosophy of the best minds which have been devoted to the elucidation of the subject."[15] Even the "fellow servant" doctrine, barely a half century old, was described by its defenders as hoary with age. They claimed that the traditional defenses were the best means of preserving justice and of providing a safeguard against employee carelessness. They generally pictured the worker as most often to blame for an accident and on occasion suggested that he threw himself into a machine in order to collect damages.[16]

The opponents of the expanded liability laws also raised constitutional questions. In the Congressional debates of 1906, for example, the controversy centered around three basic points. The first dealt with the legality of Congress to single out certain extra-hazardous occupations, making them, in effect, the objects of "class" legislation. The second involved the power of Congress to regulate the master-servant relations or to interfere with the freedom of contract. Both of these points had also been made in the various states and as in the case of federal legislation were generally unsuccessful arguments. The third issue, and the one upon which the courts ultimately declared the 1906 Act invalid, concerned inappropriate inclusion of intra-state operations in a bill designed to regulate inter-state commerce.[17] The victory, however, was short-lived. The law was easily amendable to satisfy the court and the pressures from the White House down to pass a new law were too great to overcome. The mood in Congress and in the nation had changed so in two years that by 1908, when a new and even more liberal version was discussed and passed one of the Senators grumbled "that men of all parties here or elsewhere, are tumbling over each other in the effort to appear as its chief advocate."[18]

While the United States government was passing this far reaching liability bill, it was ironically, also declaring the futility of the liability system. On March 27, 1908, the federal government inaugurated a compensation program for its own employees. In spite of the limited scope of the bill, never before had so many workers come under the protective principle of workmen's compensation. And regardless of the fact that the government was acting in its capacity as an employer, the action seemed to be an important stimulant in the whole compensation movement. According to I.M. Rubinow, an activist in and student of the movement, a "large interest in the problem grew up" as a result of the federal law, weak as this was.[19] A number of states now moved more rapidly into the field. New York set up what was probably the most ambitious investigation commission — the Wainwright Commission. The American Association for Labor Legislation took upon itself the task of coordinating efforts in the various states and set up a series of National Conferences on Workmen's Compensation, composed of the newly appointed state investigators and interested parties. The first of these conferences, meeting in Atlantic City in 1909, made little headway. Only three states had by this time appointed a commission and the handful of delegates parried with each other, seemingly in search of a leader. Within a year, however, the second and third conferences had many more delegates and they expressed few qualms about the essential and immediate importance of the cause which they sponsored.[20] By 1910, moreover, the movement had much stronger backing from both labor and business groups. Gompers now referred to the modifications of the liability laws as "tinkering and trifling with measures of great import," as nothing but "transparent pettifogging."[21] Ralph Easley, executive secretary of the National Civic Federation, declared that while progress should be slow, "it is desired if possible to avoid prolonged experimentation."[22] The National Association of Manufacturers seemed reluctantly ready to accept the inevitable but was still hopeful of preventing a compulsory program by prodding the businessmen into initiating voluntary systems throughout the country. The NAM's industrial Insurance Committee declared that the "national reputation" was at stake in this matter: "We have succeeded in other directions not only in equalling Old World nations ... but in surpassing them. We can and must excel European nations in this direction."[23] By 1910, then, something approaching a consensus on the compensation principle was definitely forming. If nothing else, all the weaknesses of the liability system were being exposed in every quarter.

As a means of coping with the dislocations caused by accidental injury, the liability laws and all other components of the American system had long since proved their disutility. To begin with, the settlements in court were rarely swift. Even where the employee ultimately received damages he had no source of income during the litigation, when he most needed medical attention and when the physical discomfort alone made adjustment difficult. President-elect Taft singled out the delay in the courts as one of the gravest injustices in the whole system. If we could "remove from the courts nine-tenths of those suits brought for recovery of damages," declared Taft, we would confer a great benefit on labor "for in such cases the old rule that 'He who gives quickly gives twice' applies."[24] In many cases, the suits dragged on for months or years. At the very time Taft made this appeal, the suit involving an explosion on the steamship Tioga in 1890 was still pending. After numerous reports and eleven volumes of testimony taken by a Commissioner for the Federal Courts in Chicago, no decision had been reached. All the damage has been done, declared William Hard in one of his more moving appeals.

> "The widows who were forced to beg, they have begged. The children who failed to get an education, they have failed to be educated. . . . Everything connected with the case is finished. Except the case itself. The only thing that survives is that thin legal emanation from the dead body of a human problem long since resolved into its elements. The ghost of the Tioga affair still goes soft-footing along the corridors of the Federal Building but the Tioga affair itself breathed its last warm, human breath many years ago."[25]

Although juries were returning more verdicts favorable to the worker and awarding him higher damages, the payments were more than likely inadequate. Charity offices were still flooded with applications from injured workers who had "won" their suits or settled out of courts. There were, to be sure, very substantial awards but these, though they caught the public eye, were far from common. In a special study of fatal accidents in Erie county, for example, the Wainwright Commission produced figures that bore out the recent findings of the United States Labor Department: out of 103 married men killed and whose cases were closed, only eight received more than $2,000; thirty-eight of the beneficiaries obtained nothing; in forty-three cases less than $500 was paid.[26]

The lawyer, of course, had a claim on the money awards too. Though his fees varied with the type of settlement, they usually amounted to somewhere between 25% and 50% of damages. In one small sample of fifty-one negligence cases studied by the New York Commission, fourteen of them were resolved with the lawyer getting more money than the client.[27] This type of drain on the injured workers' compensation, however, was merely symbolic of the more serious faults of the entire liability system. The problem lay not only in the failure of American industry to make provisions for industrial accidents but also in the inefficient distribution of these expenditures. Of all the money spent on accidental injuries more wound up in the pockets of the lawyers and insurance companies than in those of the injured worker. Out of the $23,500,000 gross premium receipts of ten New York Insurance companies between 1906 and 1908, for example, workers received $8,500,000 or about 36%.[28]

Although dissatisfaction with the Employer's Liability was widespread not all critics agreed that the liability concept should be scrapped. Both employers and employees concentrated their fire on the current abuses of the laws or upon the barnacles that encumbered the system.[29] Yet had the laws and the system of administering them been corrected by removing all the defenses of the employer, or by regulating the lawyers fees, or by establishing some type of non-profit insurance, the inherent defects of liability would have remained. For one thing, the determination of guilt in a case of personal negligence (or the degree of guilt where "comparative" negligence prevailed) often required a metaphysical turn of mind. In many instances, where explosions or fires destroyed evidence and witnesses, an accurate assessment of fault proved well nigh impossible. But the most serious indictment against the liability laws issued from that fact that negligence, as it was commonly understood, played a small part in the vast majority of accidents in the modern factory or mine. Experience in both Europe and America demonstrated that roughly half the accidents were "unavoidable." They were called "risks of the trade" and they resulted from defects of equipment that eluded the most careful inspection and from the irreducible imperfections of the human manipulator. Production

demands created inherently dangerous situations, in other words, in which
ordinary human miscalculation conspired with unpredictable malfunctions
of a machine to make "negligence" an almost meaningless abstraction.

In short, unless the very essence of the liability law be changed, the
worker would still have no definite legal claim in the majority of accidents.
Herein lay the "radical" change proposed by the compensation system. In
the hope of eliminating one type of insecurity over which the worker had
no control, the advocates of workmen's compensation rejected far more
than the extreme notions of individualism manifest in the common law
defense of the liability laws. They rejected that more moderate
individualism that held the worker accountable for every mishap that could
not be traced to the employers' or fellow servants' misconduct or
carelessness. It was not fair they argued, that the worker bear the whole
burden of injuries sustained as a result of the unavoidable hazards of his
occupation. Nor was it fair, they claimed, to equate personal responsibility
with personal negligence when the latter may well have been the product
of excessively long hours or other harmful working conditions. This
recognition by itself, though, was not so radical. It was accepted outright
by all those who pinned their hopes on a reformed American system. It
was even vaguely conceded by employers who maintained that wages were
already calculated to cover the risks of a hazardous job. But the
proponents of compensation rejected voluntarism, too, and with it the idea
that indirect governmental intervention posed a threat to self-reliance.

Had the American system been working according to theory, the
compensation proponents would have had less solid ground to stand on.
But several basic ingredients were believed to be missing. "Legislate as we
may in the line of stringent requirements for safety devices," declared
Charles McCarthy, "the army of the injured will still increase. . . ."[30] The
New York State Commission argued that "were the laissez-faire system of
political economy working without friction," a worker would receive wages
high enough to cover the risks of his occupation. "But," concluded the
commission, "that theory does not work out."[31] In theory, announced
Roosevelt, wages would always include an allowance for risks and "in
theory, if employees were all experienced businessmen, they would employ
that part of their wages which is received because of the risk of injury to
secure accident insurance. But as a matter of fact, it is not practical to
expect that this will be done by a great body of employees."[32]

There were two principal abstract objections to the compensation
principle. Both employers and employees were reluctant to accept the idea
that accidents were not caused by avoidable negligence. From this premise

workers reasoned that without the high punitive damages incurred through the liability laws, the employer would relax his efforts to provide safer machinery. W.L Carter, President of the Brotherhood of Locomotive Firemen and Enginemen stated that prevention is far more important than compensation. "Instead of accepting as inevitable (in accordance with the theory of workmen's compensation) the thousands of deaths and injuries that come to railroad employees," wrote Carter to Ralph Easley, "cannot the Civic Federation at the coming term of Congress advocate legislation that will greatly reduce this slaughter?"[33] And from the same premise, businessmen often argued that compensation would simply lead to more worker carelessness, and possibly even encourage him to get hurt in order to collect the money.

Laboring men also objected to the compensation principle on the grounds that it would deprive the worker of his rights to sue the employer. And employers argued that the law would be a confiscation of their property in violation of due process. "For if a liability be created by law based upon no misconduct of the employer," declared the President of the NAM, but upon the alleged hazard of industry and the mere accidental fact that the employee is in the service of a particular employer at the time of injury, without respect to his own conduct ... the enforcement of such an alleged obligation would take the property of one man and arbitrarily give to another."[34]

Actually the compensation principle was considered by its proponents as a redistribution rather than a confiscation of property: the employer excused from the costly damages in a relatively few cases was being asked to spread this money over the vast majority of accidents in small but definite amounts. An element of compromise was also present in that the employer was not being forced to compensate for the total cost of the disability. Payments would range from 50% to 66% of the costs and only for specified periods of time. The workers were reminded that while they might be losing the right to gamble for high stakes, they were gaining the right to something definite.

When the Wainwright Commisssion concluded its lengthy investigation it paved the way for the passage of a bill that was a carefully worked out compromise of the employer and employee interests. Indeed the National Civic Federation helped in the preparation of the bill. The New York State Compensation Act, the first of the state laws, was thus modest in terms of amount and duration of benefits, waiting period, and coverage. Actually a highly modified and experimental version of the English Compensation Act of 1906, the new law applied only to certain specified hazardous industries.

As in the English law, the worker made no outward contribution; it was believed that in receiving only partial payments and in suffering the discomforts of the accidents, his contribution was sufficient. The law was compulsory in relation to the employer while it left the worker with the alternative of selecting compensation. And finally, like the English Compensation Act, there was no provision against the possible insolvency of the employer. That is, it neither forced the employer to take out private insurance or combine in mutual associations, nor did it provide any state insurance system.[35]

The Commission had not only made every effort to get widespread public approval of the bill but the sponsors of the new measure took every precaution to insure its constitutionality. The employers were guaranteed a right to sue, and though the employers were compelled to come under the law, the sponsors felt that by selecting only extra-hazardous industries and only those that had no interstate competition, there would be no question of a proper exercise of the state's police powers.

Thus it came as something of a shock when the New York Court of Appeals struck down the new act in the famous Ives decision of 1911. Though only eight years had passed since the Maryland law sank into oblivion by the same process, so much had changed that the Ives decision had the makings of a *cause celebre*. It caused a flood of inquiries to pour into the offices of the National Civic Federation. It was the chief topic of conversation at the American Academy of Political and Social Science in 1911. It was widely reported in both the American and English press. Florence Kelley jeopardized her status in the Socialist Party because in a fit of pique, she endorsed the non-socialist ticket in the hopes of defeating Judge Werner of the Court of Appeals. "I regard that decision as infamous," she said "and Judge Werner as a terrible enemy of the working class."[36] The decision also gave Charles McCarthy a chance to beat the superior drum of Wisconsin Progressivism[37] and for Teddy Roosevelt, it seems to have triggered an impassioned plea for the recall of judges. In a series of bitter exchanges with C.H. Betts who accused the former President of inviting revolution and anarchy, Roosevelt declared that if the people did not object to the Ives decision as a "flagrant and wanton" abuse of power, they would be "unfit for self-government." "It was simple nonsense," wrote Roosevelt, "to suppose that this country will tolerate permanently a line of action like that you are upholding on the part of the Court of Appeals."[38]

The court decided that even though making an employer liable for those injuries arising out of a "necessary risk or danger of the employment" may be economically sound, "it is at war with the legal principle that no employer can be compelled to assume a risk which is inseparable from the work of the employee, and which may exist in spite of the degree of care by the employer far greater than may be enacted by the most drastic law. . . . "[39] The court further could find nothing in the police power of the state to justify taking away the employer's property without his consent and without any negligence on his part. Workmen's Compensation, in the words of the court, "does nothing to conserve the health safety or morals of the employees, and it imposes upon the employer no new or affirmative duties or responsibilities in the conduct of his business.[40]

The court was not without its supporters. One of them contended that the risks of the ordinary business are no greater than when men worked for themselves, and the police power should not be invoked to abridge the employer's freedom unless the "public welfare absolutely demands it."[41] These new conceptions of liability, complained W.S. Thomas, are a return to medieval times when the workers "were dealt with as incompetent wards of the state." We were "treading on dangerous ground" in the attempt to follow Europe, he said. "We are in danger of sacrificing the nation's birthright."[42]

"As a layman," wrote Seth Low, "I confess myself to have been shocked by the proposition that 'due process of law' means process of law when the Constitution was adopted."[43] Many legal experts were also taken aback at the decision. Ernest Freund stated that in a questionnaire sent to some of the most prominent legal minds in the country, he received two replies that favored the Court and seventeen that disagreed.[44] Many of the critics refused to accept the idea that accidental injuries did not constitute a matter of public welfare sufficient to invoke the police powers of the state. Some, however, significantly took a somewhat different tack. P.T. Sherman, Legal expert of the National Civic Federation, complained that the Court did not really understand the compensation principle at all. Otherwise it would have discovered the "private justice" inherent in the law instead of voiding it as an unwarranted assumption of police power.[45] Sherman argued, in other words, that the new measure did not have to be considered as one of public or social welfare but rather as a readjustment of the injustices in the various doctrines of the liability law, much as "comparative" negligence made a readjustment of "contributory" negligence. The employer then was not being deprived of his property without due process; but was being forced to share, according to the dictates of "private justice," the burdens for which both he and the employee were responsible.

But whether the Court failed to see workmen's compensation as a more just relationship between employer and employee or refused to regard the Act as a necessary regulation to protect the social welfare, was for the moment overshadowed by the fact that the Court nullified the first piece of social security legislation. Initially, the Ives decision threw the movement into disarray. It was feared that the New York Court would set a precedent or that other state legislatures in expectation of similar treatment by the courts would water down their legislation. Others, however, expressed confidence that New York did not have so much influence on the rest of the country and that the United States Supreme Court could still act as a liberal counterbalance. Gompers felt that the less fuss made about the decision the better.[46]

The decision did have its effect. Illinois redrafted a compulsory bill that had already passed the Senate, and reverted to an "elective" plan, the type that most other states were to adopt. Yet more striking than anything else, the decision bore testimony to the basic strength and resiliency of the compensation movement. Indeed, the New York Court of Appeals went out of its way to applaud the social merits of the bill and invited a Constitutional amendment. Judge Werner went so far as to publicize this point by sending the *New York Times* the full text of the opinion. "The high character of the work performed by the (Wainwright) Commission," he wrote to Louis Wiley of the *Times,* "and the obvious necessity for some rational reform in the matter of compensating workmen for injuries, entitles the advocates of the law to the frankest and fullest discussion of the subject and that is the point of view from which I tried to treat it."[47] The advocates in New York State went right ahead to amend the Constitution in order to get a truly compulsory bill. Other states were inclined to skirt this compulsion through the "elective" method or what Brandeis referred to as "elective obligatory" and what another referred to as "hocus pocus" compulsion.

NOTES

[1] *Journal of Social Science,* No. 40 (1902), p. 50ff.

[2] NCCC, *Thirty-Second Annual Report* (1905), p. 576.

[3] J.G. Brooks, "Report on German Workingmen's Insurance," NCOCC, *Thirty-Second Annual Report* (1905), pp. 453-454.

[4] Illinois, *Report of the Industrial Insurance Commissioner to the Governor of Illinois* (Springfield, 1907), pp. 4-12.

[5] James R. Burnet, "Critical Opinions upon Recent Employers' Liability Legislation in the United States," *Journal of Social Science,* XL (December, 1902), p. 55.

[6] C. W. Post, "Who is Owner?" National Association of Manufacturers, *Proceedings of the Tenth Annual Convention,* (1905), p. 289.

[7] "Industrial Slaughter and the 'Enlightened' Employers," *American Federationist,* XIV (August, 1907), p. 548.

[8] *Charities and Commons,* XVII (1907), p. 419.

[9] Rubinow, *Social Insurance,* pp. 157-159.

[10] Irene Osgood to C.R. Henderson, November 23, 1908, ILR, AALL MSS.

[11] U.S. Congress, House Committee on the Judiciary, *Hearings on H.R. 17036, Employers' Liability,* 60th Cong., Sess. (1908), p. 162.

[12] Davis R. Dewey to J.R. Commons, June 10, 1908, ILR, AALL MSS.

[13] Stephen D. Fessenden, "Present Status of Employers Liability in the United States," *U.S. Dept. of Labor Bulletin,* No. 31 (November, 1900), pp. 1157-1210; New York Bureau of Labor Statutes, *Seventeenth Annual Report* (1899), p. 6ff.

[14] *Ibid.*

[15] U.S. *Congressional Record,* 52nd Cong., 2nd Sess. (1893), p. 1360.

[16] U.S. *Report of the Industrial Commission on the Relations and Conditions of Capital and Labor,* VII, pp. 329, 906; U.S. *Congressional Record,* 52nd Cong., 2nd Sess. (1893), pp. 1424-1425, 1479-1481.

[17] U.S. *Congressional Record,* 59th Cong., 1st Sess. (1906), XL, pp. 4601ff.

[18] U.S. *Congressional Record,* 60th Cong., 1st Sess. (1908), XLII, p. 4359.

[19] Rubinow, *Social Insurance,* p. 159.

[20] National Conference on Workmen's Compensation, *Proceedings of July 1909; Proceedings of January 10, 1910, Proceedings June 10, 1910, passim;* Henry Seager to Gertrude Beeks, December 28, 1910. NYPL, NCF MSS, #125.

[21] American Federation of Labor, *Report of Proceedings,* XXX (1910), p. 39.

[22] National Civic Federation, *Ninth Annual Report* (1910), p. xiii.

[23] NAM, Proceedings of the *Fifteenth Annual Convention* (1910), p. 228.

[24] National Civic Federation, *Ninth Annual Meeting* (1908), p. 227.

[25] William Hard, "Pensioners of Peace," *Everybody's Magazine,* XIX (October, 1908), p. 52.

[26] New York Commission on Employer's Liability, *Report,* p. 20.

[27] *Ibid.*

[28] *Ibid.,* p. 30; NCWC, *Proceedings of 1909,* pp. 14-16.

[29] NAM, *Proceedings of the Fifteenth Annual Convention* (1910), p. 26; New York Commission on Employer's Liability, *Report* (1910).

[30] McCarthy, *Wisconsin Idea,* pp. 156-157.

[31] New York, Commission on Employer's Liability, *Report* (1910), p. 7.

[32] U.S. *Congressional Record,* 60th Cong., 1st Sess. (1908), XLII, p. 1347.

[33] W.L. Carter to Ralph Easley, December 6, 1911, NYPL, NCF MSS #125.

[34] James A. Enery, "Legislative Facts and Tendencies," NAM, *Proceedings of the Fifteenth Annual Convention* (1910), p. 130.

[35] E.H. Downey, *Workmen's Compensation* (New York, 1924), pp. 142-162.

[36] Florence Kelley to Julius Gerber, November 21, 1913, Tamiment Institute, Socialist Party MSS. Bx A69.

[37] McCarthy, *The Wisconsin Idea,* p. 257.

[38] C.H. Betts, *Betts-Theodore Roosevelt* (Lyons, N.Y., 1911), p. 9.

[39] Quoted in: Harry A. Willis and Royal E. Montgomery, Labor's Risks and Social Insurance (New York, 1938), p. 195.

[40] *Ibid.,* p. 165.

[41] Walter S. Nichols, "Argument Against Liability," *Annals of the American Academy* XXXVIII (July, 1911), pp. 159-163.

[42] *Ibid.,* p. 165.

[43] Seth Low to Wm. J. Moron, May 8, 1911. CU, Seth Low MSS, Bx. 98.

[44] U.S. Congress, Senate, *Hearings before the Employer's Liability and Workmen's Compensation Commission,* Vol. I, 62nd Cong., 1st Sess., 1911, p. 20; see also: Ernest Cawcroft, "Workingmen's Compensation," *American Federationist* XX (Nov., 1913), p. 916; U.S. Congress, Senate, *Hearings before the Employer's Liability and Workmen's Compensation Commission,* Vol. I, 62nd Cong., 1st Sess., 1911, pp. 3-11.

[45] P. Tecumseh Sherman, "Compensation Law and Private Justice," *Annals of the American Academy of Political and Social Science,* XXXVIII (July 1911), pp. 151-158; "Executive Committee Minutes," March 28, 1911, p. 6, NYPL, NCF MSS. #125.

[46] "Executive Committee Minutes," March 28, 1911, pp. 14FF. NYPL, NCF MSS, #125; Gertrude Beeks to Claud Pollard, Dec. 1, 1911, NYPL, NCF MSS #125; Ralph Easley to F.H. Norcross May 18, 1911. NYPL, NCF MSS #125; Compensation Dept. Minutes, May 26, 1911, NYPL, NCF MSS.

[47] Judge William E. Werner to Louis Wiley, March 27, 1911. NYPL, NCF 1795, #125.

CHAPTER VI

WORKMEN'S COMPENSATION: SOCIAL WELFARE AND INDUSTRIAL WARFARE

Not until the passage of the compensation act did any sizeable portion of the workforce feel the effects of a socially just security system. The laws were far from ideal, but the relative ease with which they were passed revealed a public sentiment strongly enough in favor of the principle to press for their extension into nearly every state in the Union by 1917. Whether enthusiastically sponsored or bitterly fought, the new principle of compensation was regarded as a significant innovation by the men who lived through the movement. Workmen's Compensation was a truly radical departure, for it absolved the worker of the total burden from injuries arising out of his employment, and in addition invoked the power of the government to impose that burden on someone other than the injured worker.

But certain aspects of this "radical" departure require fuller comment to make a more precise estimate of the nature and degree of boldness involved. When it is examined as the alternative to the American system of the early Progressive Era it does not appear to be so great a leap forward. Even before the compensation acts, many social reforms signaled a generous concession to the idea that both public and private sectors of society should obviate the necessity of the injured worker to fall upon charity. Further, by the Progressive Era, the very issue of the individual's self-reliance, apart from the reinterpretation of it, had declined in importance.

Industrialization had not only rendered self-reliance, in its old-fashioned sense an untenable ideal; it had created a set of circumstances in which the problems of the individual — be they his lack of self-reliance or his insecurity — were no longer pre-eminent. The individual's needs were being overshadowed by the needs of organizations — by society as a whole, on the one hand, and by the union and business enterprises on the other. In a sense, the clash over the compensation movement took place between the advocates of compulsory collectivism, who were inclined to define the problem in social terms, and the proponents of voluntary collectivism who saw the problem in the light of their respective group interests.

But in reference to the "radical" character of workmen's compensation, a more interesting and fundamental point has to be raised because the movement achieved success not by running roughshod over its American system opponents but by bringing them into the fold. And the question is whether the workmen's compensation principle, by being able to pull together the two diverse and heretofore antagonistic approaches of the American and European systems, lost something in the bargain.

Evidence indicates that the combined efforts of the two organizations most responsible for promoting workmen's compensation – the American Association for Labor Legislation and the National Civic Federation – left the meaning of the movement somewhat ambiguous.

Although the two organizations were able to reach a consensus on certain basic points, they carried their different outlooks into the interpretation of what they had jointly accomplished. For the American Association for Labor Legislation, workmen's compensation was a piece of social welfare legislation. For the National Civic Federation, it was in essence an extension of the liability system.

* * * * *

The workmen's compensation movement drew its most eloquent and enthusiastic spokesmen from the ranks of the "unorganized"; that is, from men who neither belonged to labor unions nor actively engaged in business. They were experts and they claimed to represent the public. Like a Crystal Eastman in New York or a Charles Henderson in Illinois, they might often be found on the various state investigating commissions as a ballast to the members representing business and labor. And when they spoke they preferred to use the platforms provided by the social service societies that flourished during the Progressive Era. To be sure, there were "retired capitalists" in these societies, and perhaps as the labor leaders charged, they were only posing as "public-spirited" citizens. Many labor leaders held executive positions in the groups also. Gompers, for one, had no difficulty in ticking off a score of such organizations to which he belonged. The spirit of most of the societies, nonetheless, continued to reflect that of the men and women who composed the core.

Of the two leading organizations in the compensation movement, the American Association for Labor Legislation best illustrates the influence of the experts – that is, of the professors, the journalists, statisticians, social workers, and lawyers. While the AALL enlisted the support of the businessmen and union officials, this seems to have been more an attempt to give the organization an appearance of impartiality. "We must not even seem to represent any one interest," wrote Henry Farnam in his advice to an organizer, "hence we must have representatives both of the employers, employees, and the general public, such as economists, officials, legislators, etc."[1] Farnam also warned that the title of the organization was not to be construed as having any particular connection with unionism: "They can expect nothing from us nor need they fear us."[2] More important, despite the impressive list of business and union names on the letterhead, it was men like Seager, Farnam, Commons, Henderson, Andrews and Osgood who did the bulk of the work. And their financial support came largely from the same sort. "Our most liberal supporter," wrote Andrews, "has always been a professor of Political Economy at one of the better universities."[3]

In the early years, the organization also fed upon the rather sizeable donations of the Russell Sage Foundation, a society of unimpeachable middle-class outlook. Finally, in addition to the pamphlets published for the benefit of members or the general public, they reached their audience through the propaganda printed in the *Survey,* once the voice principally of charity workers and social workers, now also the unofficial organ of the American Association for Labor Legislation.

Ideologically, the first champions of workmen's compensation were a mixed group. Their rather diverse set of attitudes included the socialism of Isaac Rubinow and the anti-socialism of Seth Low. Men like Edward Devine, who had no patience with collective bargaining "nonsense," worked alongside of John R. Commons, who studied the union movement with considerably more sympathy. Some, like Frederick L. Hoffman, might be considered pro-business; others, like Robert McDonough, pro-labor. There were Taft Progressives, Roosevelt Progressives and Wilson Progressives.

Whatever their differences in ideology, by and large they were apt to be unusually disturbed about the texture of society generally and social disorganization particularly. This should come as no surprise. While the composition of the social service groups was changing in favor of working professionals as opposed to the "idle rich," they contained many of the same types who, in the late nineteenth century, expressed a similar concern for the chasm between classes, the isolationism within urban areas, and that separatist, self-seeking life encouraged by modern industrial relationships. Indeed many of these older charity reformers and social workers still held positions of prominence in the Progressive societies. Holdovers like Charles Henderson, John R. Commons, Edward Devine, Richard Ely, John G. Brooks, probably feeling more at home with the current leadership, had in the '80s and '90s given intellectual structure to the fears expressed by those field workers who daily met with the hostility and suspicions of the poor. And what may have been the most striking and fundamental philosophical innovation to affect the social scientists of the late nineteenth century — the concept of organic society — had hardly disappeared. The evidence of a more highly organized conflict between labor and business gave them greater cause for concern, but rather than challenging the ideal of an organic society, seems more to have confirmed the corollary notion of the government's role in resuscitating the social organism. In a sense, the friendly visitor and the neighborhood associations were giving way to the imperatives of reducing social tension through the instrumentalities of the state.

When, for example, the American Association for Labor Legislation met in December 1907 with the American Historical Association, American Political Science Association, and American Economic Association, the mood was anything but cheerful. Speaker after speaker drummed upon the theme of social discord in America. Frederick Jackson Turner, dwelling upon his favorite topic, noted that despite some evidence to the contrary, sectionalism had by no means spent its force. Another expert elaborated upon the growing virulence of the racial conflict. T. N. Carver of Harvard claimed that conflict, whether in society or within the individual, was the controlling fact of life, inescapable and inevitable. According to him and Robert Hoxie, economic conflict was the most fundamental. In reference to the generally favorable reaction of the convention toward a host of proposed governmental activities ranging from direct primaries to social insurance, Edward Devine commented later that the "radicalism" of the meeting should not be entirely disassociated from the "pessimism." He noted in particular that the responses to Seager's discussion of social insurance were not only warm but that many of the listeners were prepared to go much farther. But by no means were all participants disturbed to the point of futility concerning the possibility of allaying social conflict. Henry Seager was not; nor was John R. Commons, who also spoke for most of those in the American Association for Labor Legislation. Agreeing that economic discord was basic, he suggested that governmental intervention could bring about a reconciliation.

It was this same combination of fear of social disharmony and faith in the government to protect society's interest that led many of the reformers into the workmen's compensation movement.[4] If the kind of social conflict generated by the liability system did not quite acquire the drama of a Coxey's Army or the violence of a Pullman strike, it had a constancy and a festering quality. As in the case of other problems of worker security, much of the discontent did not come to surface. However, the liability system provided its critics with ample ammunition. The most obvious disturber of the peace between employers and employees issued from the very nature of the liability system.[5] To settle the case in court necessarily involved inflammatory charges and countercharges of employer negligence and employee carelessness. Except in those states that had modified "contributory negligence," neither side could afford to compromise. Latent bitterness often lead to exaggerated claims and counterclaims which charged the atmosphere with hostilities that endured beyond the life of the case.

If the case were handled by the insurance company, the results were even more damaging because it had no stake whatever in the aftermath. The rise of the liability insurance company, according to one critic, merely "introduced a new element of barbarism in the relation between the employers and the injured employee."[6] Though the insurance companies denied having anything but the best interests of the workers at heart, their contracts with the employers were construed in many cases as preventing the employer from giving any aid to the injured worker prior to the settlement of the case. Seth Low complained publicly that such was the case about a stipulation in his own policy and recalled his frustrating efforts to aid one of his injured workers.[7] A New York manufacturer, in explanation of the usual insurance contract, complained that, "If the employer should give money to the injured employee or his family, or should provide him with a nurse or a doctor, or should even visit the employee to inquire about his condition, it might be taken as an indication that the employer considered himself liable for the injury and thus embarrass the insurance company in its efforts to settle or litigate the injured employee's claim."[8] This and other numerous testimony given to the New York State Commission led it to conclude that the only employers who manage without friction under the liability laws are those who neither insure nor pay attention to their legal liabilities, but "take care of their injured workers."[9]

This concern for class conflict was partly inspired by the fear of the middle class caught in the cross-fire of the battles between organized labor and organized business. But social conflict was also only one of the numerous impediments to the kind of society that the compensation advocates envisioned. And it was in their rather all-inclusive defense of the larger social group that these advocates lent a special meaning to the compensation movement. In a sense, it was their totally "social" outlook that distinguished them.

Anyone who had been taught by Richard Ely, declared Charles McCarthy, would understand and accept the philosophy of the Wisconsin Compensation Act. Those who had traveled to Germany, he remarked, well knew that the state "must protect and invest in the life and happiness of the individual in order that the greatest prosperity might come from it and that security, peace and happiness are the best foundations of good government and prosperity."[10] For these early advocates the problem was rarely reduced to the insecurity or the costs to the injured worker. It was not simply an industrial problem; it was a social problem and the costs were "social costs." The social costs might be lowered standard of living, or wasted production, or the social burdens of pauperism. With thousands of families living in extreme poverty, concluded the New York State Commission, "the State suffers through the lowered standard of living of a vast number of its citizens and the public is directly burdened with the maintenance of many who become destitute. This then we find out to be the most serious objection to our present system of employer's liability."[11] On many occasions, however, the reformers were thinking of the moral tone of society, of "civic righteousness."[12] For example, the debasement of the legal profession to a vulgar squabble for profits was often cited as one of the more unfortunate results of the liability system. Lawyers were characterized as playing a morbid game, in which the ambulance chasers with their uncanny knowledge of an accident raced with the employer's attorneys, who had the advantage of proximity, to win the ear of the worker. And when the case came to the courtroom, witnesses would perjure themselves, and juries, because of their sympathies for the worker, often strained the evidence.

If truth was defiled by the self-seeking lawyers and ignorant or weak witnesses and jurors, another moral value was jeopardized when responsibility for the injured worker was shifted to the wrong parties. In much the same way that the early charity reformers railed against indiscriminate charity because it was a subsidy to businessmen who failed to pay proper wages, so the advocates of compensation claimed that the real paupers were not the workers forced to seek the charity but all those people who neglected their duty.[13]

The actual placing of the responsibility for the cost of accidental injuries remained somewhat unclear even among the reformers. They agreed, as did the latter-day apostles of compensation, that the worker certainly should not bear the whole brunt. But whether this remaining cost should fall upon the employer or upon the public or both often got tangled up with the probability that the costs ultimately devolved upon the consumer. In general, the economic realities of the situation did not trouble its advocates. Carroll Wright, in 1902, dismissed all discussions involving the "intermediate" burden as irrelevant, since the consumer, rightfully so, was going to pay in the form of more expensive articles. The purpose of the law, declared Wright, is to "protect society against. . .economic insecurity," and if "economic insecurity is to be guarded against by employer's liability laws or any other laws, it seems to me wise from an economic and ethical point of view that society should pay the bills."[14] The Wainwright Commission, in much the same spirit, believed that the economic burden "should be shared by those who profit by such work, that is by the employer, who ultimately will shift that burden to the consumer."[15]

The ultimate responsibility, then, seemed to lie with the society as a whole rather than with special groups. It was not merely a case of society assuming the responsibility for its own protection, or paying for the rewards it received from the workers, but also that the worker should not be considered apart from the larger social group. If the reformers were inclined to identify with society as a whole rather than any special interest group, they were also apt to conceive of the individual worker in the same way. Instead of picturing him exclusively as a member of an industrial organization or of a trade union, they referred to him as a "soldier" of the "industrial army" or as a "veteran of peace." A figure of speech, perhaps, but one that implied not only the similarity of dangers in war and peace, but also a certain close relationship between the worker and the state. "We give a badge of honor to a soldier who has served or suffered in his country's battlefield," wrote Frank Lewis, "but we brand with the stigma of disgrace the soldier of industry who has suffered in health or in limb in the industrial life of his generation."[16] Governor Hughes of New Jersey declared that "We shudder at the carnage of war, but we give too little attention to the perils of our industrial army and to the useless sacrifice of life and productive efficiency which is the result of preventable accidents in industry."[17]

It was then, in the broadest sense, a problem of "social" welfare for which the reformers invoked the police power of the state. Workmen's Compensation, while offering immediate and direct relief to the wage earner, was not to be considered "class" legislation.[18] It offered protection to society as well as the worker. While forcing an immediate financial imposition upon the employer, the ultimate cost was recognized, and in most cases without regret, to fall upon the consumers. Edward Devine, perhaps better than anyone, captured the spirit and philosophy that he and his friends brought to the compensation movement. "'We' who can save them," he wrote in 1909, "are but the 'we' — men, and women and children — who are to be saved. This is no paternalistic enterprise but, on the contrary, of the very essence of Democracy."[19]

Naturally, the participants in the "class" conflict to which the middle class addressed itself, did not approach the compensation movement with as great a concern for the public interest. Businessmen and laborers had immediate and specific interests to protect which prevented them from rushing into the movement with the enthusiasm of the representatives of the public. Moreover, relatively little of the reluctance had anything to do with desire to preserve old-fashioned virtues of self-reliance. Financial gains and losses, and the effect of a compensation program upon the number of accidental injuries were two of the principal points carefully considered. For the worker especially these were the heart of the matter; an additional accident was more than a statistic, and a change in the payment could spell the difference between comfort and misery as a disabled person. He had to determine, therefore, whether the uncertain but relatively large sums obtained through the courts offered more protection than did the certain but partial payments of a compensation system. His efforts thus far on behalf of more liberalized liability laws were paying off handsomely in terms of more opportunities to bring suit and larger sums from the juries. There was even some talk of regulating lawyers' fees, thus suggesting a way of eliminating one source of waste in the liability system. Some workers had hopes of expanding the liability laws so that nearly all accidents would be covered, and to some extent this hope fed on the notion that the vast majority of accidents were caused by employer and fellow servant negligence.

Businessmen had a roughly similar dilemma. Many of them were as convinced as the workers that accidents were caused by someone's personal negligence and by and large they were inclined to place the blame on the worker. As a result, the employer, for all his complaints against the liability laws, especially the current trend toward their liberalization, was not encouraged to think that they could be indefinitely expanded. Thus, at first glance, the compensation idea, while reducing the size of the payments, would force the employer to pay for many more accidents than under current liability laws and probably under any expanded law.

Aside from the European experience, there was nothing that could be presented as definite proof that both employers and employees would really gain from compensation. Proponents of the new measure reasonably suggested that the employees would benefit by getting the money currently going to insurance companies and lawyers and that the smaller fixed sums would not necessarily be to the detriment of the worker who might ordinarily win large damages. If the worker, for example, were the victim of "gross and willful" negligence, he more than likely would have recourse to the courts. On the other hand, employers were assured that compensation merely made a redistribution of the current monies already spent by the employer and that additional costs would either be minimal or passed on to the consumer. But neither of these appeals took into account special issues raised by the workers and the employers. Not all businessmen took out insurance or permitted the accident cases to come to court, so the redistribution argument was inapplicable. Hazardous businesses with relatively low profit margins would be in a weaker position even if the over-all cost were minimal, while larger enterprises or those with higher profit margins would be in a better position to absorb whatever additional costs there might be. Companies doing an interstate business could not be impressed with the notion of passing on the cost to the consumer if their competitors were not so imposed upon. The fact that liability laws differed from state to state and that within the states they did not affect all industries the same way presented still another variable in the calculations. Railroad operators, for example, were generally more favorable to the workmen's compensation principle because in most states they had been the first of the industries to feel the burden of the expanded liability laws. Conversely, railroad workers were on the whole far less willing to risk what they already had for the promises of a new system.

For the employer as well as for the employee, then, the terms of acceptance had to do largely with the amount of compensation to be paid, the duration of the payments, and the number and types of accidents to be covered.[20] Organized laborers generally insisted upon the retention of an alternative remedy in the common law of liability, but were of the opinion that if the payments under compensation were high enough a suit would rarely be initiated by the worker. Although the controversy over the retention of the right to a suit involved abstract questions of law, the unions qualified their position, once they were assured that the awards under the compensation laws were adequate.[21] Employers, on the other hand, generally pushed for legislation that would not undercut their attempts to pass the costs on to the consumer. Miles Dawson declared that any attorney who argues in favor of workmen's compensation must prove that the employer has the opportunity to shift the burden: "Upon no other economic or legal proposition has any kind of an act of this type a ghost of a chance to be sustained by any court in the United States."[22] Thus the employers spent a good part of their energies in making certain that legislation throughout the states was as uniform as possible; and in order to avoid unfair competition within the state they often promoted the strict compulsory rather than the elective obligatory laws. The Wainwright Commission, after reading the letters of more than two hundred businessmen in New York State, concluded that economic questions were far more important than any other in determining the employer's opinions about workmen's compensation. "Practically all employers," declared the Commission, "would, from the standpoint of their own interest, heartily favor a compensation system if it could be so worked out that the expense to the employer would be no greater than under the present system."[23]

Most of these conflicts of economic interest were resolved one way or another through the provisions of the compensation acts. In most states, the employers won a two-week waiting period; that is, they paid no compensation to any worker who recovered from an injury within that period of time. In Colorado the employer received an additional week of grace, whereas in Oregon he enjoyed no waiting period at all. With the exception of a few states such as California, Massachusetts, New York and Ohio which provided for compensation of two-thirds of the worker's wages for disability, the payments amounted to fifty percent. The duration of the payments, however, varied considerably. In a few states, the compensation was given for the duration of the disability, but in most cases payments were limited to periods varying from 240 to 550 weeks. In most states in addition, the employer contributed toward funeral expenses of the deceased, and paid survivor's benefits that were somewhat less liberal than those paid to the injured worker.[24]

Immediate economic self-interest goes far in accounting for the attitudes of businessmen and workers toward compensation. There were, however, other considerations — though they were not entirely divorced from the realm of economics. Both business and labor were well aware of the broader implications of the compensation movement. This, too, affected their willingness to join the movement; more important, their group interest orientation was the basis for their distinctive interpretation of Workmen's Compensation.

The middle class, of course, did not have a monopoly on social consciousness any more than it had a monopoly on the compensation movement. Certain elements of labor and business, for example, quite early joined together for reasons similar to those that motivated the middle-class reformers. The National Civic Federation, in fact, in claiming a reduction of the class conflict as its raison d'etre, deserves some credit as being the first nation-wide organization to give such singular distinction to this problem. One of its early representatives of the "public" in rather poignant foreshadowing of Woodrow Wilson's New Freedom speech delared it was time to consider the "inoffensive people who are neither organized workmen nor organized capitalists, and who have the misfortune in all conflicts between these two forces to be ground between the upper and nether millstones."[25] The addresses of labor and business representatives likewise celebrated the virtues of coming to an understanding; of getting to know one another better; of trying to find those areas of conflict that resulted from ignorance and unfounded suspicion rather than from any basic conflict of interest. One employer glowingly spoke of restoring "that 'old time personal touch with employees.'"[26] And Mark Hanna, the first President of the National Civic Federation announced that the "division of the people into classes is against the spirit of democratic institutions."[27]

Similarities between the National Civic Federation, and say, the American Association for Labor Legislation did not end with a common desire to create a greater social harmony. They had an overlapping membership of which Seth Low, Frederick Hofmann, Ernst Freund, Louis Brandeis, and Henry Seager were only a few of the examples. On occasion, as in Massachusetts, the two organizations found themselves competing for the allegiance of the same men in an attempt to start a new chapter.[28] Their efforts in the Workmen's Compensation movement overlapped also and there were several attempts to join forces.[29] The two groups in fact were often confused in the minds of public; both societies were continually receiving the correspondence of the other. And to make matters worse — or perhaps better — the lady secretary of each organization ultimately married her boss.

But there were differences. The rhetoric binding labor, business and the public in a promise of social harmony very clearly suggested the peculiar orientation of the National Civic Federation. Indeed the essential ingredient of the bargain was a recognition of the legitimacy, durability, and power of the competing elements. Thus in calling together the first annual meeting in 1901, Ralph Easley, a founder and Secretary of the National Civic Federation, invited the "largest leaders of labor in the country" to sit down with the "largest leaders of capital". At this and subsequent conferences, the giants of the organized industrial community gave each other pledges of mutual respect and lashed out against their common enemies: the anti-union employers in the National Association of Manufacturers and the socialists in the labor movement. Gompers could be heard to assure the businessmen that his brand of unionism sought neither to tear down the capitalistic system nor to dismantle the trusts.[30] And

Senator Mark Hanna, and others representing capital, gave their continued support to the idea that organized labor had the right to exist, and that only by their recognition could the industrial conflict be prevented from turning into a revolutionary conflict the outcome of which would result in the control of industry, "either by despotic capital, or by despotic labor, or by the state."[31]

While the alliance in the NCF was a precarious one as well as a peculiar one, it was a practical one because the NAM in its antiturst inclinations threatened the giants of the NCF, and the socialists in their theory of statecraft threatened the structure of craftunionism. This, in turn, suggests that another element of the accord between business and labor within the NCF was the elimination of the government as a force in settling the disputes between capital and labor. Indeed, the first major policy pronouncement — a repudiation of compulsory arbitration — gave fair warning of their negative attitude to the most powerful instrument of the general public. By joining hands for the benefit of the public interest, they also reinforced their shared hostility to public power; harmony was to come through a kind of self-regulation which also protected and indeed strengthened their respective group interests, vis-a-vis the "third party."

If, in substance, the NCF compromised the public's interests, the organization of the NCF similarly left the representatives of the public interest in an ambiguous position. From the form of the letterhead, where the names of each group appeared in different columns, to the actual decision-making process in which there had to be a consensus among the three segments, the NCF had built into the structure its conception of society. Had the public members been so inclined, they could not have run the organization as they did in the AALL. Although, on the other hand, they were probably less inclined to move as rapidly toward radical departures in the American system. In spite of the overlapping membership, the general complexion of the NCF had a wealthier and more successful tone; there were more retired capitalists, and the contributions came in larger sums. Perhaps there was a hint of envy in Andrews' demurrer that the AALL could get along without the fancy names and the big money of the NCF, but there was also an element of truth in his belief that the names and money of the NCF often proved a drag upon the organization.[32] The public sector then, like the business and labor sectors, smelled of success. In a sense, the NCF was a coalition of the establishments of society.

It was not solely for its initial rejection of governmental interference, however, that the National Civic Federation deserves attention, but also its manner of finally accepting that interference. It was a case of joining hands again, in which the participants in the social conflict formed a partnership against the "public".

"The life of the employers is at stake in this matter," declared Edwin Wright of the Illinois Federation of Labor, as he began to explain the absence of any representatives of the public on the new Illinois Compensation Commission. "If we build up conditions so high that he will have to leave the state or abandon his property, he cannot afford to pay wages to the workingmen. We, on the other hand, have all we have to lose; we have not only our trade, but we have our lives at stake, and the public has no voice in it. Organized capital, through the Manufacturers' Association, and so forth, has a voice. Organized labor has a voice, but if the public has any voice at all, it does not amount to a great deal in the State of Illinois."[33]

With somewhat less contempt for the public interest, other labor leaders and businessmen were also prone to view workmen's compensation as the solution to an industrial problem more than a social problem. In doing so they tended to downgrade society's responsibility. They may have differed quite strongly as to the relative responsibility of the employer and employee, but they seemed anxious to confine this responsibility to the "family". From the worker's point of view, the industrial accident was to be considered, much as the breakdown of machinery, as a cost of production; and while it was clearly recognized that, as such, it would be transferred to the consumer, discussion of this facet of the problem was almost always in terms of the employer's burden, or of the burdens of employer and employee. Employers and their spokesmen were equally aware of the shifting of this burden to the consumer, but they too preferred to speak of this as an employer's burden or, taking into consideration the essential compromise with the compensation principle, as a burden jointly shared by the worker and employer. Senator Sutherland, in a luncheon speech before the National Civic Federation, declared that it is not fair that the injured worker "should be a burden upon the community." "He has got to be cared for by somebody," protested Sutherland, "and it is far more just that the industry should care for him within reasonable limits, than the community at large. Of course you know it is shifted there."[34] The workers and businessmen, according to one employer, were "joint partners in production" and they were to "share the burdens of the accident for which they are jointly responsible."[35] Another referred to the compensation acts as "average justice" in which the employers and employees divide the costs equally among themselves.[36]

In essence, these views were variations of the "Private Justice" theme expressed by P. T. Sherman in his criticism of the Ives decision, and they resembled, too, the earlier "Natural Justice" sentiments of William Willoughby; namely, that workmen's compensation was really an extension of the liability law, particularly in its concept of contributory negligence. Both business and labor, by accepting a compulsory compensation system, were in effect conceding the power and perhaps the responsibility of the public to enforce certain conditions between capital and labor; yet neither side, particularly those associated with the National Civic Federation, did much to encourage a broad interpretation of that power and responsibility. Samuel Gompers, more than anyone else, was most articulate in defining the new system as narrowly as possible. "It contemplates the theory of two free contracting parties," wrote Gompers, "each of which is to incur part of a burden inseparable from an industry. . . . Compensation is given as a result of an isolated occurrence in which the employer and the employed are directly concerned. . . . The connection with it of society in general is not even secondary, for that position belongs to the industry in which the employer and the employee in any given case are engaged."[37] With similar force, Gompers took exception to all the references to the "industrial army." "There is one thing to which I dissent;" he wrote, "and that is that the workmen may be regarded as enlisted men."[38]

In short, the compensation principle did not have very precise meaning beyond what was agreed to by all parties: that the worker was not to carry the full load of an accidental injury. There were in effect two rather distinct interpretations. The American Association for Labor Legislation fostered the idea that the nation was faced with a grave social problem, that it was society's responsibility to correct this problem, and that the compensation laws were social welfare measures operating under the police powers of the state. "We are here dealing with a public law," wrote Charles Henderson, "and not with private arrangements, and until we admit this principle we shall be a long way from social insurance."[39]

The interpretation of workmen's compensation as a governmentally enforced "private arrangement" would, in fact, prove to be an impediment to the social security movement. Indeed, in view of later events, the stance of the National Civic Federation seemed to be a calculated move to guard against the kind of extensive governmental intervention envisioned by the American Association for Labor Legislation.

The position of the National Civic Federation, however, was not to have a bearing on all social security programs. And one may ask again whether the initial suspicion of workmen's compensation and the restrictive interpretation placed upon it really issued from a desire to preserve the old individualism. In the case of the widow's pension movement, for example, an idea potentially more radical than either workmen's compensation or social insurance was at stake. Yet neither the National Civic Federation nor many of its business and labor members took an active part in the movement, and of those who did, some, like Gompers, were sympathetic toward the pension. In the case of the widow's pension — one in which the governmental intervention did not immediately or directly affect business and labor — the movement was left largely in the hands of the "third party." It is thus to the third party and to the division within the ranks of welfare reformers that we must turn if we are to examine a rigorous defense of the old individualism.

NOTES

[1] Henry Farnam to Metcalfe, April 26, 1909, ILR, AALL MSS.

[2] *Ibid.*

[3] John B. Andrews to Dr. George E. Tucker, Sept. 26, 1913, ILR, AALL MSS.

[4] Edward Devine, "Social Forces," *Charities and Commons* XVIII (1908), pp. 1377-1378.

[5] See for example William J. Moran, "Unbending the Eyes Justice," NCF, *Ninth Annual Meeting,* 1908, pp. 158-62.

[6] George Alger, "The Present Status of Employer Liability," Charities and Commons XVII (1908), p. 827.

[7] Seth Low to Robert Hillas, Dec. 23, 1912. CU, Seth Low MSS. Bx. 97.

[8] NYS Commission on Employer's Liability, *Report,* 1910, p. 151.

[9] *Ibid.,* p. 35.

[10] McCarthy, *Wisconsin Idea,* p. 161.

[11] NYS Commission on Employer's Liability, *Report,* p. 30.

[12] *Atlantic City Conference,* July 1909, p. 37.

[13] Frank Fetter, "Need of Industrial Insurance," NCOCC, *Thirty-Third Annual Report* (1906), p. 469.

[14] Journal of Social Science, XL (1902), pp. 70-71; see also: U.S. Congress, Senate, *Hearings before the Employer's Liability and Workmen's Compensation Commission* I Cong., Sess., 1911, p. 77.

[15] NYS Commission on Employer's Liability, *Report,* 1910, p. 48.

[16] F.W. Lewis, *State Insurance,* p. 45.

[17] Quoted in *Charities and Commons* XVII (1907), p. 759.

[18] C.H. Henderson, "Logic of Social Insurance," *Annals of the American Academy,* XXXIII, (March, 1909), p. 48. Rubinow appears to have been the major exception among social insurance proponents, in that he considered the measures as class legislation.

[19] Edward Devine, *Misery and Its Causes* (New York, 1909), p. 111.

[20] *American Federationist,* XVII (March 1910), pp. 218-220; C.H. Franklin to Ralph Easley, March 10, 1910, NYPL, NCF MSS. #125.

[21] Third National Conference on Workmen's Compensation, Proceedings of June 10, 1910, pp. 21-22; *ALLR,* III (1913), pp. 280-282.

[22] U.S. Congress, Senate, *Hearings before the Employer's Liability and Workmen's Compensation Commission* I, Cong. Sess., 1911, p. 30.

[23] *Report,* p. 110.

[24] U.S., *Bulletin of the Bureau of Labor Statistics,* (Washington, 1916), pp. 130-164.

[25] Franklin MacVeigh, "Opening Speech," NCF *Industrial Conciliation,* 1900, p. 91.

[26] National Civic Federation, *Industrial Conference, 1902,* (New York, 1903), p. 38.

[27] NCF, *The National Civic Federation: Its Methods and Aims,* (New York, 1905), p. 9.

[28] Andrews to Farnam, April 24, 1909, ILR, AALL MSS.

[29] John H. Gray to J.B. Andrews, May 7, 1910, ILR, AALL MSS; Henry Farnam to J.B. Andrews, Jan. 21, 1910, ILR, AALL MSS.

[30] Green, *National Civic Federation,* pp. 41, 106; NCF, Industrial Conciliations, *Report of the Proceedings of the Conference, December 16-17, 1901,* (New York: 1902), pp. 62-63.

[31] NCF, *Methods and Aims,* pp. 8-9.

[32] J.B. Andrews to Henry Farnam, March 18, 1910; Farnam to Andrews, March 19, 1910, ILR, AALL MSS.

[33] *Third National Conference on Workmen's Compensation,* June 1910, p. 25.

[34] "Executive Committee Minutes," March 28, 1914, NYPL, NCF MSS #125.

[35] Emery, "Legislative Facts...," NAM, *Proceedings of Fifteenth Annual Convention,* 1910.

[36] *Monthly Bulletin* (Dec. 1913-Feb. 1914), p. 13.

[37] American Federationist, XVII (1910), pp. 596-597.

[38] *Journal of Social Science,* XL (1902), p. 50.

[39] Charles Henderson to George Sutherland, Nov. 29, 1914, NYPL, NCF MSS #127.

CHAPTER VII

THE WIDOW'S PENSION MOVEMENT

As the workmen's compensation movement shifted into second gear around 1909, the widow's pension movement had barely shifted into first. In that year, Theodore Roosevelt called together the White House Conference on Dependent Children which resolved that poverty should be no bar to the maintenance of the family. The Conference also declared that aid to families should be given "preferably in the form of private charity rather than public relief."[1]

Within two years, the pension movement had gained such momentum that its opponents could barely marshal their forces against it. In a reference to the first state-wide law passed in Illinois in 1911, Sherman Kingsley said that "some of the legislators since have been asking 'when in thunder' it went through."[2] By 1913, 20 states, most of them in the mid and far West, had passed a pension law. In Colorado, where the bill was put to a referendum, the pension won by a thumping two to one majority.

The pension movement was essentially an attempt to provide for the dependent mother what the workmen's compensation movement was beginning to provide for the worker struck down by an industrial accident — a measure of social justice.

Dependency in motherhood, however, presented so different a set of circumstances from the case of the injured worker that the two movements are more a study of contrasts than of similarities. The workmen's compensation movement represented a minimal consensus reached by advocates of the two main currents in social welfare history, the voluntary-collective and the compulsory-collective approaches. The compromise embodied two different notions of compulsory-collective responsibility, both of which were far removed from the idea of charity, and neither of which carried that idea of social justice to the point of rejecting the value of the worker's making some contribution to his own security. By contrast, the widow did not figure much in either of these two main currents because she was not the average worker, and traditionally she was the client of either the private or public charities. The debates over the pension were not a contest between labor and capital or between these two and the representatives of the "third party." The argument took place

141

largely within the latter group — among social workers, journalists, lawyers, and professors, many of whom had ties with the AALL.

A settlement was reached which in many cases was less than that achieved by workmen's compensation, because the pension was something between charity and social justice.

However, the widow's pension advocates raised more fundamental questions about the relationship between work and pay and in doing so forced their critics, many of whom supported social insurance, to attack the pension with old-fashioned arguments of individual responsibility.

* * * * *

The widow's pension (or more accurately, the dependent mother's pension) movement, addressed itself to a problem that was small in numbers by comparison with unemployment, accidental injury, illness or old age. But the small size and manageability of the problem worked to the widow's advantage. In addition the awareness of her plight was heightened as a result of the publicity that the compensation movement gave to this particular by-product of fatal industrial accidents. And the resolution of her problem became all the more compelling with child labor and compulsory education laws having the effect of depriving the family of needed income.

In essence, the widow's pension movement summoned the nation to a defense of the most fundamental and cherished unit in society, the family. "Home life" declared the White House Conference, "is the highest and finest product of civilization."[3] The movement evoked the most basic and universal sympathies among a people whose concepts of motherhood and childhood were as yet unsullied by knowledge of the Oedipal syndrome and one of whose favorite songs was "Be It Ever So Humble, There's No Place Like Home." No other social welfare problem provided such a rich opportunity for florid and poignant oratory. If the rhetoric of the workmen's compensation movement turned macabre, that of the widow's pension slipped into mawkish sentimentality. The following specimen, delivered by a member of the Indiana State legislature in 1913, was by no means unusual:

> We make an awful mistake when we assume as we often do, that we can add or take away from a mother's love, because a mother's love is part of the mechanism of the soul, and it receives no abridgement from any known condition. It is a jeweled diadem placed upon the brow of a finite creature that the world may honor and obey. We know it to be imperishable, because it bears the impress of an undying perfection, and it is cherished as life's chiefest beatitude, wielding empire over the domain of human tenderness.[4]

There were sure to be cases in which society agreed that the "jeweled diadem" should be wrenched from its object: in families where the parents were mentally or morally incompetent to raise children. But there were many families whose poverty made it almost impossible to keep the members together. If not wandering the streets in pursuit of illegal gain or stunting their development in some dingy factory, the children of such homes were often placed in orphanages or foster homes. The pension advocates asked why the State could not give aid to the mothers, in order to prevent the dissolution of the family. And since the State subsidized foster care, they asked why the public funds could not be diverted to the real mothers. "In their desperate loneliness," wrote Clara Cahill Park of the Massachusetts Commission "they are gathering by the tens and thousands to ask for the custody of their own children.[5]

The unusually warm response of the community to this question during the Progressive Era was not only understandable but in keeping with the preferential treatment historically accorded the widow and particularly the dependent child. In the latter, the reformers of the 1870's and 1880's saw the possibility of breaking the vicious chain of dependency. Although public aid carried with it a host of dangers and in itself, according to the reformers, might lead to pauperism, no one disputed the State's obligation to protect the dependent child. They attacked only out-door relief and relief in the almshouses where little but pauperism could flourish. They urged therefore that the children be put in orphanages or in foster homes. Much of the activity was motivated by a desire to protect society; as in the case of other reform activities there was a soft side also. The foster home idea, for example, was an attempt to maintain at least the semblance of home life. Moreover, however strongly relief officals condemned out-door relief to the able-bodied adult, they were often inclined to make exceptions for the dependent mother and child, who because of their roles in forming the family unit, had a legitimate excuse for their dependency.[6] And even some of the reformers were willing to admit that if the only alternative were to send the child or the parent to the Almshouse, it would be best to give aid in the home. In the late nineteenth and early twentieth century, efforts to maintain the unity of the family continued in a variety of ways, from the rather dramatic but unsuccessful attempts to revive out-door relief in New York City, to quieter and virtually unrecognized moves in San Francisco and Los Angeles to interpret the laws so liberally that children were, in effect, returned to their parents with the aid of public funds. Scholarships were available for indigent school children in Oklahoma, and some states incorporated into their compulsory education laws, provisions for clothing and books.[7]

If the widow's pension movement was the culmination of an historic concern for her helplessness; it was also a new eruption of the controversies that had historically accompanied all efforts to aid her. Indeed, over the years, the widow had become, precisely because of her special circumstances, a focal point in the debates over the respective merits of public and private charity. In a sense, her plight both clarified the dispute and heightened it at the same time. Regardless of her essential moral health, the widow did not fully share in the benefits derived from the enthusiasms over social justice. These were principally showered upon the wage earner. The widow had little to gain from better working conditions, postal savings banks, higher wages; nor could she fall back upon an employer or a union. Her status as a non-worker, then, required that she be taken care of by some social agency – as opposed to a special interest group – and that she receive some form of charity. And if her family was to be kept intact, there was no question that the relief had to be a direct payment in the home – however much one might argue against the evils of out-door relief to the able-bodied adult male.

The question, then, had been whether the pension should come from the private or the public charity systems. A number of relief officials and welfare workers, particularly those in the settlement movement maintained that the widow required less of the personal attention usually associated with private relief and more of the money obtainable through public charity. The established private charities, led by the charity organization societies, however, generally stood their ground and argued that public relief was administered by inexperienced or corrupt politicians, and that private pensions were inherently less dangerous to the widow's spirit of self-reliance. As the private charities became more professionally oriented they probably had an even greater incentive to have the widow become the recipient of expert counsel.

There was still another reason for the private charities' insistence that the pensions be given under their auspices. That a few of the charity reformers, in recognition of the mothers' special problem, condoned public out-door relief is probably less important than the hope and strategy growing out of that same recognition. "This is the class of cases," wrote Robert Treat Paine in 1894, "which has always been used most effectively by our Overseers of the Poor in advocating the necessity of out-door relief. Taking from the Overseers this class of case would greatly facilitate its total abolition, or great reduction." Paine therefore appealed to the churches and private agencies to expand their widow's aid programs in order to vitiate the necessity of public relief.[8] Thus with something of a vested interest in the dependent mother, the private charities were inclined to fight all the more in order to keep her away from the public relief roles.

The fact is that these appeals for greater private relief met with relatively weak response until the eve of the pension movement. Even in New York City, where the established charities were strongest, efforts to provide the widow with sufficient aid faltered upon the inability to mobilize resources or upon the reliance on conservative relief principles presumably repudiated years before.[9]

As the widow's pension movement got underway, these private programs became far more ambitious. The first line of defense against the pension movement was an attempt, by showing the adequacy of private relief, to prove that new outlays of public money were unnecessary. Studies and investigations made by the Russell Sage Foundation and the NYAICP were offered as proof that no important problem existed, that few of the children in foster homes or orphanages were there merely because of the poverty of the family.[10] Charity officials pointed with pride to the continuing efforts to expand their relief activities and the positive results achieved by their new efforts. David F. Tilley flatly declared that he knew of no families in Massachusetts broken up solely because of poverty.[11]

Advocates of the pension movement, however, did not agree with the optimistic assessments made by the established charities. Both the Massachusetts Commission and the New York Commission produced figures in direct contradiction to those presented to the charity organizations. The Massachusetts Commission, for example, declared that nearly two-thirds of the institutionalized children could be with their own families were funds made available.[12]

The widow's pension movement threw the social workers into something resembling a state of shock. It was, for one thing, instigated by many people who were outside of or little known to the social work profession. "Who are these sudden heroes of a brand new program of state subsidies, that they have grown scornful," of traditional forms of benevolence? asked Edward Devine with no attempt to conceal his contempt.[13] One of them, who thought of himself as the "father" of the mother's pension movement, was, according to another opponent of the pension movement, "a man named Henry Neil, who sits on the border and breaks in whenever he can, who is not at all a safe or wise person, putting it mildly,"[14] Among the pension supporters, however, were respected newspapermen like William Hard, editor of *Everybody's Magazine* and Theodore Dreiser, who, as editor of *The Delineator*, had been instrumental in promoting the White House Conference, as well as the pension movement. There were, in addition, many prominent judges, such as Ben Lindsey and Merritt Pinckney, who presided over the newly created juvenile courts and made arrangements by which children were taken from their mothers. Also among the supporters were the members of many women's clubs, Mother's Congresses, and labor unions. And some of the "sudden heroes," like Lillian Wald, came from the ranks of social work.[15]

Although the private agencies might have delayed the pension somewhat, it is improbable that any greater success in handling the widow problem could have prevented it; for in the challenge posed by the pension movement the question involving the adequacy of the private charity became an issue of scondary importance. The reformers were ever ready to point to the widow's degradation whether forced to surrender her child or allowed to keep him through the "good graces" of the community. They rejected all forms of charity, private and public, as totally inappropriate; they were determined to grant the widow a measure of social justice.

> It is a recognition by the State, declared Judge Lindsey, that the aid is rendered, not as a charity but as a right – a justice due mothers . . . it is a recognition for the first time by society that the state is responsible in a measure for the plight of the mother and acknowledges its responsibility by sharing the burden of her poverty that is created largely by the conditions that the state permits to exist.[16]

If the widow were to achieve an immediate solution, the advocates had no alternative but to propose what to the established charities seemed like old fashioned out-door relief. For the same reasons the widow could not participate in the remedies advanced under the rubrick of social justice in the late 90's, she could not in any real sense be a part of any social insurance scheme. Very simply, without employment she could make no contribution to an insurance fund whether administered by the State, the union, or the employer. And in the absence of any broad social insurance program under which she might be provided through her husband's coverage, there remained only the possibility of direct aid from the government.

The established charities and particularly the stalwarts of the charity organization societies stated over and over that the pensions were nothing more than a form of old-fashioned, out-door relief. "Their champions may 'run the chromatic scale up' in asseverating that their provisions are justice and not relief,"[17] declared Mary Richmond, dismissing the rhetoric of the advocates. She agreed that a pension properly so-called, was given in justice, but would give a fixed and stated sum to all widows with children regardless of need. William Hard, the sharpest tongued advocate of the pensions, lost no time in responding to the objections raised over labels applied to the new laws. "No claim to the name of pension?" he asked. "One might as well 'sharply challenge' a prickly pear because it isn't a pear. Some unacademic enthusiastic upright soul called it a pear because it happened to remind him of a pear, though it is really a cactus berry. It makes a distinguished salad just the same."[18]

Actually both the opponents and the advocates of the Widow's pension fully appreciated the importance of language in transforming what was once considered a gift of charity into an act of justice.[19] All the euphemisms used in reference to the laws, complained Mary Richmond, are already being taken up by shrewd politicians who may give them a significance and a power of popular attraction that their originators never intended."[20] Edward Devine, though brushing aside all real distinctions between out-door relief and the pensions, had to admit that the new names made a difference — a "purely subjective difference, a change in the point of view of the observer." The whole process, he declared, was an exercise in "self-delusion."[21] But from the point of view of the pension advocates this subjective difference was crucial. It was precisely this subjective difference that the advocates were striving to create. Indeed, the principal difficulty in the movement lay not so much in getting the public to dispense funds but in convincing the whole community, including the widow herself, to accept the aid as social justice. Gertrude Vaile, whose experience with the administration of the Pension act in Denver turned her from skeptic to a rather ardent friend of the law, wrote that the state, by officially recognizing that the average woman could not be both father and mother at the same time, created a "new public attitude regarding governmental responsibility for the care of the weak and destitute."[22] More important, the law created a "psychological difference" in the applicant. "The woman who will not apply for ordinary charity until she breaks does not apply for the pension with a sense of right and dignity."[23]

A vital part of the pension campaign strategy, then, was based upon an old truth that an essential difference between charity and social justice lay in the spirit with which the aid is given or received. Unlike the workmen's compensation acts and the schemes for social insurance, the widow's pension was so closely associated with charity that the tasks of injecting it with a new interpretation were far greater. Both workmen's compensation and social insurance were, in effect, circumventions of the poor law system. The State dealt with the individual in his capacity as an employee, and the employee was in one way or another regarded as having made a contribution toward the payments. The pension, however, created a direct relationship with the recipient just as the poor law had done and no contribution on the part of the widow was involved. As such, the pension program, even though it called for an administrative agency entirely separate from the poor relief offices, was an attempt to create a non-charitable relief system under the auspices of the State whose welfare was traditionally charity. Thus, what in another case might have been an insignificant tinkering in administrative methods, was here an important element in removing all the symbols associated with charity. And what in another case might have been a semantic quibble, in this instance was a debate of enormous consequences in which the subjective interpretation of a set of intangibles might spell the difference between charity and social justice.

If the widow's pension ran the risk of being construed as one of the oldest forms of public charity, it was at the same time capable of being regarded as one of the most radical forms of social justice. And it seems that this aspect caused the opponents to shudder most. In their brief against the pension they claimed that social insurance was an acceptable method of coping with insecurity. According to Devine, "It is simply a means of getting back that of which they are now unjustly and uneconomically deprived, and a means of meeting their own share of the risk in manageable installments."[24] Social insurance was a cooperative form of self-help. The widow's pension, on the other hand, was neither a payment of a financial obligation nor did it make any comparable demands in the way of a contribution. It was thus an invitation to disaster. It was "socialistic." It was "Unamerican." One critic complained, "It is not virile."[25]

The advocates of the pension, however, were not prepared to abandon the ethic of work; they were not about to justify their measure on the grounds that mere human existence deserved the right to a comfortable and dignified continuation. Instead, they wrapped the widow in all the raiment that enabled the wage-worker to claim outside help without the taint of charity; they gave her a job and an employer. "The aid is called a pension," wrote Marie and Frederick C. Howe, "to establish the idea that the destitute mother may take from the state money which is her right, since the bearing of children is really a more valuable service to the state than bearing arms."[26] An article in the *New York Times Annalist* went so far as to suggest that the state assumes the role of a business institution in that the pension would save money in the long run through better upbringing of the children. Some of the proponents objected to the term pension because it implied a payment for services already rendered, so a number of states substituted "subsidy" or "allowance" or "aid," indicating that the services were yet to be rendered. In any event, the services were considered socially necessary because as one newspaper put the case, "healthy, well-trained children are the biggest asset that a state can have."[27] And though the laws varied, payments to the widow ceased when the children were, according to the standards set by the state, old enough to assume financial responsibility of the household. To call the pension recipient a "dependent" declared William Hard "is as monstrous as to call the Librarian of Congress a "dependent."[28]

Most of the pension critics, however, could not swallow this argument. They could not accept the notion that the tasks of motherhood conferred any special rights to the public treasury and they feared the extension of this logic as they observed the manner in which the new acts were willing to include not only widows but women whose husbands had deserted or who had been in prison, or in the case of Michigan, women who had never had husbands, or in the case of Illinois, women whose husbands were still members of the family. Their long-time objection to public charity stemmed in part from the belief that this form of relief inspired dangerous attitudes even without it being advertised as a right.

But if the critics attacked the pension with new vehemence, the arguments were mostly familiar ones.[29] Essentially, the widow's self-reliance was believed to be at stake. Unwilling to conceive of her as worker for the state, the pension would remain in the eyes of the COS a dole and as "something for nothing" and as such would thwart her independence. She would become pauperized and be taught to believe that "the public purse is inexhaustible." Bessie McClendon of the Des Moines Association Charities felt that this old argument had lost none of its relevance. "I am convinced that there is a subtle difference in the psychological attitude of the applicant towards public and towards private relief and because of the subtility it is all the more necessary to take it into account."[30]

They also maintained that it would be impossible to find public officials who could administer the program with the proper safeguards, because as Frank Persons put it "the source of the fund is so remote and impersonal."[31] And John L. Lindsay, president of the N.Y. Society for the Prevention of Cruelty to Children, claimed that in order to carry on the proper investigations the law "would require the services of municipal spies and informers, clothed with the most despotic power." And even then, it would be "impossible to prevent a host of clever mendicants from profiting at least temporarily from the system."[32]

In addition to the widow's self-reliance, they feared for the whole community's sense of responsibility. The proverbial "well-spring of charity" would dry up; social relationships would dissolve. "The enthusiast in favor of the Widow's pension," remarked C.C. Carstens, "is indifferent to the rigid enforcement of responsibilities. He is apt to hold light the ties of kinship and of those natural community relations which find their most beautiful expression in the service which one person may render to another in a time of distress. He is apt to turn easily toward the payment of a lump sum from the public treasury as a substitute for family and neighborhood responsibility . . . . "[33] And they broadened this argument to include the detrimental effect the pension might have on genuine social reform. According to Persons, it "would be a sedative to public consciousness of wrongs to be righted."[34] Mary Richmond received information from a Pennsylvania social worker who was fighting the pension "tooth and nail" because it would "play havoc with any legislation concerning workingmen's compensation."[35] Richmond agreeing wholeheartedly with this view, stated that anything that would "delay recognition by the steel companies, of the patent fact that their main industry should be the production of steel, not of widows, is — may I say it — damnable."[36]

The conflict between opponents and most of the proponents had all the markings of a fundamental clash of philosophies. Pension advocates argued that extreme poverty, far more than public aid, destroyed self-reliance by making the economic struggle seem so futile. William H. Matthews of the NYAICP claimed that widows will not make individual efforts "unless we remove from their lives today that constant crushing anxiety that not only deadens hope and aspiration in the mother's life, but also gradually lays its withering, paralyzing hand on the lives of the children creating a downward pressure on life instead of an upward energy, sapping and undermining the vigor and hope of every member of the family."[37] Occasionally they would argue, as did Peter Alliot, that the indignity of private and public charity was far more detrimental than the grant of money given as a right "because the pauperizing tendency of an act is largely governed by public opinion and if the widow's support was popularly accepted, it would not be any more pauperizing than veteran's pensions."[38]

Since many of the pension supporters, perhaps because of their non-professional approach, did not regard the dependent mother as incompetent or on the brink of moral collapse, they were not so impressed with the necessities of exhaustive intensive investigations and the "following through" processes characteristic of private organized charities. They claimed they sought efficiency instead of the "formality, delay, officialdom, supervision and investigation," which tended to drive the widow into an unrealistic and often dangerous effort to remain self-supporting. She would either force her young ones to work, or go to work herself, thereby depriving the children of her attention — or what was worse, take in boarders.[39]

Thus according to friends of the pension, the meagre amounts of private charity, the uncertainty of their payments and the attitudes resulting from the nature of the act itself all conspired to leave the widow financially, and psychologically and spiritually depressed. And when opponents of the pension warned that public relief dissolved family ties or weakened the personal relationships among members of the community by absolving relatives and friends of their responsibilities, the pension advocates often replied, as did the majority of the Massachusetts Commission, that forcing the widow to beg from relatives or from private agencies not only pauperized the widow but through her embarrassment actually built a wall between the giver and the taker.[40] As for the effect of charity on the donors William Hard again minced no words: "Mr. Carstens would improve the situation by whipping up the businessman in his capacity as philanthropist. I would whip up that same man in his capacity as taxpayer. From his own standpoint, incidentally, and for the good of his own soul, since he has to pay the bill anyway, and ought to pay it, I would have him do so in a manner least calculated to tempt him toward thinking that he is performing an act of moral grandeur when he is really performing an act of elementary civic routine."[41]

For all of the intensity in the debate and the real differences of opinion, the philosophical dispute should not be exaggerated. A number of the supporters of the widow's pension were no more in favor of extending the logic to the wage earner than was Mary Richmond or Frank Persons. There seemed to be genuine agreement that for the wage worker contributory social insurance was the ideal. And there was considerable consensus that the widow's pension did not, in fact, fully implement the standards of social justice.[42] Supporters, however, considered it at least a "step forward" while the enemies considered it a "serious step backward." But it seems unlikely, even here, that their respective views stemmed entirely from a fundamentally diverse set of opinions concerning the effect of public aid on the individual. Most of the psychological principles presented by supporters of pension had for years found favor with its critics. And pension supporters did concede that public aid degenerated into the "disgraceful condition that existed in New York City up to 1878 and that still exists, though in lesser degree, throughout the rest of the State."[43] The most basic quarrel, it seems, was over the specific nature of the dependent widowhood.

Pension supporters declared her morally and mentally healthy — at least until proven guilty. They believed she would respond favorably to the money and in light of her need and the needs of society there was no point in waiting for a comprehensive social insurance scheme. Pension critics, on the other hand, were inclined to regard the widow as so personally responsible for her plight or so damaged by her experiences, or so susceptible to the temptations of a public gift that she required the kind of careful, individualized attention of the established charities.[44]

Moreover, a long-standing antipathy toward the charity societies ignited many of the fiery encounters between the contenders. It may have been that the established charities were too close to the type of widow that had come under their care and quite likely they had taken a proprietary interest in the widow's case. But for whatever reasons, they placed themselves in a position of favoring a modern yet distant proposal for social insurance while attacking the "step forward" with some of the most archaic weapons in their arsenal. And what little reserve of good will they had, after so many years of being the scapegoat in the anti-charity crusades, was virtually lost. Both Mary Richmond and Edward Devine felt that the sentiment in favor of the pension sprang in part from a prejudice against the charity organization societies and the social case-work method. "Who are these brash reformers," asked Devine, "who so cheerfully impugn the motives" of old-fashioned givers, of the conscientious directors of charitable institutions, of pious founders of hospitals and all manner of benefactors?"[45] To a considerable degree they were correct in thinking that pension campaign was combined with a rather vindictive and personal attack upon the COS. The investigating commissioners in New York singled out the "charity workers that dominate the New York School of Philanthropy and the Russell Sage Foundation" as the principal source of the opposition and echoed the currently fashionable charge that the COS was some sort of Charity Trust. That the widows still suffered from inadequate aid was all "the more serious in light of the fact that the private charities have had exclusive control of the field for more than thirty-six years."[46] Charity organizationists frequently found themselves ridiculed and their methods branded as the "third Degree" or as the "blood red tape of charity." But certainly not all the antagonists were "brash reformers."

In the early days of the movement a rather large body of social workers eyed the new pension with a good deal of skepticism. The most frequently voiced objection and the one which for a while, united the skeptics with the more hostile critics had to do with the administration. On one level it was that constant and frustrating search for the honest politician who would not exploit the funds for political purposes. Charles Henderson, for example, warned that unless the pension fund in Chicago be carefully watched it would become "another kind of spoils for low politicians."[47] And George F. Damon, Superintendent of the Kansas City Provident Association, though admitting that the law worked well, still expected "to see politics creep in sooner or later."[48] Many of them also were concerned that the administrators would be poorly trained for their work and in Illinois where the law was passed hastily without the prior consultation of the social workers their concern was amply justified. Yet if this issue created a united front against the pension it was also an issue upon which some of the social workers could reach an accommodation. In Chicago they were able to work out an agreement with the Judge of the Juvenile Court, in whose hands the chief responsibility lay. Graham Taylor claiming to speak for the "best informed social workers in Chicago," said that they felt the idea of a pension was a good one if properly administered.[49] And Jane Addams saw no reason to object to the law if "it can be administered with the help of the same charity-experts, who would otherwise be determining upon the relief for the same families."[50]

Generally speaking, settlement or group workers were quickest in accepting the new laws or less rigid in making demands in administration. But as the financial inadequacies of the established charities became too obvious to hide from public view, particularly during the depression of 1914-1915, and as the "irresistible tide of public sentiment" made itself felt, many of those closely connected with the COS found that resistance to the laws was, at best, bad public relations, and, at worst, unreasonable negativism. In the west where the private charities were not so well organized – where principles of charity organization had been watered down – there the pension movement ran roughshod over its opposition. The purity and the strength of the New York COS were of little influence and no help to Gertrude Vaile out in Denver. Believing in the principle of public pensions, yet convinced the particular Colorado Bill had many faults, she had to think twice about campaigning against it "as it would bring me into direct opposition to the people with whom I must heartily and tactfully work if I am to be of any further use in the charities situation here."[51] But even in the East and particularly in New York, where the established charities had so long fought the revival of out-door relief, the COS found itself increasingly isolated and subjected to abuse from members of its own family. Homer Folks, a vigorous opponent of widow's pensions in the 1890's, still had hopes in 1912 that the private charities should make an effort to expand their own pension programs. "But I think they should realize," he warned, "that this is the last call for dinner."[52] Frederic Almy of the Buffalo COS thought it safer for the present to rely on private charities, but acknowledged their inadequacy. He agreed that the methods of private charity — "A stupid fear of spending," and a "stupid fear of pauperizing — has made us penny wise and pound foolish." He feared the reopening of public relief, but conceded that the "curse of the old name is something and the new and better associations will make it easier to keep up the new and better standards."[53] A year later Almy was still having an "anxious time" on the widow's pension. But clearly he was breaking. He said he did not share Miss Richmond's concerns for the lack of competent supervision: "I am no special friend of supervision."[54] Paul Kellog, editor of the *Survey*, and one time student at the New York School of Philanthropy, admonished both Persons and Devine for having presented arguments that were ten or twenty years old. The American political scene had, he reminded them, changed greatly since Josephine Shaw Lowell's day when public officials "conceived public action merely in terms of ward politics and doles." Kellog felt that the charity workers had not fully faced up to the real needs of the widow and though a few leaders in the COS had become prominent spokesmen for social insurance, the majority of the COS people had been dragging their feet even in the field of workmen's compensation "and it was their field." So long as charity organizations "limited themselves to negative pronouncements on particular measures which may be half-baked," wrote Kellog, they "will be placed on the defensive continually while they should be the be the leaders in constructive proposals."[55]

Although members of several other of the established charities in New York had initially met the pension movement with hostility, their position was far less rigid than that of the New York COS.[56] C.L. Sulzberger, a trustee and former president of the United Hebrew Charities, expressed the attitude with which most of the established charities finally gave into the movement. Modern standards of control are fine, he said, "but a hungry widow cannot eat a friendly visitor."[57] And as the New York COS continued its battle against the pension, the other established charities found themselves unable to support what they increasingly saw as an unreasonable position. Bailey Burrit of the New York AICP publicly complained that the private charities were being subjected to abusive and unfair criticism, but privately conceded that they encouraged the misrepresentations. "Must we not arouse ourselves at once," he wrote to Edward Devine, "in order to remove any suspicion of smug feeling that we are at present adequately dealing with the problem and arm ourselves forthwith to deal with it, or failing this, to admit that we cannot in order that some other agency official or otherwise may undertake to cope with it?"[58]

With the passage of the New York Widow's Pension Law in 1915, the battle was over. If there were any lingering doubts about the capacity of the private charities to handle the widow these were cast away by the relief burdens imposed during the depression of 1914-1915. The success of the pension in other areas, the persistent demands for social justice, the mounting attacks on the charity organizations were too great to overcome.

It would be easy to dismiss the Charity organization position as a vain and stubborn attempt to resist the inevitable but inadvertently it was of considerable benefit. Without resistance the pension movement may have been less effective. It may have simply turned out as the accumulation of previous efforts to expand public relief to the widow. Without the challenge there would have been less opportunity to publicize the difference and to focus national attention on the problem. At the very least the struggle cleared the air somewhat. Despite all of the personal hostilities engendered by the debate, it forced into open forum an articulate discussion of the values in American society. It encouraged more precise definitions of charity and social justice; it raised more probing questions about the effect of public aid on the individuals. This is not to say that the social workers did not also extract their pound of flesh. They imposed certain demands upon the administrative safeguards which in some cases sucked the spirit out of the pension. In Massachusetts, for example, the funds were distributed through the Poor Law offices, making the pension virtually indistinguishable from earlier forms of out-door relief.

Although their opposition gave rise to a kind of vendetta against their own methods, the vehemence of the attack did have some salutary effect. It shocked them into a more critical self examination.[59] There was too great a tendency among Eastern charity workers, wrote William Matthews, "to slam the doors shut in the face of people who have become thoroughly dissatisfied with much of our private relief work and who honestly feel that there can come improvement only as we change some of the methods which we have worshipped and clung to for so long."[60]

Most important, while the debates over the pension temporarily dramatized the splits within the social work profession, the case workers and the group workers were thrown closer together on the question of social insurance. There seems little reason to doubt that the social insurance movement gained a more solid and enthusiastic support of the case workers. In a sense, it was the only way in which they could redeem themselves. Not until the advent of the pension movement, had so many pronouncements in favor of social insurance issued from the charity organization societies. And after a long and bitter campaign, Robert DeForest had had enough of the widow's pension. There were more important issues, he said. It was now time "to secure harmony and cooperation in larger matters."[61]

NOTES

[1] White House Conference on Child Health and Protection, *Dependent and Neglected Children* IV, C-1 (New York, 1933), p. 59.

[2] Sherman Kingsley to Frank Persons, February 17, 1912, CSS COS MSS.

[3] White House Conference, *Dependent Children*, p. 9.

[4] *Indianapolis Star,* Jan. 28, 1913.

[5] *Survey* XXX (April 12, 1913), p. 74.

[6] *Lend A Hand,* XI (1893), pp. 517, 532; Paine, *Seventh Episcopal,* 1881, p. 98.

[7] Abbott, Child and State, pp. 230-238; Laura Thompson, *Laws Relating to Mothers' Pensions in the United States, Canada, Denmark and New Zealand,* U.S. Dept. of Labor, Childrens' Bureau, Bureau of Publications No. 63 (Washington: 1919), pp. 7-9; Emma O. Lundberg, *Unto the Least of These* (New York and London, 1947), p. 124.

[8] Robert Treat Paine, "Pauperism in Great Cities," *Lend a Hand,* XII, (1894), p. 201.

[9] Watson, *Charity Organization,* pp. 511-512; *Charities Review,* VIII (March 1895), p. 5.

[10] *Public Pensions to Widows with Children: A Study of their Administration in Several American Cities,* 1913.

[11] Massachusetts, *Report of the Commission on the Support of Dependent Minor Children of Widowed Mothers,* (Boston, 1913), pp. 35-36.

[12] *Ibid.,* pp. 10-13

[13] Edward T. Devine, "Pensions for Mothers," *ALLR,* III (June 1913), p. 200.

[14] Sherman Kingsley to Frank Persons, Feb. 17, 1912, CSS, COS MSS.

[15] Edith Abbott, *The Child and the State,* Vol. II, (Chicago, 1938), pp. 230-238; Memos entitled "Mother's Pensions," "The Situation in the States," December 30, 1912 and January 13, 1913, CSS, COS MSS.

[16] Ben B. Lindsey, "The Mother's Compensation Law of Colorado," The Survey, XXIX (February 15, 1913), p. 715.

[17] Mary Richmond, " 'Pensions' and the Social Worker," *The Survey,* XXIX (Feb. 15, 1913), p. 665.

[18] William Hard, "Pensions for Mothers," *American Labor Legislative Review,* III (June 1913), p. 230.

[19] *Ibid.,* p. 231; Homer Folks, "Making Relief . . . ," N.Y. Charities Aid Association, *Report* 1934, p. 5.

[20] Mary Richmond, "Motherhood and Pensions," *Survey,* XXIX (March 1, 1913), p. 778.

[21] Edward T. Devine, "Pensions for Mothers," *American Labor Legislation Review,* III (June, 1913), p. 194.

[22] Gertrude Vaile to William Matthews, Jan. 29, 1915, CSS, AICF, MSS.

[23] *Ibid.,* Gertrude Vaile, "Administering Mother's Pensions in Denver," *The Survey,* XXXI (Feb. 28, 1914), p. 674.

[24] Devine, "Pensions for Mothers," *op. cit.,* pp. 200-201; see also: NCOCC, *Thirty-Ninth Annual Report,* 1912, pp. 491-492; C.C. Carstens, "Public Pensions to Widows with Children," *The Survey,* XXIX (Jan. 4, 1913), pp. 465-466.

[25] *The New York State Commission on Relief to Widowed Mothers Report* (Albany, 1914), p. 130.

[26] Frederic C. Howe and Marie Jenny Howe, "Pensioning the Widow and the Fatherless," *Good Housekeeping,* LVII (Sept. 1913), p. 283.

[27] Clipping from *Republican Press* (Marion, Ill.) Feb. 1, 1915, CSS, COS MSS.

[28] William Hard, "The Moral Necessity," *Survey,* XXIX, p. 773; see also: "The Needy Mother and the Neglected Child," *Outlook,* CIV (June 7, 1913), pp. 280-283; Theodore Roosevelt to Mrs. Clara Cahill Park, quoted in *New York Times,* Jan. 9, 1912.

[29] Edward Devine to Frank Persons, Feb. 8, 1912, CSS, COS MSS.

[30] Bessie A. McClenahan to Edward Devine, Oct. 2, 1912, CSS, COS MSS; also see Robert W. DeForest to William Colne, 1912, CSS, AICP MSS, pp. 15-17.

[31] Persons, *A Serious Step Backward*

[32] Clipping from *New York Times,* ca Feb. 1912, CSS, AICP MSS, 15.7.

[33] C.C. Carstens, "Public Pensions . . . ," *The Survey,* XXIX (1913), p. 462.

[34] Frank W. Persons, *A Serious Step Backward* (N.Y., 1912).

[35] Quoted in a letter signed by Mary Richmond, Jan. 7, 1913, CUSSW, RSF MSS.

[36] Quoted in a letter signed by Mary Richmond, Jan. 7, 1913, CUSSW, RSF, MSS.

[37] William H. Matthews, "Widows' Families, Pensioned and Otherwise," *The Survey,* XXXII (June 6, 1914), p. 270.

[38] Peter Allcot to W. Frank Persons, Dec. 7, 1913, CSS, COS MSS.

[39] N.Y. State *Commission-Widows,* p. 51.

[40] Mass., *Report on Widowed Mothers,* pp. 22-25.

[41] William Hard, "The Moral Necessity of 'State Funds to Mothers,' " *The Survey,* XXIX (March 1, 1913), p. 171.

[42] Rubinow, *Social Insurance,* pp. 437-438; Merritt Pinckney, "Public Pensions to Widows . . . ," *Child,* I, pp. 43-47.

[43] New York *Commission-Widows,* p. 114.

[44] Untitled Paper by Mary Richmond, Nov. 5, 1910, CSS, COS MSS.

[45] Devine, "Pensions . . . ," *op. cit.;* Richmond, "Motherhood and Pensions," *The Survey,* XXIX, p. 114.

[46] New York *Commission Widows,* p. 79.

[47] Charles R. Henderson to W. Frank Persons, Feb. 16, 1912, CSS, COS MSS.

[48] George F. Damon to W. Frank Persons, April 18, 1912, CSS, COS MSS.

[49] Graham R. Taylor to W. Frank Persons, Feb. 15, 1912, CSS, COS MSS.

[50] Jane Addams to Frank Persons, Feb. 20, 1912, CSS, COS MSS.

[51] Gertrude Vaile to Mary Richmond, Sept. 25, 1912, CSS, SOC MSS.

[52] NCCC, *Proceedings,* 1912, p. 487.

[53] Frederic Almy, "Public Pensions to Widows: Experiences and Observations which Lead Me to Oppose Such a Law," *Child,* I (July 1912), pp. 52, 53-54.

[54] Frederic Almy, to Persons, June 14, 1913, CSS, COS MSS.

[55] Paul Kellog to W. Frank Persons, March 7, 1912, CSS, COS MSS.

[56] *New York Times,* Oct. 13, 1912; John Kingsbury to Thomas Cullen, Feb. 27, 1912, CSS, AICP MSS; New York COS Executive Committee Minutes, June 5, 1912, CSS, COS MSS.

[57] New York *Commission-Widows,* p. 119.

[58] Bailey B. Barritt to Edward Devine, Feb. 25, 1914, CSS, AICP MSS.

[59] Mary Richmond, "Pensions and the Social Worker," *The Survey,* XXIX (1912) pp. 665-666; Mary I. Breed to W. Frank Persons, Jan. 30, 1914, CSS, COS MSS.

[60] Matthews to Vaile, April 10, 1915, CSS, AICP MSS.

[61] Robert DeForest to W. Frank Persons, Jan. 6, 1915, CSS, COS MSS.

CHAPTER VIII

THE HEALTH INSURANCE MOVEMENT, 1912 – 1917

With the widow's pension and workmen's compensation movements well underway, the American Association for Labor Legislation set out to attend to "larger matters." In 1912 it organized the "New Committee on Social Insurance," and called for a National Conference on Social Insurance to meet in 1913. *The Survey* proclaimed that it was now time for the government to expand its role; to protect the citizen against misfortune as well as against violence and fraud.[1]

The American Association for Labor Legislation was not destined to repeat its workmen's compensation successes, but the failure to achieve legislative results in the areas of old age, unemployment or health insurance hardly bears testimony to an enduring American attachment to rugged individualism. In their appeals for social insurance, advocates found responsive audiences among many sectors of American society.

In an atmosphere generally favorable to social reform and apparently favorable to some type of modern social welfare reform, the American Association for Labor Legislation took the path of least resistance and focused upon health insurance. The problem of sickness took precedence over other sources of worker insecurity for a number of reasons. It not only trapped large numbers of people in a "vicious circle" of poverty and sickness, but health insurance was a logical follow-up to accident and occupational disease compensation.

In what appears to have been an impressively organized campaign, paying proper deference to the medical interests, the American Association for Labor Legislation managed to mobilize sufficient resources to introduce health insurance bills in several state legislatures and to win approval from a wide variety of individuals and organizations. If Americans in 1917 remained committed to a strictly defined notion of individual responsibility, it is difficult to square with the fact that so many people declared in favor of health insurance and that to quite a number of them as well as to others, health insurance was imminent.

* * * *

The mood of the social insurance movement had changed rather rapidly toward the end of 1912. When in late 1911 and early 1912 New

York State considered the amending of its constitution to permit a compulsory workmen's compensation law, a question arose as to how broad the new amendment should be. Henry Seager felt it should be so worded as to allow for all forms of social insurance. "I think we can be certain this country is going to follow the countries of Europe," he wrote. "It is in the air."[2] Others, however, shared John B. Andrews' opinion that it would be better to concentrate on accident compensation because of the hostilities already provoked by the amendment and because of the "present remoteness of old age, sickness and unemployment insurance."[3] But within a matter of months a new temper was apparent. One observer, in reference to the progress being made on the Workmen's Compensation Acts, stated "that there is danger that what is said today may be out of date tomorrow."[4] Jane Addams paid her tribute to what was probably the most important new factor, Theodore Roosevelt's 1912 campaign. The social reform measures she had been working on for years, she said, "never before seemed to become so possible of fulfillment as at the present moment."[5] William Kent, one of the successful progressive candidates in the election did not think the defeat of the party so disastrous: "We have gotten the humanitarian issues before the people and they are bound to stay there until recognized."[6] And within a little more than a year, John B. Andrews had seen enough to announce "that when we once get underway in America, we are willing to move much faster than they are in Europe."[7]

In part, the receptivity to social insurance was a by-product of both the widow's pension movement and the workmen's compensation movement. In the case of the former social insurance became a more urgent requirement if only for the fact that it offered a more "rational" and more safe method of dealing with insecurity. The workmen's compensation was an even more effective stimulant. For one thing, it tended to put a premium on the younger worker who was less susceptible to accidental injury; consequently it intensified the problem of unemployment as well as aged dependency, because many of the older workers found themselves at a serious disadvantage when looking for work.

Second, the compensation acts gave rise to new insurance systems which were important in laying the foundations for any future social insurance program. Contrary to many of the predictions that the new laws would not be an additional financial burden on the employer, they did in fact tend to raise costs — especially in those states with elective measures, where the element of uncertainty caused the insurance rates to go up several times. Several states, therefore, went into the insurance business in order to provide the employer with a cheaper form of protection against the new liabilities. Even where the state did not hold a monopoly — where it competed with various forms of private insurance, it generally engaged in far more strict regulation of the private forms. In addition, while some employers were reluctant to buy the government insurance, they were in the process of forming their own mutual insurance associations.

Perhaps, even more important, the workmen's compensation movement, by reopening the still unhealed wounds suffered by the private insurance companies, managed to subdue what were potentially the most formidable opponents to social insurance. Organized labor was probably most insistent upon striking a blow at the "cold blooded, sordid, greedy influences" of the private insurance companies,[8] but few people shed any tears of sympathy for them. Seth Low did not favor the demands of labor for a state monopoly of accident insurance, but he said his own observations of the behavior of the insurance companies toward the injured worker made it easy for him to understand labor's desire to eliminate the private companies from the compensation system.[9]

Employers, and especially those within the National Association of Manufacturers, who had some dealings with the private companies through their liability policies, were in most cases very much dissatisfied with the handling of worker injuries and with the rates charged. The investigations made by the NAM's Industrial Insurance Committee revealed that a vast majority of their membership preferred that an alternative method of insurance be developed.[10] According to the chairman of the California Industrial Accident Board, employers in that state felt that the liability companies had "dealt very harshly with them as to rates."[11] A. G. Hardwick, Secretary of the Niagara Falls Employers Association, wrote that the "powerful influence" of the insurance companies was proving to be one of the greater obstacles to social justice. "I have attended many conferences upon this subject," he said, "and each has proved fruitless, and the consequence is a weariness in the attempt to work against the entrenched monied interests."[12] The insurance companies were able to exert their pressure throughout the storms of public protest, but their methods had, at the same time, driven a wedge into the business community which under other circumstances might have presented a more solid front against the encroachments of governmental interference.

Social insurance proponents also felt they might be able to reap some benefit from the outbreak of the European war. Although the European conflict disrupted all the plans for the United States to be the host nation of the 1915 International Congress on Social Insurance, the war did dramatize the urgent need for what the new nationalists were now calling "social preparedness."[13] "In the world's crisis of clashing nations where the efficiency is the test of endurance," warned a prominent insurance commissioner, "those found most efficient, most enduring, and most patriotic are those having the most extensive and far reaching systems of social insurance." If the war comes, he continued, the nation would not be defended by the wealthy few "but it will be the common people whom we have for half a century neglected."[14] From American businessmen in Berlin, came the opinion that the hundreds of thousands of German soldiers doing battle for the fatherland "may trace their health and capacity to the timely and proper treatment received with the aid of sickness insurance."[15]

From the point of view of social security proponents, America had neglected the victims of aged dependency, unemployment, sickness and invalidity and all of these misfortunes were regarded as properly coming under an insurance program. "When we classify the causes of poverty," declared *The Survey,* "we enumerate the various kinds of insurance."[16] The social security movement, however, did not advance on all fronts with equal promise, nor for that matter was it the intention of the social insurance advocates to divide their energies in all directions.

The movement for aged security had perhaps the most consistent vitality. For years enthusiasm had been widespread. A number of states had established investigating commissions, and there were numerous bills introduced into the state legislatures.[17] In a number of cities in Massachusetts and in the state of Arizona, where an old age pension proposition was put before a referendum, the measure won resounding victories.[18] In Arizona the legislature passed a pension act in 1915, but it was declared unconstitutional.

Acitivity on the federal level was also encouraging. Various pension bills were introduced in Congress and federal civil service employees had managed to create a lively and reasonably well organized agitation for civil service pensions. Yet the movement for old age security remained a rather diffuse affair. The American Association for Labor Legislation did not attempt to marshal the energies of the movement, so it remained seriously split between the advocates of a pension and those favoring a contributory or insurance system.

The projected costs of old age security tended to be a drag on enthusiasm and more than likely the Civil War pensions, distributing more than 150,000,000 dollars to nearly a million people, were able to blunt any sense of urgency.[19]

The American Association for Labor Legislation gave somewhat greater priority to the problem of unemployment. In 1912 it established the American Congress on Unemployment as an offshoot of the International Congress on Unemployment and sponsored a National Conference of Unemployment in 1914. While the problem of unemployment was an old one, and often regarded as extremely serious, national interest was sporadic. The movement seemed to gain a steadier momentum after the passage in 1911 of the British Unemployment Insurance Act, but discussion and enthusiasm generally rose with the valleys in the labor market and declined with the peaks. Thus in 1914, in the midst of a recession a number of special bodies, such as the Chicago Mayor's Commission on Unemployment, the Oregon Committee on Seasonal Unemployment or the Commission of Immigration and Housing of California explored the merits of unemployment insurance. It was also on the agenda of the United States Industrial Commission of 1915 as well as of several state and city commissions in California, Massachusetts and New York. In spite of the fact that bills on unemployment insurance were introduced and discussed in state and federal legislatures, the movement had not yet gotten off the ground.[20] Many of its most active proponents agreed with one employer that the question of unemployment was "perhaps the most important as well as the hardest that civilization requires shall be solved." Definitions of unemployment were still vague, statistical information remained in a rather primitive stage, trade union machinery, which had formed a basis for the governmental program in Europe, was often too informal.

The movement's leaders, therefore, concentrated on educating the public and providing as best they could, groundwork for a system of unemployment insurance. With some success the social insurance advocates waged a campaign to set up a network of public employment bureaus or labor exchanges throughout the country. In 1900 there had been fifteen such offices in thirteen cities of seven states. By 1910 the number had increased to fifty-five bureaus in fifty-three cities of twenty-one states and by the end of 1917, there were 181 bureaus in 152 cities of forty-two states (including D.C.).[21] The growth of the employment bureaus probably exaggerates the strength of the unemployment insurance movement. While many of their proponents generally conceived of them as necessary machinery in any future system of unemployment insurance, the bureaus also held out the hope of obviating the necessity for insurance in that they would bring workers and work together. Even in the American Association for Labor Legislation some felt as did John R. Commons that unemployment was an avoidable contingency of life and could be eliminated if the employers were induced to find more rational uses of manpower and production.[22] Or as the Washington *Times* put it: "To organize the productive means so that they will be kept at work .... There is managerial capacity enough in the world to solve the riddle, if only it were set to work."

It was in the area of sickness or health insurance that the social security movement was most promising of success and the area which the American Association of Labor Legislation focused upon in its 1913 Conference of Social Insurance. It is only in light of more recent social welfare history that one might be surprised to learn that health insurance was thought to be the "next step." In the context of the progressive era, however, health insurance appears to have been an appropriate follow-up to widows' pensions and workmen's compensation.

Sickness was first of all more definable and more persistent than unemployment. Health insurance was both less costly and more urgent than old age insurance. Moreover, sickness had for some time been blamed for a host of moral, mental and social evils. During the nineteenth century, insanity, crime and pauperism were frequently diagnosed in terms of an organic disturbance and traced back to an unhygienic environment. In the progressive period, the connection between sickness and poverty and dependency was even more fully explored. Medical social service, which had become a leading specialty in the professional social work, reflected both the broadened social outlook of the medical profession as well as the heightened interest in sickness among the professional social workers.[23] Doctors, in addition, had become more aware of the possibilities of preventive medicine – of the need to improve standards of living, diet, housing, sanitary facilities, medical check-up, early diagnosis. Progressive commentators spent less time pondering whether sickness caused poverty or poverty caused sickness and more time discussing the "vicious cycle of poverty and sickness."[24] The United States Public Health Service estimates revealed rather dramatically how illness could become a drain on the income – $500,000,000 lost annually in wages, $180,000,000 spent on medical care. A study made by the United States Immigration Commission in 1909 reported that out of more than 30,000 charity cases sickness was a factor in 38.3%. The reports of charity societies were even more startling. The New York Association for Improving the Condition of the Poor spent 60-80% of its relief money on cases caused largely by sickness. The New York Charity Organization Society discovered that in a sample of 5,000 cases of family dependency about three-quarters were due mainly to sickness.[25]

In sheer numbers, sickness far outstripped accidental injury. The figures cited by the Immigration Commission show that sickness was a factor in six and one-half times as many cases of dependency as were accidental injuries. But numbers alone did not make for urgent atmosphere surrounding the health insurance movement. Other misfortunes may have been more numerous or more capable of producing social unrest, but neither old age, unemployment nor an accidental injury were contagious. There was still some talk of tramps and vagabonds contaminating the morals of a community, but no one doubted that sickness posed a public health problem. And while all the available evidence demonstrated that the poor had shorter life spans and were more susceptible to the cholera and tuberculosis, the rich were aware that these diseases could spread easily in thickly populated urban centers. One of the most "popular" causes of the day was the fight against tuberculosis. The campaign that had begun when the New York Charity Organization Society established its Committee on the Prevention of Tuberculosis in 1902, was in full swing by 1913. The National Association for the Study and Prevention of Tuberculosis, which had propagandized the poverty and sickness theme, was of inestimable value in making the American public as receptive to health insurance as it was.

Equally important in preparing the way for health insurance was the workmen's compensation movement. For one thing, it established a major precedent for compulsory medical attention. In addition to compelling the employer to provide for loss sustained as a result of injury, the workmen's compensation laws also required in varying degrees that the employer be charged with some of the medical expenses accruing from the accident. In Connecticut the employer was obliged to pay for "reasonable" expenses, in California he was to cover the cost for the first ninety days, in Iowa he was expected to assume the doctor's bills for two weeks or up to a maximum of $100.[26]

Although both the opponents and proponents of health insurance relied primarily upon the experience in Germany and England for evaluating the specific machinery under which the system would operate, the workmen's compensation laws did provide some native experience with several different types of medical insurance carriers. Thus even before health insurance, America had some brush with the questions of the doctor-patient relationship, malingering, adequate pay and adequate medical service in an arrangement where the patient did not directly pay the doctor.

Workmen's compensation laws, moreover, led rather naturally to the question of compensation for occupational diseases, and this in turn opened up the problem of sickness in general. Although in virtually all states an accident was defined as a sudden and violent product of an industrial situation, this was for all practical purposes the only basic distinction that could be made between many an industrial disease and an industrial accident. Increasingly the distinction was regarded as an artificial one. In Massachusetts, where the compensation law applied to personal "injury" sustained in the performance of duty, the courts rather liberally interpreted the new act so as to include some of the more well-known and predictable diseases associated with certain occupations, such as "painter's palsy," "matchmaker's Phossy-jaw," and "mine-worker's bends."[27] Other states had accomplished the same thing by amending the compensation laws to include occupational diseases, and the federal government enacted the Kern-McGillicuddy Act, conferring the benefits of this principle upon federal employees.

Not all the active proponents of health insurance, however, were eager to push the question of occupational disease as an extension of workmen's compensation. One reason was that with certain notable exceptions the occupational disease was still so imprecisely defined as to include illnesses that were caused largely by factors outside of an industrial situation. Therefore, to some it seemed unfair to hold the employer as responsible for this type of affliction as for an accident which more directly and more clearly issued from conditions of employment. According to this reasoning, health insurance would provide a more just solution because the worker would be making a definite monetary contribution to the health insurance fund. In addition, it was felt that a campaign for occupational disease compensation siphoned off reformist energies into seeking the solution of a relatively insignificant aspect of workmen's health and would present workmen's compensation boards with the difficult task of distinguishing between an occupational disease and an ordinary illness. Rather than tackle this problem which merely confused the whole issue of worker's health, declared the economist, Selig Perlman, it would be better to concentrate on illness in general. In fact, wrote Perlman, the very vagueness of an occupational disease would be an invaluable "talking point in an argument in favor of constitutionality of a general compulsory sickness insurance law. . . ."[28]

The American Association for Labor Legislation, however, continued to promote compensation for occupational disease. The organization collected statistics, kept tabs on court interpretations, and wrote articles and pamphlets. The AALL had, in addition, successfully agitated for a federal Commission on Occupational Diseases in 1913, prepared the bills introduced and sponsored by Senator Kern and Congressman McGillicuddy, and kept up a constant pressure on congressmen until its passage in 1915. John B. Andrews had since 1910 supported the inclusion of occupational diseases in the compensation acts. He did not put much weight on the distinction between the sudden and violent nature of an accident and the gradual deterioration from an occupational disease. The fundamental similarity remained, namely that both arose out of the specific conditions of employment and it was therefore unfair to make the worker contribute more for one than the other. Moreover, whatever the difficulties in defining the occupational disease, the campaign for it had become useful in the health insurance movement. This type of compensation, he wrote, marked a "natural transition" in the public mind from accident compensation to sickness insurance, "and as such might be regarded as an 'entering wedge.' "[29]

On the whole, the proponents of health insurance had a proper regard for the necessity of easing the public into acceptance of the new measure. In what appears to have been a better organized campaign than that for workmen's compensation, the American Association for Labor Legislation went about its task confidently and patiently. While its committee on social insurance worked on a preliminary standard bill for health insurance during 1913 and 1914, the organization stepped up its educational campaign and strove to allay the suspicions and head off the criticisms of likely opponents. One of the main targets of this effort was the medical profession, about whom health insurance advocates had few illusions. "Many of the physicians," wrote Andrews, "are not exactly what we would call social minded."[30] Yet the hope of courting favor with influential members of the profession and medical societies was not an unreasonable expectation. Doctors were not entirely immune to the infectious reformism of the progressive period. With the growth of hospitals, clinics, dispensaries, public health boards and medical social work, came the rise of the organization doctor, the salaried doctor and the "social minded" doctor. In addition there were many doctors whose practices were small or whose patients were virtually charity cases, and these members of the profession might welcome a scheme that would expand business and at the same time assure them payment for their services. The Federation of Medical Economic Leagues, for example, had no quarrel with the idea of compulsory health insurance. On the contrary, its main concern was that under the bill prepared by the AALL doctors would not get their fair share because it excluded coverage for the most indigent. "What is to become of him! Is he to be an object of medical charity at the expense of the physician as at present. . .?"[31]

Actually it was the strategy of the health insurance proponents to remain vague and flexible on those provisions of the bill that would directly affect the doctor. In order to avoid some of the mistakes of the English health insurance movement, they sought to enlist the medical community by giving its representatives an opportunity to help in the formulation of the standard bill. In a speech before the State Medical Society of Wisconsin, John R. Commons invited the doctors to join the movement early in the game when they would have considerable influence rather than to wait until they would either lose prestige or be forced into rebelling against what was sure to come.[32]

In the late summer of 1914, John B. Andrews began to intensify his efforts to sound out possible support among doctors and to cultivate sympathy where possible. He wrote to a number of leading medical men in some of the main industrial centers, and had interviews with Dr. Theodore Sachs of Chicago and Dr. Bardeen, head of the Wisconsin University Medical Department. With the able assistance of Ida Cannon, head of the Social Service Department of the Massachusetts General Hospital, prominent medical men were called together to discuss the subject of health insurance.[33]

There appeared to be many untapped reservoirs: in New York City a committee of prominent physicians who were agitating for occupational disease compensation; at the University of Wisconsin, the Medical Department was taking an "advanced stand" on the state's role in medical care; at the University of California, several prominent medical professors had championed the cause; in Washington, D.C., Dr. B. S. Warren, the U.S. Surgeon General, an ardent friend of health insurance, had been appointed to investigate the question under the auspices of the United States Industrial Commission.

The results throughout the year and the next grew steadily more encouraging. Dr. Charles McIntire, Secretary of the American Academy of Medicine, notified John B. Andrews in December that the Academy's Journal would now be called the *Journal of Sociologic Medicine,* and expressed the hope that it would live up to the "broader implications of its new name."[34] The AMA *Journal* which, for several years, had been periodically reporting on insurance activities here and abroad, was paying considerably more attention to the movement. "The failure of many persons in this country at present to receive medical care," declared one writer, "constitutes the best argument for a change to the more effectual provision for medical attention offered by health insurance."[35] In 1915, Dr. Alexander Lambert, Chairman of the Judicial Council of the American Medical Association, became the principal medical advisor to the AALL. In the same year his Judicial Council had issued a report highly sympathetic to health insurance.[36] And toward the end of the year the American Medical Association moved closer to establishing a formal endorsement of health insurance. Dr. Frederick R. Green, Secretary of the AMA's Council of Public Health and Instruction, offered to create a special three-man advisory committee so that the AMA could take official part in the activities of the American Association for Labor Legislation. "Your plans," wrote Green, "are so entirely in line with our own that I want to be of every possible assistance."[37]

In the meantime, the health insurance movement was arousing considerable interest and gaining converts in other quarters. By December of 1915, the American Association for Labor Legislation had printed up 13,000 copies of its draft bill on health insurance in order to meet the demand. One state, California, had already established a social insurance commission and, in the fall of the year, began focusing, as was its intention, upon health insurance. A variety of private organizations also were beginning to set up their own special committees and commissions on social insurance or offering their cooperation to the American Association for Labor Legislation. Among the more powerful social welfare organizations to lend their support was the Russell Sage Foundation, and in November, William T. Cross, Secretary of the National Conference of Charities and Correction, responded to the urgings of many of the members and offered the cooperation of this prestigious group.[38] By the middle of 1916, nearly every national organization dealing with socio-economic problems discussed the question of health insurance, and more than forty groups officially investigated the subject.[39] Health insurance committees were booming in charity organization societies, chambers of commerce, actuarial societies and medical societies. In Detroit the newly formed American Association of Industrial Physicians and Surgeons set up a social insurance committee as its first official act.

In the earliest days of the health insurance campaign, the AALL had not only been in its most serious financial straits but the working membership had dwindled as well. "There are only a few of us who care for the association," Andrews had written in December, 1913, "and we are nearly driven to death by work."[40] Now the organization seemed to be thriving. If it could have used more money and if the active members were still overworked, it at least was able to enlist many more people in the cause. With the introduction of the Mills health insurance bill in the New York legislature in 1916, the AALL was able to put together a speaker's bureau to explain the new measure before charity societies, business groups and civic organizations. Among the speakers were Frederick Almy, Secretary of the Buffalo Charity Organization Society; Pauline Newman of the Women's Trade Union League; James Jenkins, Jr., Executive Secretary of the Brooklyn Board of Charities; Dr. Louis J. Harris, Chief of the Division of Industrial Hygiene of the New York Department of Health; Dr. G. S. Goldwater, formerly the New York City Commissioner of Health and now Superintendent of the Mt. Sinai Hospital; and Dr. Philip F. Jacobs, Assistant Secretary of the National Association for the Study and Prevention of Tuberculosis.

Whatever the strain on the proponents of health insurance they were now working in the heady atmosphere of success. As they looked back upon their earlier efforts for workmen's compensation they saw many parallels in the health insurance movement. Indeed if anything the health insurance movement appeared in better shape in 1916 than workmen's compensation did in 1909. They began to talk of its inevitability. An enthusiast from California predicted that by the end of the European War there would be a social revolution "such as the world has never seen before. We will surely be influenced by it and compulsory insurance is sure to come."[41] Even Rubinow, who was not ordinarily given over to excessive optimism, declared that victory could not elude a movement growing so fast. "One almost begins to feel," he wrote, "that it is growing too fast."[42]

Although not every desire to investigate the movement could be recorded as a vote of confidence there were enough favorable responses to have encouraged the most hard-headed realists. What was one to think when even that "thoroughly reactionary" body, the National Association for Manufacturers, had come out in favor of compulsory health insurance? The resolution adopted by the NAM in 1916 did not endorse the bill proposed by the American Association for Labor Legislation, but the businessmen put their stamp of approval on some of the principles behind it. The Industrial Betterment Committee, whose report was adopted, proposed that all types of insurance carriers, including private ones, should be allowed to compete under health insurance and the committee expressed a preference for a voluntary system. But the committee also acknowledged the difficulties in relying upon the initiative of employers and employees and accepted the necessity of indirect or direct compulsion. "It has been well said," stated the report "that the state should move cautiously and tentatively in the direction of the experiment; but as the evolution of the modern state plainly shows, it must move. It must often subordinate the independence of the individual to the general good."[43] However cautious the endorsement it came as a welcome, if surprising, portent to the leaders of the movement. "The report of the Committee on Industrial Betterment," wrote one of them, "seems almost too good to be true."[44]

Actually the position of the NAM was largely the work of the Chairman of the Industrial Betterment Committee, Ferdinand C. Schwedtman. Schwedtman had been active in social welfare causes for some years now. In 1910 he and A. Parker Nevins, the NAM's legal counsel, had gone to Europe to investigate the workmen's compensation laws. Their report was instrumental in getting the NAM to support the new welfare program. Schwedtman's efforts on behalf of social welfare legislation did not cease with the success of the compensation movement. On the contrary he seems to have assumed the role of keeper of the NAM's social conscience, and guardian of its public image. He had hopes that the NAM would become the "recognized standard bearer of righteous American industrialism."[45] Two years before the NAM accepted his committee's report, he had begun prodding the Board of Directors to adopt a constructive platform on the question of social insurance in order to aid the movement "instead of opposing it as has so often been the tendency of manufacturers in the past."[46] At the same time he had urged the general membership of NAM to be more progressive in their attitudes toward social insurance. "Social legislation is not going to stop at workmen's compensation and accident prevention, nor ought it to stop there."[47]

Schwedtman's progressivism was obviously not typical in the NAM. He was forced to move cautiously because, as he put it, the average manufacturer "naturally belongs to the more conservative class of people."[48] Yet the delegates assembled in May 1916 had approved of the committee's work. Moreover, a survey of the NAM membership conducted by the Industrial Betterment Committee had led it to conclude that "a large percentage of our members favor sickness insurance." The returns from a questionnaire showed that only 197 out of 564 respondents objected to the state or federal government taking action with reference to social insurance.[49]

In those states where health insurance proposals were given an official airing, the reaction of witnesses was reassuring if in some cases more expected. Most of those who testified before the California commission were sympathetic and the commission itself, though it did not recommend a specific bill, had declared in favor of a constitutional amendment enabling the passage of a health insurance act.[50] Furthermore, the commission's poll of social workers and economists belonging to the

National Conference of Charities and Correction and the American Economic Association revealed that a heavy majority were in favor of compulsory health insurance. Out of 675 replies to the commission's questionnaire, 87% favored a bill, 9% made no comment and only 4% opposed health insurance.[51] The hearings before the New York and Massachusetts legislatures, where bills had been introduced, produced similar results. In one session in October which lasted until 11 o'clock in the evening, the Massachusetts Commission of Social Insurance had to move its hearings to the largest room in the State House in order to accommodate the large audience. Dr. Carroll Doten of MIT reported that the enthusiasm for health insurance was much greater than earlier comparable hearings on workmen's compensation and the opposition was much milder.[52] In New York, where Senator Ogden Mills had introduced a health insurance bill, there was virtual unanimity in support of the principle of health insurance among those who testified before the legislative hearings.[53] The activities in the legislatures had also been given a wide coverage by the press and in many cases a cordial and sympathetic reception. The *New York Globe, New York Herald*, the *New York Sun*, and the *Press* all looked favorably upon the proceedings in the legislature.[54]

There were, of course, expressions of disapproval, but these were easily interpreted as signs of the essential health of the movement. That private insurance interests had taken the time and effort to appear before the legislators meant at least the issue was too important and lively to be dismissed with indifference. Insurance companies in New York, for example, were urging their agents to join the New York Insurance Federation, one of the principal organs of opposition. The Great Eastern Casualty Company was making an appeal to its agents to help defeat the "pernicious and un-American" legislation, warning them that "THE NEED IS PRESSING."[55] In addition, it was believed even by the enemies of health insurance that the open opposition of the insurance companies did more good than harm to the movement. Miss Gertrude Beeks of the NCF believed their very presence in the debate was helpful to the social insurance advocates.[56] In the opinion of Frederick Hoffman, "the insurance companies are either *persona non grata*, or their motives are suspected. The casualty companies particularly have been fighting state insurance and have made themselves throughly disliked and throughly misunderstood."[57]

Many of the objections, moreover, seemed to indicate either tacit approval or grudging acceptance of some compulsory health measure. On the hearings in Albany, Olga Halsey, of the American Association for Labor

Legislation, noted that most of the criticism of the proposed bill dealt with details rather than principles.[58] In California hearings, James Mullen, editor of the *Labor Clarion*, objected to compulsory health insurance, but mostly for reasons that it would become a precedent for compulsory arbitration. At the same hearings, A.R. Maloney, President of the California Insurance Federation, made a most strenuous objection to the whole concept of social insurance but then agreed to reconsider the idea if only the private insurance carriers were permitted to compete for the business.[59]

The failure of any of the legislatures to pass any of the bills was not considered as a major setback or even any setback at all. Advocates of the measures had not regarded this phase of the movement as anything more than educational. By any account their efforts were successful. Interest in the subject remained high. Rubinow alone travelled 20,000 miles through six states, delivering one-hundred lectures to some 50,000 people. Articles and books on the subject continued to pour from the press and much of the discussion remained favorable or at least open-minded. In Ohio, the State Board of Health under the leadership of E.L. Hayhurst issued its widely circulated and highly commended report in favor of health insurance. Public investigation commissions had been set up in Massachusetts and California. By 1917 the legislation had been introduced in twenty states. In addition to the many prominent individuals supporting the measure, there were many local organizations such as the Social Welfare Council of Buffalo, the New York City Department of Health, New York Consumers' League endorsing it. So also did the Massachusetts, Ohio, Wisconsin, Nebraska, New Jersey and Missouri State Federations of Labor.

Among the national organizations that endorsed health insurance were the National Conference of Charities and Correction, the American Public Health Association, The National Association of Manufacturers, the National Association of Industrial Accident Boards and Commissions, and the American Medical Association. Otto Geir, Chairman of the Section on Preventive Medicine and Public Health of the AMA, declared that the medical profession "is looking upon this legislation as inevitable and it but remains for them to adjust themselves to this scheme of things."[60] And at the AMA Convention, March, 1917, Dr. Alexander Lambert reported that blind opposition to health insurance by the medical profession would be useless; it would leave the doctors helpless "if the rising tide of social development sweeps over them."[61]

NOTES

[1] *Survey,* XXIX (March, 1913), p. 827.

[2] Minutes of the Workmen's Compensation Department, December 8, 1911. NYPL, NCF MSS, WC #125.

[3] John B. Andrews to Pauline Goldmark, January 5, 1912, ILR, AALL MSS.

[4] A.A. Mowbray to John B. Andrews, August 21, 1912, ILR, AALL MSS.

[5] Jane Addams to Theodore Roosevelt, November 20, 1912, Swarthmore College, Jane Addams MSS, Bx. 4.

[6] William Kent to Jane Addams, November 15, 1912, Swarthmore College, Jane Addams MSS, Bx. 4.

[7] John B. Andrews to Andrew Faruseth, January 31, 1914, ILR, AALL, MSS.

[8] Staley, *Illinois Federation of Labor,* p. 480; see also Green, *The National Civic Federation and Labor,* p. 263.

[9] Seth Low to Robert Hillas, CU, Seth Low MSS.

[10] NAM, *Proceedings of the Fifteenth Annual Convention,* 1910, pp. 221-222.

[11] J. Pillsburry to John B. Andrews, January 8, 1912, ILR, AALL MSS.

[12] A.H.G. Hardwicke to Lewis B. Schram, December 12, 1912, C.V. Seth Low MSS, Bx. 97.

[13] Irving Fisher, "The Need for Health Insurance," *American Labor Legislation Review,* VII (March, 1917), p. 10.

[14] U.S. House Committee on Labor, *Hearings of the Commission to Study Social Insurance and Unemployment,* (1916), p. 25.

[15] *American Labor Legislation Review,* VI (June, 1916), p. 217.

[16] *Survey,* XXIX (March, 1913), p. 827.

[17] Rubinow, *Social Insurance* (1913), pp. 404-413.

[18] "Old Age Pensions Poll a Strong Vote," *Survey,* XXXV (November 27, 1915), p. 197; Abraham Epstein, *Facing Old Age* (New York, 1922), pp. 318-320.

[19] U.S. Bureau of the Census, *Historical Statistics of the United States, Colonial Times to 1957* (Washington, D.C., 1960), p. 741.

[20] Henry Malisoff, "The Emergence of Unemployment Compensation," *Political Science Quarterly,* LIV (June, 1939), pp. 237-258; Feder, *Relief* pp. 220-245; Stewart, *Unemployment Benefits,* pp. 80-84, 57.

[21] Shelby M. Harrison, *Public Employment Offices* (New York, 1924), p. 624; Stewart, *Unemployment Benefits,* pp. 34-35.

[22] Malinoff, ". . . Unemployment Compensation," *op. cit.,* p. 242.

[23] Roy Lubove, *The Professional Altruist,* Chap. 2.

[24] Kelso, Poverty, pp. 157-167; U.S. House Committee on Labor, *Hearings . . . on Social Insurance and Unemployment,* p. 34; Joseph P. Chamberlain, "Sickness Insurance and its Possibilities in Mining and Railroading," *Survey,* XXXIII (January 16, 1915), pp. 423-424.

[25] American Association for Labor Legislation, "The Need for Health Insurance in America," 1916.

[26] *The American Labor Yearbook* (1916), p. 296.

[27] John B. Andrews, "Compensation for Occupational Diseases," *Survey,* XXX (April 5, 1913), pp. 15-19. John B. Andrews, "Occupational Disease Compensation: Some Recent Verdicts," *Survey,* XXXIII (July 18, 1914), p. 415.

[28] John B. Andrews to John R. Commons, November 23, 1914, ILR, Cornell University, AALL MSS.

[29] John B. Andrews to John R. Commons, November 23, 1914, ILR, Cornell University, AALL MSS.

[30] John B. Andrews to Katherine Coman, August 7, 1914, ILR, AALL MSS.

[31] Letter from officer of the Federation of Medical Economic Leagues to Olga Halsey, February 2, 1916, ILR, AALL MSS.

[32] John R. Commons, "Social Insurance and the Medical Profession," read before the 68th Annual Meeting of the State Medical Society of Wisconsin, October 7, 1914.

[33] Katherine Coman to John B. Andrews, August 4, 1914; John B. Andrews to Coman, August 7, 1914, ILR, AALL MSS.

[34] McIntire to Andrews, December 14, 1914, ILR, AALL MSS.

[35] *Journal of the American Medical Association* (October 30, 1955); see also Morris Fishbein, *A History of the American Medical Association, 1847-1947* (Philadelphia, 1947), p. 281.

[36] *Journal of the American Medical Association,* LXI, No. 1, p. 74.

[37] Frederick R. Green to John B. Andrews, November 11, 1915, ILR, AALL MSS.

[38] James Jenkins, Jr. (Executive Secretary of the Committee on the Prevention of Tuberculosis, Brooklyn Bureau of Charities) to John B. Andrews, November 20, 1915, ILR, AALL MSS.

[39] Irving Fisher, "The Need for Health Insurance," *op. cit.,* pp. 11-12.

[40] Charles R. Henderson to John B. Andrews, December 4, 1913, ILR, AALL MSS.

[41] G.H. Richardson to John B. Andrews, December 26, 1915, ILR, AALL, MSS.

[42] Rubinow, "Social Insurance," *The American Labor Yearbook,* 1916, p. 289.

[43] "Report of the Industrial Betterment Committee," NAM, *Proceedings,* 21st (1916), p. 36.

[44] Letter from doctor at Mt. Sinai Hospital to John B. Andrews, May 17, 1916, ILR, AALL MSS.

[45] "Report of the Industrial Betterment Committee," NAM, *Proceedings,* XIX (1914), p. 57.

[46] Ferdinand C. Schwedtman to John B. Andrews, June 11, 1914, ILR, AALL MSS.

[47] "Report of Industrial Betterment Committee," *op. cit.,* p. 57.

[48] Ferdinand C. Schwedtman to John B. Andrews, August 10, 1914, ILR, AALL MSS.

[49] "Report of the Industrial Betterment Committee," NAM, *Proceedings,* XXI (1916), p. 33.

[50] *Survey,* XXVII (December 30, 1916), p. 376.

[51] Rubinow, "20,000 Miles . . . ," *Survey,* XXXVII (March 3, 1917), p. 632.

[52] *Survey,* XXXVII (October 14, 1916), p. 41.

[53] *Survey,* XXXV (March 11, 1916), p. 691.

[54] *Globe,* January 29, 1916; *Herald,* February 9, 1916; *Sun,* January 17, 1916; *Press,* January 17, 1916.

[55] *Survey,* XXXV (March 11, 1916), p. 691; Rubinow, "20,000 Miles . . ," *Survey,* XXXVII (March 3, 1917), p. 632.

[56] Gertrude Beeks to Otto Eidlitz, December 30, 1914, NYPL, NCF MSS.

[57] Minutes of the Social Insurance Department, December 20, 1916, NYPL, NCF, MSS.

[58] Olga Halsey to F.C. Huyck, March 16, 1916, ILR, AALL MSS.

[59] *Survey,* XXXVII (December 30, 1916), p. 375.

[60] Otto P. Geir to Gertrude Beeks, March 19, 1917, NYPL, NCF MSS, Social Insurance #102.

[61] Fishbein, *The American Medical Association,* p. 296.

CHAPTER IX

HEALTH INSURANCE MOVEMENT ANALYZED

Although the fate of the health insurance movement was not yet sealed by 1917, time actually seemed to be running out for it. Social reformism in general had more than likely already passed its peak and the glowing reports about the health insurance movement did not always take into account some of its evident weaknesses. Opposition in certain quarters was no doubt a healthy sign but the resistance that issued from the National Civic Federation played a critical role in preventing any legislative successes.

In a sense, the National Civic Federation after having come out in full support of workmen's compensation, reverted to type as might have been foreseen by their interpretation of that particular compulsory collective program. As the principal carriers of the voluntary collective idea, the members of the National Civic Federation were not, despite their rhetoric, strictly or rigidly defining individual responsibility or self-reliance. Their system was merely one of the less progressive ways of helping others to help themselves. In keeping with the requirements of an industrial age, the voluntary-collective system also exemplified those welfare trends in which the needs and rights as well as the responsibilities of individuals were giving way to the needs, rights and responsibilities of the group — in this case the union and the corporate enterprise. Thus the opposition to social insurance can be seen as a joint effort of two normally antagonistic segments of society to protect their respective group interests against encroachments of the public.

In turn, the social insurance movement, as well as its dualistic features, can be regarded in part as a reaction against the voluntary-collective programs, not only because they were inadequate but because they were somewhat hostile to the public interests as well as to the interests of the individuals they were designed to serve. From the point of view of social security proponents, a compulsory-collective program could best guarantee both social welfare and self-reliance.

* * * *

As early as 1911, with the publication of Frederick Friedenburg's critical analysis of the German Insurance Program, some of the heretofore

177

repressed hostilities toward the German system were beginning to come to
the surface if not always into the open. P.T. Sherman privately bemoaned
the fact that Americans "have been accustomed in the last few years to
hear only what is favorable about the German system, because by general
consensus of opinion it is the best system."[1] By 1916, there were few
restraints, if any. "Some little girl" goes over to Germany, complained
Frederick Hoffman, "and comes back with a new wonderful report; it
could be gotten up after fifteen minutes.... Is it not preposterous?"
Hoffman still felt that you could "flim-flam anybody if you have been to
Germany."[2] But Frank Dresser of the National Association of
Manufacturers warned the Social Insurance Conference that foreign systems
were coming under increasing attack and the day of blandly accepting them
as unqualified successes was over.[3]

In this regard, the European war cut both ways. Although it had
stimulated the drive for social preparedness, it revived the older cries
against German absolutism. As a result of the war, admitted Henry Seager,
"the very examples that we have cited as proving value and need of labor
legislation are beginning to be turned against us as evidence of their evil
tendencies and dangers."[4] Seager also took note of the fact that the whole
reform impetus seemed to be slowing down. And Rubinow in a more
reflective mood was displeased by what he felt was a reactionary trend
even in the compensation acts. Instead of their getting better, he thought
that those enacted after 1915 were actually weaker. In addition, he
observed that the cheaper magazines were no longer giving as much
coverage to social issues.[5]

That private insurance carriers and certain business organizations had
become more vocal and highly organized in their attempts to thwart the
social insurance movement was perhaps not so threatening. Their
opposition was anticipated, and might have proved no more potent an
obstacle than it had been for workmen's compensation. But some of the
support for the health insurance movement proved to be rather superficial.
Organizational endorsements, in some cases, turned out to be
unrepresentative of the rank and file, and some of the sympathy for health
insurance was only as strong as the belief in its popularity and
inevitability. There were, for example, soft spots in the medical profession.
Dr. William S. Gottheil, a member of the special social insurance committee
of the New York County Medical Society, remarked that most of the
doctors were still unfamiliar with health insurance but that the trend
seemed to be toward an "uncompromising opposition" to the bill
introduced in the New York legislature. Gottheil further noted that the
medical men who were the most active in the health insurance movement

were institution men and medical employers while the most energetic proponent, Rubinow, was not even a practicing physician.[6] Other doctors had complained that a few men in leadership positions in the AMA had rammed the measure down the throats of the whole membership.[7]

A more ominous sign was the role played by the National Civic Federation and the labor and management interests within the organization. Although the public position of the NCF remained one of open-mindedness until 1917, this was in most respects a cover for a deep-seated hostility freely expressed among friends, and with the passage of time, more frequently displayed before the public. Like many other organizations of the period, the National Civic Federation established formal procedures for active involvement in the social insurance movement. In 1914, it sent a committee overseas to study the latest English measures in social welfare reform and in 1916, it established a permanent Social Insurance Department. But these activities in reality supplied the organization with greater ammunition to criticize the new movement and permitted a more coordinated opposition to it.

Actually, more than a year before the National Civic Federation initiated its investigation into social insurance, the case against it seemed already closed. In response to a request for information on the subject, Miss Beeks wrote that the organization had none. "It is, however, regarded by our experts as being very dangerous legislation and it would be hardly applicable to conditions in this country in any event."[8] Thus it would seem, as was so often charged, that the three-man committee that traveled to England in 1913, and found the old age pension wanting, might have saved themselves a trip.[9]

To a considerable degree the official position of the National Civic Federation was tempered by the apparent popularity of the movement. Unwilling to buck the tide, they concentrated their fire upon the details rather than the principle of the bills introduced in the several state legislatures. In New York, for example, their strategy was to approve of a state investigation commission, but to strongly attack the bill during the hearings. If the AALL, which had prepared the legislation, were to propose amendments, then the NCF was to have argued that these could not possibly have been made in so short a time.[10] Several opponents felt that this strategy was ill advised and that the Civic Federation should make a more fundamental stand against the measure. Walter Drew warned that proponents of health insurance were already claiming victory on the grounds that the only opposition they encountered dealt with specifics.[11]

The American Association for Labor Legislation and the National Civic Federation, uneasy collaborators in the early years of the workmen's compensation campaign, were now taking such disparate paths that those who held dual membership in the two organizations found it ever more difficult to pay dual allegiance. Whatever the official position of the National Civic Federation, individual members had their own positions to consider as well as those of their respective business and labor circles. Although Samuel Gompers remained a vice president of the AALL until 1915, when he resigned in a huff, his relations with the organization had been strained for several years as a result of a number of issues related to social insurance. In 1912, for example, he was enraged because some members of the American Association for Labor Legislation had circulated a petition of protest against the "reactionary" union men appointed to the United States Industrial Commission. "You should all be thoroughly ashamed of yourselves," he wrote to Andrews, "and you will have cause to be for this piece of stupidity and arrogance."[12] The specific issue over which Gompers resigned had to do with the AALL's penchant for sponsoring government by commission instead of government by elected representatives, but the question of social insurance was involved and would sooner or later have brought a severing of the relationship.

Conservative labor leaders tended to be cautious in their opposition to social security so long as the rank and file, encouraged by the socialists, demonstrated support for some form of governmental welfare program. Although the American Federation of Labor periodically endorsed the idea of national old age pension, the executive committee did what it could to discourage the enthusiasm. In 1907, a year in which the annual convention first directed the executive committee to investigate the subject of compulsory life insurance and old age pensions, Gompers declared that labor in the United States "asks for no old age pensions and the like from government, federal or state. . . ."[13] The following year, the executive committee, acting upon the request of the previous convention, reported that it would be a long time before the public would approve of the old age pension and that the laboring man should carefully consider the pitfalls of such a program.[14]

By 1913 Gompers had successfully secured his leadership against the socialists who for years had been challenging his control within the American Federation of Labor. His affiliation with the National Civic Federation, which in 1911 threatened to topple his regime, no longer made him so vulnerable. Thus by the time the health insurance campaign was in full swing, the labor members of the NCF, including the three hand-chosen by Gompers to sit upon the Social Insurance Department were somewhat freer to make a closer identification with the National Civic Federation and to strike out more boldly against social insurance. Some, like George W. Perkins, president of the Cigar Makers' Union, seem to have shifted ground somewhere around 1913 or 1914. Perkins' earlier pronouncements led the American Association for Labor Legislation to believe that he was among the friends of the movement;[15] but ultimately he became an active propagandist for the opposition. "I feel quite sure," wrote Perkins, "that I have succeeded in checking the enthusiasm of many and in turning some from this compulsory health insurance measure."[16] Several labor leaders, including Gompers, carried their fight to Congress where Meyer London was holding hearings on his resolution to set up a congressional investigation into the subject of social insurance. Gompers maintained he could not even tolerate the government's studying a compulsory program. When at one point London reminded Gompers that many prominent labor leaders – including Lennon and O'Donnell, both officers of the AF of L and A.G. Garretson, President of the Railway Conductors – approved of sickness insurance; Gompers reminded the Congressmen that his views had always prevailed any time the subject had come up within the American Federation of Labor.[17]

The case of Frederick Hoffman, however, provides a more interesting example of both the strain of dual allegiance and the way in which the National Civic Federation members were hedging their bets. Hoffman resigned from the American Association for Labor Legislation two years after Gompers, in 1917. Perhaps his rise in the ranks of the Metropolitan Life Insurance Company had something to do with his resignation since he had recently become vice president. But it is not his resignation that needs explaining; rather it is his remaining in the American Association for Labor Legislation that seems strange.

To suggest that he indulged in espionage and subversion, would be to romanticize and inflate the nature of his "duplicity." Yet he did more than simply give his name to the letterheads of the two organizations; he was active in the NCF's social insurance department and a member of the special committee of the AALL which drafted the health insurance bill. And he claimed – and there is reason to believe his claim – that he stayed on in the AALL as long as he did only to prevent the radicals from carrying their notions to excess.[18] For several years prior to his resignation, Hoffman insisted that his mind was still open on the subject of health insurance and would point to his endorsement of occupational disease compensation and the state insurance program set up under the Washington state compensation system as proof of his progressive leanings.[19] Nonetheless he became increasingly testy as the health insurance movement took shape. While the social insurance committee of the AALL was in the process of developing the standards for a health insurance measure, he periodically protested the necessity of such legislation as well as its compatibility with the American system of government. He also voiced his objection to setting up a state commission to investigate the subject of health insurance and when the social insurance committee had sent him a draft of the proposed bill, he opposed introducing the "ill-digested and ill considered" measure. Hoffman questioned not only the fundamental principles behind compulsory social insurance, he had attacked certain features of the proposed bill as too radical. "No one to my knowledge," he wrote, "has ever proposed a compulsory sickness scheme for this country including contributions by the state." He complained, too, that the committee went about its tasks in so haphazard a manner that it did not provide the opportunity for a genuine exchange of views.[20]

If there had ever existed any possibilities for a fusion of the two organizations, it was unthinkable now that the American Association for Labor Legislation had taken so forceful a stand on health insurance. Generally the members of the AALL were referred to as "that bunch," a group of do-gooders whose sole strength lay with the radicals and socialists. When at a luncheon meeting of the National Civic Federation, it was suggested that the NCF should work with the AALL rather than against it, the idea was turned down as out of the question. "Look at that Committee!" sputtered Ralph Easley in a reference to the men who had written the draft of the health insurance bill. Easley concluded his argument by declaring that Miles Dawson who, in addition to being a "crazy actuary" was also a rake and the whole matter was dropped.[21]

Members of the American Association for Labor Legislation lost no time in noting the irony of the labor leaders' meeting in concert with some of their bitterest foes; that Lucius Sheppard, a senior vice president of the Order of Railway Conductors of America, was "glad to introduce" the NAM's legal counsel, A. Parker Nevin, who denounced social insurance as a piece of "class legislation."[22] The National Civic Federation not only brought labor and business together on this issue; as if to cap the equality of and the harmony between labor and business, it could even boast of two social insurance foes by the name of George W. Perkins, one a cigar maker, the other a money maker.

"The National Civic Federation," declared John Andrews, "is progressing backwards."[23] Yet given the organization's approach to workmen's compensation, its position on health insurance was reasonably consistent and could have come as no surprise. Workmen's compensation was rarely if ever considered a facet of social insurance. Unlike the American Association for Labor Legislation, or for that matter even the National Association of Manufacturers,[24] the NCF had kept these questions distinct even in its investigations. The NCF interpretation of the Compensation Acts, be it remembered, confined the role of the government to that of readjusting an historic legal claim within a purely industrial context or to that of settling a matter of "private justice" between the employer and his employees.

"Morally and legally," declared one member of the National Civic Federation, workmen's compensation was "based not upon the duty of society but upon the duty of industry to the worker."[25] However, no such narrow interpretation of social insurance was possible since problems of old age, sickness and unemployment were not litigable nor were they so much the hazards of industry as they were the hazards of life. To have called upon the government in these cases was to make them problems in which the public had a primary interest and for which the public assumed a more direct responsibility. Yet neither the businessmen nor the unionists of the National Civic Federation had any intention of delivering up these problems to the public.

At times, their reasons would seem to place them in the company of men who rose in defense of the old-fashioned virtues of the Republic. They pictured the reformist effort as a gratuitous assumption of guardianship over men quite capable of taking care of themselves. Indeed, one of the principal themes, and one even the social insurance advocates admitted to be effective, was that neither business nor labor asked for this legislation, that it was being forced down their throats, by "moral uplifters," "do-gooders," and "otherwise disengaged intellectuals."[26] According to Ralph Easley, the measure had the support of "academicians and social reformers, who honestly believe that they know better than the wage earners themselves what the wage earners need."[27]

Time and time again union men argued that social insurance was class legislation, a kind of charity in disguise, a form of paternalism that curbed the individual's liberties and damaged his moral fibre. The relationship that would be established between the person insured and the state was "not one contemplated under a government made up of free and equal citizens."[28] One labor leader conceded that social insurance could work smoothly – but in Germany "where the people are drilled into submission."[29] The *American Federationist* reminded its readers of the virtues of "red blooded rugged independence."[30] The social do-gooders

were anxious to do things for the workers, Gompers fumed, "anxious to do
everything but that which is essential — get off their backs and give them
an opportunity to do things for themselves."[31] Their attempts in this
direction were not only condescending; they were impossible of fulfillment.
"The principle involved," wrote Gompers in what sounded more like
existentialism than trade unionism, "is the realization of one of the
difficult, important and heartbreaking facts of life — the limitations upon
our capacity to help our fellows. No one can transmit to another his
knowledge of the results of his expression. The act of learning is necessarily
personal — it is bound up with the loneness of each life."[32]

Lest the opponents of social insurance be taken for advocates of a
kind of free wheeling individualism, it should be pointed out that the issue
over individual rights, security and responsibility was virtually over-shadowed
by the concern for the rights, security and responsibility of their special
group interests.

Conservative union leaders issued an historic warning against any
aggrandizement of governmental power that interfered with industrial
relations. "Our first concern . . . in considering any proposition," declared
Grant Hamilton on the proposition of health insurance, "is will it interfere
with organization for freedom."[33] Specifically, labor leaders feared that
government would be in a position to withhold benefits from men guilty of
"bad conduct." The laboring man must consider, warned the executive
committee of the American Federation of Labor, "whether this fact and
the fear of its result may not take the heart out of some men who seek to
defend, protect or to promote their rights and interests."[34] Compulsory
insurance would undermine the union movement, Gompers declared time
and time again. Government insurance of necessity would exert control
over a labor force that requires absolute freedom to organize. "This," he
said, "is the meat of the whole matter."[35]

It was not that critics of social insurance refused to recognize the
"public interest," rather they defined it narrowly and in such a way that it
was best served by leaving the solution of certain problems to organizations
of those whose interests were immediately and directly affected.

What was often called the "public interest" was in their view merely
fiction for another set of organized special interests and the "public" was
in reality a "third party," clamoring for a place in the sun.

Though much of the campaign against health insurance took the form
of highly personalized attacks upon the men behind the movement, these
attempts to discredit the do-gooders, the moral uplifters, the "disengaged
philanthropists," were all endeavors to drive home the points that the

promoters of social insurance were an effete group presumptuously speaking in the name of the public. It was not only that they had never met a payroll or never performed any kind of work that would enable them to speak for the public as a whole, but that they also failed to recognize that everyone represented some special interest. No one segment of society could ever really claim to be the exclusive preservator of the public interest. As Grant Hamilton, a member of the AF of L Legislative Committee, stated the case, the "social reform element permits itself to be largely classed with that mythical portion of society euphoniously denominated the 'public.'"[36] According to Gompers, the social reformers and intellectuals were undoubtedly motivated by a desire to improve human welfare; but they were also looking for jobs as "experts" and their solutions to social ills almost invariably involved the creation of a governmental machinery that would require their services.[37] And Ralph Easley pointed out that health insurance was being promoted by "physicians who regard it as a means of generally increasing their income."[38]

The union and business rhetoric of individualism, antipaternalism, and freedom must also be examined in the rather specific context of the kind of welfare programs they were offering as alternatives to social insurance. Needless to say, private welfare systems did not embody the expansive collectivism of public insurance. But they were collective enterprises, nonetheless. They did not have the force of governmental law behind them, but with the force of economic law they were often coercive. They did not invoke the paternalism of the state, but they were paternalistic, demanding in return for protection, loyalty to the sponsoring organization.

The dual role of the group welfare plans continued to command the attention of the interested parties during the Progressive Era. Indeed, if anything, the efficiency ethic of the period gave greater weight to the practical motives for these plans. Even before the publication of Taylor's *Principles of Scientific Management*, in 1913, employers were beginning to expand their experimentation with welfare as a stabilizing influence among the work force. The business institutions adopting old age pensions, remarked one employer, "have not done so from sentimental considerations but rather from the consideration of economy and efficiency."[39]

The National Civic Federation, proud of its successful effort in stimulating the philanthropic spirit among its business membership, nonetheless, found the growing enthusiasm something of an embarrassment. The Federation was founded on the idea that a peaceful coexistence could obtain between organized labor and organized capital. Yet a number of the employers were obviously using their philanthropies to weaken the unions.[40] Although the Federation's welfare department tried to discourage welfare work that would offend their labor membership, there was always a recognition that employer benefit systems would flourish only so long as they brought results to the employer. Gertrude Beeks claimed that the NCF never cared to talk about the profits of welfare work but under the circumstances confessed, "we must talk not only about the employers' obligation but also the value of the work."[41] While aware of the union hostility toward compulsory programs, Miss Beeks, in advising an employer, reserved judgment on the question of compulsion. It was, she said, a debatable point since if employees are not forced to join a benefit plan those who need it most will not join.[42]

Actually the trend in the Progressive Era was away from the compulsory form of employer welfare systems. Of the 389 sickness insurance funds examined by the United States Commission on Industrial Relations in 1915, only 29 were listed as compulsory.[43] Of the 21 pension plans offered by railroad employers, none were compulsory. And many employers described their accident policies as voluntary.

The new vogue of voluntary systems, however, did not indicate any change in the purpose of employer welfare schemes, and, in fact, in some cases only a questionable change in form. For one thing, many benefit programs were voluntary in name only. Employers resorted to a variety of pressures to induce their employees to join the relief association.[44] One student of employer welfare work discovered that although only 10% of the establishment funds examined were officially compulsory, "a considerable number of the remaining nine-tenths" were in fact also compulsory.[45] Joining the relief association was in these cases frequently made the condition of employment or advancement or possibly the receipt of other forms of employer largesse.

On the whole, the employees were winning a greater voice in the operation of the funds to which they made contributions, but their power was rarely commensurate with their financial investment. One government study for example revealed that workers were officially given "exclusive management over only 89% of the funds to which they were the exclusive contributors. It is true that workers were officially granted control over 52% of the funds in which employers supplemented the employees' contributions, yet the study found that even in these cases of "exclusive" employee management, the employers "very frequently" were exercising influence in the administration.[46] In those systems where management was shared equally by employees and employers, the latter rarely paid anything like half of the costs. Where the employer gave a specified percentage of total contributions, it amounted in two-thirds of the funds to less than 50%. In many instances, the employer only paid for the administrative expenses. In other companies the employer might make up deficiencies or make a small token payment.[47]

Neither the remnants of compulsion nor the subtle forms of fiscal manipulation, however, tell the whole story of employer intentions. The purely voluntary and non-contributory systems had virtues of their own in accomplishing similar purposes. Frederick Hoffman tried to minimize the importance of these ostensibly more liberal strategies. "Never mind," he said, "what the ulterior motive would be such as allying the men to the industry. It does not cost the men anything."[48] Yet the issue was difficult to ignore, least of all for the businessmen who contemplated the advantages of the truly voluntary benefits. Employers in the National Civic Federation were divided on the question, but a number of them were arguing "that employees will be more loyal to a company if not required to contribute. . . ."[49] Their reasoning was not obscure. Since voluntary systems gave the company undisputed control over the management of the fund; there was no danger of incipient unionism that some employers observed in the systems where workers shared in the administration. Moreover, the employer was free to dispense the benefits to those workmen who caused the least trouble.

Welfare work designed to insure worker loyalty continued to take a variety of forms. Some steel corporations encouraged their employees to buy company financed housing or rent company owned homes. The Steel Corporation and the Youngstown Sheet and Tube Company inaugurated a stock subscription plan for those who rendered "faithfull service." The Steel Corporation had a stock subscription and special bonuses for the corporation employees who had "shown a proper interest in its welfare and progress."[50] The Ford Motor Company, through its profit sharing plan, not only safeguarded the interests of the corporation but presumed to regulate the daily lives of the employees. One Ford worker who forced his wife to keep boarders, jeopardized his chances for admission to the profit sharing plan. The corporation investigator warned him either to reform his ways or lose the bonus.[51]

Of all the security measures, the most effective was the old age pension because the worker did not receive the benefits until after many years of employment. He thereby built up an equity in the pension, which as time passed he would be less likely to jeopardize. According to one employer, "The pension attaches the employee to the service and thus decreases the liability to strike.... When the employees realize that unsatisfactory conduct may at any time lose them not only their present position – a loss which in such a labor market as ours might be easily made good – but that it entails further the loss of a very valuable asset, the employee's right to a pension, the incentive is greatly increased."[52]

In much the same spirit labor leaders promoted union superannuation benefits. In most of the national unions, membership in the benefit funds was compulsory and the benefits stopped with no reimbursement, when the worker left the union.[53] Old age pensions, though most capable of serving the interests of the organization, were still not the most common form of union benefit. Unions were expanding other less costly but valuable welfare measures.

Organized labor was still divided over the merits of welfare, but the U.S. Commissioner of Labor reported in 1909 that the fear that high dues would drive people away no longer prevailed. The labor leaders who had "come into authority since 1880," maintained that benefit features "have helped to retain" the membership through periods of trade depression "and that they were a source of strength rather than weakness."[54] One student of the labor union movement remarked that the strength of the union organization "is usually in direct proportion to the development of their insurance systems. Thus not only is insurance a prime support in the collective bargaining of the union; but it insures control in the exercise of that function. The infrequency of railroad strikes may be attributed to the almost perfect control of the head officials over their membership."[55]

It is more than sheer coincidence that the most persistent and aggressive opposition to social insurance was to be found among the large businesses and the well established craft oriented labor unions that composed the National Civic Federation. No business, no union would welcome any measures that hampered freedom of operation but it was only the most powerful business and labor interests, with a vested interest in welfare, who were most eager to avoid competition from the government. Neither the middling size businesses of the National Association for Manufacturers nor the newer, less stable and ethnically mixed unions had so well developed systems of welfare nor were they in so strong a position to develop them.[56]

The effect that social insurance would have upon the private plans may not have been the most critical issue, but it was widely recognized as an important one. "The conservative labor leaders are opposed to it" [health insurance], wrote Ralph Easley, "as they have their own health insurance organizations."[57] Miss Beeks agreed and thought this factor to be "one of the strongest arguments against" social insurance.[58] The fact that social insurance advocates time and time again tried to reassure both businessmen and trade unionists that governmental insurance did not stifle the "voluntary" collective plans, is also an indication that this was an important consideration.[59]

That private welfare plans were to be protected against governmental competition was apparent even before social insurance entered the picture. Despite the fact that the National Civic Federation heaped praise upon the Brandeis voluntary governmental insurance idea as an acceptable American answer to the problem of worker insecurity, the scheme was not really an especially popular one among employers who had their own benefit systems. When Secretary of the New England Civic Federation was approached on the matter of enlisting employers to act as agents for the Massachusetts Savings Bank system, he said that employers with their own programs, whose "chief motive is to bind the employer to the company," were not about to undermine this asset. He advised that help would more than likely come from companies that could not afford to establish a pension system. Labor leaders, as well as businessmen, were zealous in safeguarding their benefit systems. In accounting for the widespread opposition of certain unions to social insurance, one of the labor journals listed as important, "the loss of influence of labor organizations that have directed their efforts toward the same purpose contemplated by the bills for social insurance."[60] When Warren Stone was asked if this were true of the railroad brotherhoods, he answered, "Yes we are opposed to it because we have our own insurance."[61] These may have been woefully inadequate in most cases, but even the desire to protect a potential bore heavily upon their attitude. In fact Gomper's earlier opposition to workmen's compensation issued in part from his hope that the unions would be able to provide all the necessary aid to injured workers. In objecting to the concept of the worker as part of an "industrial army," Gompers in 1902 declared that "there is more being done, and that more will be done, by workingmen, organizing in their trade unions and by the establishment of funds in those unions to protect them in case of non-employment, in case of illness, in case of accident — yes, and even in the superannuation benefit."[62]

More was being done now. Virtually all local unions had some type of benefit feature and though not all were successful in serving either the members or the organization, many unions were receptive to the encouragements of the AF of L leadership. In response to all the union requests for information and advice on setting up benefit features, the AF of L executive council in 1914 put together and distributed a standard outline for the basic policies and procedures for the administration of such funds.[63]

To describe these critics of social insurance as being motivated largely by the desire to preserve freedom and individualism is not only to miss the collectivistic, paternalistic and coercive elements within the "voluntary" private insurance systems. It is also to distort the context within which the promoters of social insurance operated and consequently the meaning and the character of their efforts.

Whatever the ironies in a situation in which powerful business and labor interests combined against public regulation of welfare in order that they could, so to speak, carry on their industrial battles more efficiently, the policy was seriously questioned by the social insurance advocates. John B. Andrews took strong issue with a bargain struck between representatives of organized labor and organized capital in New York when they declared their agreement "makes it a clean fight between the two parties solely interested and shuts out the self-appointed third party whose interest has been guessed at, but never satisfactorily defined."[64]

This kind of power was not only "socially dangerous" in itself, wrote Selig Perlman, but becomes the source of great antagonisms between employer and employee. Perlman, who was commissioned to investigate employer welfare funds for the USIRC, had, as did numerous other social insurance advocates, misgiving about the effectiveness of employer welfare work in creating employer-employee harmony. "Our interest in this subject [employer welfare]," he explained to Ida Tarbell, "springs first upon its relation to industrial unrest."[65]

They conceded that in certain instances employers managed to establish welfare projects that were beneficial and acceptable to the workers. But they often heard complaints from workmen and their leaders, angry about attempts to undermine the union, suspicious of even the most harmless efforts to make life in the factory a bit more pleasant. Perhaps more than anything else it was the outbreak of strikes that caught the eye of social insurance proponents. Observing the elaborate welfare work of such companies as Pullman or the Ludlow Steel Mills, and noting the attendant friction, social insurance advocates were prone to advise that employers concentrate on higher wages and better working conditions, "leaving welfare work to the public."[66]

With so much of the public interest at stake there was no question in the minds of social insurance proponents that the government should take command of the situation. To those who raised a special objection to the idea of public contributions to the proposed health fund, the Surgeon General of the United States answered for many of his colleagues when he maintained that the public had a duty as well as a "right to be a contributor on the ground that sickness insurance is a measure distinctly for its own welfare."[67]

Business and labor interests, admitted Ernst Freund, may legitimately desire "to be left undisturbed in the peaceful settlement of their disputes." But, he argued, the issue was not one of a dispute between two parties — it was a social issue. "Legislation," he would remind them, "is not litigation. When legislation is demanded an appeal is made to the public to stand above the parties."[68]

That the social workers and professors of the AALL were constantly under attack seems to have reassured them that they were anything but "disengaged intellectuals." They were occasionally "abused by both industrial warring classes," remarked John Andrews, but "this association has a very special function to perform, and its activities have always proceeded from the *general welfare* point of view.[69]

While social insurance proponents sprang to the defense of the social welfare, social responsibility and social rights, they were not unmindful of the individual's welfare, responsibility and rights. The concept of social insurance undoubtedly put to rest the notion that workers should bear the entire burden of their security. Health insurance, as one advocate remarked, signified that American society was now dealing with the "lamentable failing of our old individualism."[70] The kind of attachment to self-reliance that would preclude any interference by the public — even at the risk of widespread individual and social suffering — was regarded as fetishism. Many advocates could have agreed with D.L. Cease, one railroad leader who looked upon the reverence for self-reliance as both impractical and inconsistent. He would prefer to see healthy and sturdy "mollycoddles," he wrote:

> than the most ferociously independent and self-reliant super race of tubercular, rheumatic and malarial cripples, tottering unsocialistically along the socialized highways, reclining self-reliantly upon the communal benches of the public parks and staring belligerently at the communal trees, flowers and shrubbery, enjoying defiantly the social light of the great unsocialized light of the sun, drinking individualistically the socialized water bubbling from the public fountain in adversity even eating privately the communistic bread provided in the communistic almshouses, and at last going expensively to rest, independently and self-reliantly, in a socialized or mutualized graveyard full of little individualistic slabs erected to the memory of the independent and self-reliant dead.[71]

Social insurance advocates, however, were not about to scrap every concern for the individual's willingness to contribute to his own support. Henry Seager, noting that the voluntary insurance benefit programs were not being utilized to any great extent by wage earners, attributed this circumstance partly to "a lack of prudence and forethought on their part."[72] Joseph P. Chamberlain specifically requested that the investigation into the British and German health insurance programs try to determine whether they "interfere with the independence and sense of self help of the individual or if on the contrary they interest the individual more, and give him a more direct voice in the operation of the insurance and of the fund."[73] Indeed among the social insurance proponents were a group more than capable of lecturing the rest of the community on the virtues of the Protestant ethic. In their opposition to widow's pensions, social workers like Edward Devine and Mary Richmond did most to evoke memories of traditional arguments on behalf of self-reliance. From their point of view the pension was outdoor relief and capable of tempting the poor into a life of idleness, thriftlessness and insobriety.

A social insurance program for the poor, however, was hardly comparable since the principle distinction between the pension and the social insurance idea was that in the latter the individual made a contribution to the fund. As Devine had earlier remarked, social insurance provided the individual recipients with "a means of meeting their own share of the risk in manageable installments."[74] Not all proponents of social security favored contributory over non-contributory systems, but within the American Association for Labor Legislation there was a distinct preference for the former. There was never any serious question that the new social welfare measures sponsored by the Association would be anything but insurance. Collective responsibility was shared responsibility. "The employee," declared B.S. Warren in his report for the Industrial Commission, "should in no sense be a ward."[75]

Frequently, the contributory system was hailed as a form of compulsory thrift or compulsory self-help. Lee Frankel, still convinced in 1908 that American workmen were capable of voluntarily ameliorating the problem of economic insecurity, nonetheless refused to reject the European compulsory insurance as inimical to self-reliance. "To my mind," he wrote, "it is immaterial whether the form of insurance in vogue is compulsory or not. The fact remains that through one system or another it has been possible to bring to the workman himself the recognition of his ability to do things for himself."[76]

The Massachusetts Old Age Commission of 1910 as well as that state's

Social Insurance Commission of 1917 declared in favor of social insurance partly because it was a form of compulsory thrift. The 1917 Commission, sympathetic to the standards of health insurance proposed by the AALL, declared that every citizen had a duty to prepare for old age, sickness and invalidity. "If he fails to make such provision the social structure suffers and if his failure is complete the state supports him. In theory then, all citizens should be compelled to make such provision."[77]

Although a compulsory collective system may have struck the opponents as antithetical to self-reliance — because of both the compulsion and the monetary contribution of the state — this progressive generation of social welfare reformers found self-reliance compatible with social security. In a sense they were extending the logic of an earlier generation of welfare reformers who believed that helping the poor to help themselves presented no contradiction. The individual-social ethic may have continued to confound its critics, but its disciples remained firm in the belief that individual responsibility and collective responsibility were inseparably bound, each growing fat upon the other. The opportunity to improve the individual's health and sense of security was considered a positive force in fostering economic independence. To those who believed that sickness was the route by which "most paupers travel to their doom,"[78] or that "disease and poverty are skeleton twins in the household,"[79] health insurance could scarcely be conceived of as an influence corrupting self-reliance. By the same token, the concern for self-reliance hardly precluded the advocacy of a program of social security. From the reformer's point of view, the threats to self-reliance made social security an imperative.

The concept of self-reliance, to be sure, had undergone a transformation, perhaps greater under public than under private collectivism. The individual was not asked to rely as much on his own financial resources in sharing the burden of his security. But welfare reformers were claiming that a public contribution made for a more equitable distribution of the costs because society had permitted harmful conditions to exist. To ask the individual to pay his fair share did no violence to his self-reliance. To have asked him to pay more would have pauperized society.

In regard to the compulsory aspects of social insurance, its defenders could not disagree perhaps with Gompers when he argued that it was easier to resign from a union or a company than it was to resign from the United States. But social insurance proponents contended that leaving one's union or one's employment was never easy and even less so when one would be surrendering contributions already made to the union or company fund.

The point was an important one. The welfare reformers were not arguing the theoretical merits of the case so much as the practical ones. And in practice, the "voluntary" collective measures had a questionable record insofar as the preservation or the promotion of individual self-reliance was concerned. The private schemes, in the eyes of the social insurance advocates, were objectionable not simply because they were weapons in an industrial warfare that threatened the social order. The private systems offered only a minimum of security to those covered and nothing to the vast majority of workers. As a system, the voluntary-collective plans were therefore incapable of coping with a situation that daily pushed many respectable men into the "abyss of pauperism." But equally significant was the belief that while offering little in the way of security, the union and company welfare plans — far more than governmental programs — deprived the worker of his mobility and independence. If the worker were to depend upon the government for his security, he could move about from job to job or union to union, or from union status to non-union status without fear of losing his benefits, or having to limit his choices to kinds of employment that offered nothing more than security. By the "so-called 'establishment funds,'" declared Selig Perlman, the employer, "succeeds in attaching the employee to himself just as the feudal lord used to have the peasant attached to himself."[80] Even the socialist Rubinow attacked company welfare systems for their "demoralizing character upon the spirit of self-reliance among the wage earners."[81] Father O'Grady, speaking before the Social Insurance Conference, noted with regret that union benefits no less than employer benefits "gave the organization too much power over its members."[82]

Thus, from the point of view of social security proponents, the broadest form of collectivism did not preclude individual responsibility but rather made it all the more probable.

NOTES

[1] P.T. Sherman to Gertrude Beeks, July 17, 1911, NYPL, NCF MSS, WC #126.
[2] Minutes of Social Insurance Department, December 20, 1916, NYPL, NCF MSS.
[3] Frank F. Dresser, "Assurance of Health versus Sickness Insurance," U.S. Bureau of Labor Statistics, *Bulletin 212,* pp. 572-574.
[4] Henry Seager, "American Labor Legislation," *ALLR,* VI (1916), p. 95.
[5] Rubinow, "20,000 Miles . . . ," *op. cit.,* p. 631.
[6] Dr. William S. Gottheil to John B. Andrews, February 25, 1916, ILR, Cornell University, AALL MSS.

[7] H.R. Strong, Publisher, *The National Druggist,* to Ralph Easley, June 21, 1916 and March 16, 1916. NYPL NCF MSS, SI #102.

[8] Beeks to Franklin Graff, January 16, 1912, NYPL, NCF MSS, WC #127.

[9] Everett Colby to Gertrude Beeks, March 10, 1915, NYPL, NCF MSS, Social Insurance #102; Beeks to Everett Colby, March 6, 1915, NYPL, NCF MSS, SI #102.

[10] Gertrude Beeks to Warren Stone, March 3, 1917, NYPL, NCF.

[11] Walter Drew to Gertrude Beeks, March 3, 1917, NYPL, NCF MSS, Social Insurance #102; see also J.T. Eagen to Easley, July 24, 1916, *op. cit.*

[12] Samuel Gompers to John B. Andrews, January 3, 1913, ILR, AALL MSS.

[13] *American Federationist,* XIV (August, 1907), p. 550; American Federation of Labor, *Proceedings,* XXVII (1907), p. 334.

[14] American Federation of Labor, *Proceedings,* XXVIII (1908), p. 102.

[15] *ALLR,* III (1913), p. 234ff; John B. Andrews to George Perkins, November 17, 1915, ILR, AALL MSS.

[16] George W. Perkins to Gertrude Beeks, March 23, 1917, NYPL, NCF MSS, SI, #102.

[17] U.S. Congress, House, Committee on Labor, *Hearings on Social Insurance,* p. 163.

[18] Minutes of Social Insurance Department, December 20, 1916, p. 3, NYPL, NCF MSS SI, #102.

[19] Frederick L. Hoffman to John B. Andrews, October 21, 1914, ILR AALL MSS.

[20] Frederick L. Hoffman to John B. Andrews, July 17, 1914, ILR AALL MSS.

[21] Gertrude Beeks to John B. McPherson, January 27, 1917; Minutes of Social Insurance Department Luncheon, December 6, 1915, p. 7, NYPL, NCF MSS, SI #102.

[22] *Survey,* XXXVII (January 27, 1917), pp. 495-496.

[23] John B. Andrews to Paul Kellog, December 17, 1914, ILR, Cornell University, AALL MSS.

[24] See for example, NAM. *Proceedings of the Fifteenth Annual Convention* (1910), p. 220ff.

[25] Untitled speech written by Walter Drew, NYPL NCF MSS, IWD #85.

[26] Gompers, "Labor vs. its Barnacles," *American Federationist,* XXIII, pp. 268-274; Royal Meeker to Ralph Easley, September 1, 1916, NYPL, NCF, MSS SI #102.

[27] Ralph Easley to J. Henry Walters, March 13, 1916, NYPL, NCF, MSS SI #102.

[28] *American Federationist,* XVII (July, 1910), p. 596.

[29] J.W. Sullivan, "Social Insurance and American Trade Unionism," Social Insurance Department Conference, NYPL, NCF MSS #102.

[30] "Self Help is the Best Help," *American Federationist,* XXII (1915), pp. 113-115.

[31] Gompers, "Intellectuals . . . ," *op. cit.,* p. 53.

[32] *Ibid.*

[33] Hamilton, "Proposed . . . Insurance," U.S. Department of Labor, *Bulletin* 212, p. 560.

[34] American Federation of Labor, *Proceedings of the Twenty-Eighth Annual Convention* (1908), p. 102.

[35] Samuel Gompers, "Not Even Compulsory Benevolence Will Do," address delivered at the 17th Annual NCF Meeting, January 22, 1917, NYPL, NCF MSS SI #102.

[36] Grant Hamilton, "Proposed Legislation for Health Insurance," U.S. Department of Labor, *Bulletin* 212, p. 559.

[37] "Intellectuals Please Note," *American Federationist*, XXIII (March, 1916).

[38] Ralph Easley to J. Henry Walters, March 13, 1916, NYPL, NCF, MSS SI #102.

[39] E.A. Vanderlip, "Insurance . . . Employers Standpoint," *op. cit.*, p. 463; see also James A. Hamill to W.R. Wilcox, January 27, 1913, NYPL, NCF MSS, IWD #85.

[40] Green, *The NCF*, pp. 267ff, 291ff; *The National Civic Federation Review*, II (March, April, 1906), p. 16.

[41] Gertrude Beeks to C.V. Carpenter, March 13, 1908, NYPL, NCF MSS, WD #113.

[42] Gertrude Beeks to George L. Cain, October 4, 1906, NYPL, NCF MSS, WD #113.

[43] Sydenstriker, "Existing Agencies for Health Insurance in the United States," U.S. Department of Labor, Bureau of Labor Statistics, *Bulletin* 212, pp. 452-453.

[44] *Survey*, XXXIV (May 22, 1915), p. 175.

[45] Boris Emmet, "Operation of Establishment and Trade Union Disability Funds," *Monthly Review of the U.S. Bureau of Labor Statistics*, V, No. 2, p. 19.

[46] U.S. Bureau of Labor Statistics, *Monthly Review*, p. 220.

[47] Sydenstryker, "Existing Agencies . . . ," Bureau of Labor Statistics, *Bulletin* 212, pp. 454-456.

[48] Minutes of the Social Insurance Department meeting, December 20, 1916, NYPL, NCF MSS SI #102.

[49] Ralph Easley to F.H. Gillett, February 28, 1912, NYPL, NCF MSS, IWD #85.

[50] Brody, *Steelworkers*, pp. 87-95.

[51] "Employers Welfare Work in Ford Auto Works," Appendix #5, August 19, 1914, Investigators Reports for the United States Commission on Industrial Relations, LC, USCIR MSS.

[52] Vanderlip, "Insurance . . . Employers' Standpoint," *op. cit.*, p. 463.

[53] U.S. Commission of Labor, *Twenty-Third Annual Report* (1909), pp. 24-26.

[54] *Ibid.*, p. 23

[55] J.B. Kennedy, "The Beneficiary Features of the Railway Unions," in Jacob Hollander (ed.), *Studies in American Trade Unionism* (New York, 1906), p. 348.

[56] Charles R. Henderson, *Industrial Insurance in the United States* (Chicago, 1909), p. 111; Mollie Ray Carrol, *Labor and Politics*, p. 108; Hoxie, *Trade Unionism*, p. 202.

[57] Easley to Ivy L. Lee, December 2, 1915, NYPL, NCF MSS, SI #102.

[58] Beeks to Lee K. Frankel, February 17, 1917, NYPL, NCF MSS, SI #102.

[59] Rubinow, "Social Insurance," *op. cit.*, p. 289; Hayes Robbins to Gertrude Beeks, July 28, 1908, NYPL, NCF MSS #111.

[60] *Railroad Trainmen*, XXXIV (April, 1917), p. 237.

[61] Minutes of Social Insurance Luncheon Meeting, December 6, 1915, NYPL, NCF MSS, SI #102.

[62] Journal of Social Science, No. 40 (1900), p. 50; see also American Federation of Labor, *Proceedings of the Twenty-Second Annual Convention* (1902), p. 135ff.

[63] Mollie Ray Carroll, *Labor and Politics*, p. 108.

[64] Quoted in letter from John B. Andrews to E.J. Barcalo, President, Associated Manufacturers and Merchants of New York State, March 18, 1916, ILR, AALL MSS.

[65] Selig Perlman to Ida Torbell, October 12, 1914, National Archives, Department of Labor, Files of the United States Commission on Industrial Relations.

[66] B.S. Warren, "Preliminary Report on Health Insurance," p. 66, National Archives, Department of Labor, USCIR files.

[67] Warren, "Preliminary Report on Health Insurance," *op. cit.*

[68] Ernst Freund to John B. Andrews, June 12, 1915, ILR, AALL MSS.

[69] John B. Andrews to William F. Cochran, July 27, 1915, ILR, AALL MSS.

[70] U.S. Bureau of Labor Statistics, *Bulletin* 212, p. 419.

[71] *Railroad Trainmen,* XXXIV, No. 3 (1917), p. 212.

[72] Seager, *Social Insurance,* p. 119.

[73] Chamberlain to John B. Andrews, June 11, 1914, ILR, AALL MSS.

[74] See pp. 278-279 this dissertation; see also Devine, "Social Forces," *op. cit.,* p. 1377; NAM, *Proceedings of the Twenty-First Annual Convention,* p. 36.

[75] B.S. Warren, "Preliminary Report on Health Insurance," *op. cit.,* p. 58.

[76] Lee K. Frankel, "Facts in Connection with Workingmen's Insurance in the United States," NCF, *Ninth Annual Meeting* (1909), p. 78.

[77] *American Labor Legislation Review,* Vol. 7 (March, 1917), p. 202.

[78] Henderson, "Logic . . . Insurance," *op. cit.*

[79] Bureau of Labor Statistics, *Bulletin* 212, p. 690.

[80] Perlman, "Preliminary . . . Social Insurance," *op. cit.*

[81] Rubinow, *Social Insurance,* p. 396.

[82] U.S. Bureau of Labor Statistics, *Bulletin* 212, pp. 758-759.

CONCLUSION

In the half-century between 1870 and 1917, American society remained true to its faith in self-reliance. But it remained true only after a fashion, as it had in the two and one-half centuries before 1870 and as it has in the fifty years since 1917.

The faith in self-reliance had no doubt served as a governor, but by no means as a brake on social change. From the end of the Civil War to the beginning of America's participation in the First World War, the doctrine of self-help demonstrated an extraordinary staying power, and, like the American Constitution, an equally extraordinary capacity to bend with the winds of change. In 1870, a social security program would have been a gross and intolerable violation of the belief in self-reliance. By 1917, social security was not only compatible with the ideal of self-help but considered necessary to fulfill it.

Americans had never carried self-reliance to the point of ruling out all forms of economic aid to the able-bodied individual. Historically, some types of private as well as public help were looked upon as proper and just, while other forms, namely public welfare, were regarded as a necessary imposition, but tolerable under conditions that would remind the recipient of his obligation to remain self-supporting. Traditionally, the doctrine of self-reliance has been flexible, its specific meaning set by the kind and degree of collective responsibility acceptable to society at any particular time. Self-reliance has not been the sole component of our social welfare codes, but rather an abstract — a goal within a broad and dualistic philosophy of "helping others to help themselves."

Under pressure from the rapid industrialization of the post-Civil War years, American society broadened its view of kinds of help individuals could legitimately expect to receive from others, and turned what was merely a tolerable and charitable form of helping others to help themselves into an imperative act of social justice.

Although the workmen's compensation movement of the Progressive Era represents the most convincing evidence of a shift in views, significant changes were taking place throughout the period under review. The great flood of philanthropic activity between 1870 and 1893, and the search for a more appropriate system of relief in the post-depression years of the 1890's were indicative of substantial modifications in the concept of self-reliance. Both the sentimental and reform philanthropies, for example, stood for a more expansive version of collective responsibility. And in the case of the former, charity was dispensed with an air of indifference to the old-fashioned ideas of self-help, while reform philanthropy, even though giving the appearance of upholding them, was actually in the process of modifying them. What has generally been described as the charity reformer's adherence to rugged individualism was really a preoccupation with the *question* of self-reliance, but not a commitment to pre-industrial conceptions of it.

Within the individual-social ethic of reform philosophy, the progressive analyses of dependency lay dormant until after the depression, when they found increasing favor among welfare and social reformers. Thus, even before the advent of the social security movement, many influential Americans believed not only that the individual's problem arose from something in the environment – for this had always been recognized – but that an environment of struggle may have been a cause of his difficulties rather than a cure for them; that in the vast majority of cases, the bitter struggle to remain economically independent had not yet weakened the individual's moral fiber so that many of those who were forced to seek relief did so through no fault of their own; and that collective responsibility should be called upon to prevent suffering and demoralization, and should be assumed in the spirit of social justice rather than charity.

Although the social security movement produced no legislation beyond industrial accident compensation and pensions for dependent mothers, this limited success can be misleading as a factor in assessing America's attachment to individual responsibility. For one thing, the health insurance movement in the late Progressive Era achieved enough momentum to encourage its supporters and to frighten many of its opponents into thinking that legislation would be produced within a year or two. Whether or not the expectations of both the friends and enemies of health insurance were realized is not a vital consideration. It seems clear that in a society strongly committed to a narrow interpretation of individual responsibility, the health insurance movement could not have come so close to fruition.

Moreover, insofar as some of the major critics are concerned, the desire to preserve this type of individual responsibility does not appear to have been the motive for opposing health insurance. No doubt many people who objected to health insurance did so on grounds that the strict interpretation of self-reliance was being violated. But for the opponents who came from the National Civic Federation, old-fashioned notions of individualism had already become a dead issue. Consequently, much of the controversy surrounding the social security movement had to do with the relative merits of the voluntary and compulsory forms of collective responsibility.

To ignore the premises of these particular opponents of social insurance is not only to understimate the extent of collective responsibility in American society, it is to deprive us of the full meaning of the social security movement.

Normally, we first think of these various welfare systems as attempts to solve the individual's welfare problem. But there were other purposes involved, for in each case the welfare systems were designed to insure the stability of the sponsoring organization. The history of the voluntary-collective programs no less than the development of the compulsory programs suggest a dual purpose: promoting the welfare of the individual and protecting the interests of the group. And the history of both the voluntary and compulsory programs further suggests that the welfare of the group was becoming increasingly more important. The result was that welfare became involved not only in the competition between the employers and the unions for the stability of their respective organizations and for the loyalty of the workers, but was also an issue in the competition between these two special interest groups, and society as a whole.

What was being debated, in other words, was not simply the question of which kind of collective responsibility provided greater security for the individual or which type did less damage to his spirit of self-reliance. Among the proponents of social security, the compulsory collective programs were regarded as the best way of preventing the social welfare from being harmed by the potentially anti-social power concentrated in the hands of organized capital and organized labor. This is not to say that the advocates of social insurance forgot about the individual's security or his self-reliance. Individualism in a modified form was still very much alive in the minds of social welfare reformers, perhaps even more than in the minds of their opponents. The progressives claimed that in helping others to help themselves, a compulsory program far more than a voluntary one would enhance individualism, and at the same time redound to the welfare of society.

Thus, extending the traditional dualism in American welfare as well as that classic version found in their late-nineteenth-century predecessors, the progressive welfare reformers proclaimed that individual responsibility was no. longer at odds with a socially just form of compulsory collective responsibility and that self-reliance was no longer the antithesis of social security.

BIBLIOGRAPHY

Manuscript and Record Collections

American Association for Labor Legislation, Cornell University, School of Industrial Labor Relations

Charity Organization Department of the Russell Sage Foundation, Columbia University School of Social Work.

Homer Folks, Columbia University, School of Social Work

Jane Addams, Swarthmore College

National Civic Federation, New York Public Library

National Women's Trade Union League, Library of Congress

New York Association for Improving the Condition of the Poor, Community Service Society, New York

New York Charity Organization Society, Community Service Society, New York

Seth Low, Columbia University

Socialist Party, Tamiment Institute Library, New York

U.S. Department of Labor, National Archives

Public Documents

Boston. *Annual Report of the Overseers of the Poor.* 1872, 1874–75, 1877, 1885–86.

California. The Commission of Immigration and Housing, *Report on Relief of Destitute Unemployed, 1914–1915.* California State Printing Office, 1915.

——. *Report of Unemployment.* San Francisco, 1914.

Connecticut. State Commission on Compensation for Industrial Accidents. *Report of the . . .* 1912.

Fessenden, Stephen D. "Present Status of Employer's Liability in the United States," U. S. Department of Labor Bull. No. 31, Nov. 1900, pp. 1157–1210.

Illinois Bureau of Labor Statistics. *Bulletin. Workmen's Compensation Act 1912.* Illinois State Journal Co., 1912.

Massachusetts. *Eighteenth Annual Report of the Bureau of Statistics of Labor, December 1887.* Boston; Wright and Potter Printing Co., 1887.

Massachusetts. *Preliminary Report of the Commission on Old Age Pensions, Annuities and Insurance, January 1909.* Bóston: Wright and Potter, 1909.

Massachusetts. *Report of the Commission on Old Age, Pensions, Annuities and Insurance, January 1910.* Boston: Wright and Potter, 1910.

Massachusetts. *Report of the Commission on the Support of Dependent Minor Children of Widowed Mothers,* January 1913. Boston: Wright and Patten, 1913.

Massachusetts. *Report of Committee on Relations Between Employer and Employee.* Boston: Wright and Potter, 1904.

Massachusetts. *Report of the Massachusetts Board to Investigate the Subject of the Unemployed.* 5 Parts. Boston: Wright & Potter Printing Co., 1895.

Massachusetts. Board of State Charities. *14th Annual Report.* Rand, Avery & Company, 1878.

Massachusetts Bureau of Labor Statistics. *Tenth Annual Report, January 1879.* Boston: Rand, Avery & Co., 1879.

Massachusetts Bureau of Statistics. *Report of a Special Inquiry Relative to Aged and Dependent Pensions in Massachusetts, 1915.* Boston: Wright and Potter, 1916.

Massachusetts, Commission on Compensation for Industrial Accidents. *Report . . . July 1, 1912.* Boston: Wright and Potter, 1912.

Massachusetts, Commission on Old Age Pensions, Annuities and Insurance. *Report, January 1910.* Boston: Wright and Potter, 1910.

Massachusetts Special Commission on Social Insurance. *Report February 1917.* Boston: Wright and Potter, 1917.

Michigan Board of State Commissioners for the General Supervision of Charitable, Penal, Pauper, and Reformatory Institutions. *Fourth Biennial Report, 1877–78.* Lansing: W. S. George & Co., 1879.

Minnesota Employees Compensation Commission. *Report to Legislature.* January 1911.

Missouri Commission on Employer's Liability and Workmen's Compensation. *Report . . . Missouri . . . to the Governor and 47th General Assembly,* January 1913. Jefferson City, Mo.: The Hugh Stevens Printing Co., 1912.

National Association of Officials of Bureaus of Labor Statistics. *Publications,* 1892–1901.

Nebraska Employer's Liability and Workmen's Compensation Commission. *Preliminary Report Nebraska . . .* 1912.

New York. *Journal of the Assembly.* 123rd Sess., Vol. III, Vol. IV. Albany: James B. Lyon, 1900.

New York. *Revised Record of the Constitutional Convention of the State of New York.* 5 Vols. May 8, 1894 to September 29, 1894. Albany: The Argus Co., 1900.

New York Bureau of Labor Statistics. *Seventeenth Annual Report* for the year 1899. Albany: James B. Lyon, 1900.

New York City Department of Public Charities and Correction. *Sixteenth Annual Report 1875.* New York, 1876.

New York City Mayor's Committee on Unemployment. *How to Meet Hard Times.* January 1917.

New York City Mayor's Committee on Unemployment. *Report.* New York City, January 1916.

New York State. *Journal of the Senate.* 123rd Sess., 1900.

New York State. *Proceedings of State Convention of Superintendents of the Poor,* 1874.

New York State Board of State Commissioners of Public Charities (of the State of New York). *Second Annual Report.* Albany: Argus Co., 1869.

New York State Charities and Association. *First Annual Report,* 1873.

Thompson, Laura A. *Laws Relating to Mother's Pensions in the United States, Canada, Denmark and New Zealand.* U. S. Department of Labor, Children's Bureau, Bureau Publication No. 63.

U.S. Commission on Employer's Liability and Workmen's Compensation. *Hearings Before . . .* appointed under joint resolution of the Senate and House of Representatives of the United States, May 10, 1911.

U. S. Commission of Labor. *Fifth Annual Report, Railroad Labor.* Washington: Government Printing Office, 1890.

U. S. Commissioner of Labor. *23rd Annual Report,* Workmen's Insurance and Benefit Funds in the United States. Washington: Government Printing Office, 1909.

U. S. Department of Labor, Bureau of Labor Statistics. *Proceedings of the Conference on Social Insurance* (called by International Association of Industrial Accident Boards and Commissions), Bulletin No. 212, December 5–9, 1916. Washington: Government Printing Office, 1917.

U. S. Department of Labor, Bureau of Labor Statistics. *Bulletin* No. 31, November 1900.

U. S. Senate. *Hearings Before the Employer's Liability and Workmen's Compensation Commission,* Vol. I, Document No. 90. Washington: Government Printing Office, 1911.

United States. *Report of the Industrial Commission on the Relations and Conditions of Capital,* Vol. XIV. Washington: Government Printing Office, 1901.

Articles and Books

Abbott, Edith. *Public Assistance.* Vol. I. Chicago: University of Chicago Press, 1940.

Abbott, Grace. *The Child and the State; Select Documents with Introductory Notes.* 2 vols. Chicago: University of Chicago Press, 1938.

Adams, Henry C. "Relation of the State to Industrial Action," American Economic Association. *Proceedings, 1885–86,* I, No. 6 (1887), 471–549.

Addams, Jane, *et al. Philanthropy and Social Progress.* New York: Thomas Y. Crowell and Company, 1893.

Almy, Frederic. "Public Pensions to Widows: Experiences and Observations Which Lead Me to Oppose Such a Law," *Child,* I (July, 1912), 51–54.

——. "The Problem of Charity, From Another Point of View," *The Charities Review,* Vol. IV (February, 1895), 169–180.

Altmeyer, Arthur J. "The Wisconsin Idea and Social Security," *The Wisconsin Magazine of History* (Autumn, 1958), pp. 19–25.

Boyd, James Harrington. "Some Features of Obligatory Industrial Insurance," *Annals of the American Academy,* Vol. 38 (July 1911), 23–30.

Brackett, Jeffrey, R. *The Transportation Problem in American Social Work.* New York: Russell Sage Foundation, 1936.

Brandeis, Louis D. "Massachusetts Savings Bank Annuity Plan," NCF. *Ninth Annual Meeting,* 1908, 80–86.

Brandeis, Louis. "Savings Banks' Life Insurance," *American Federationist,* Vol. XIV (October 1907), 777–780.

Brannon, Victor DeWitt. *Employer's Liability and Workmen's Compensation in Arizona.* University of Arizona Social Science Bulletin No. 7, November 15, 1934.

Branscombe, Martha. *The Courts and the Poor Laws in New York State, 1784–1929.* Chicago: University of Chicago Press, 1943.

Breckenridge, Sophonisba P. *Public Welfare Administration in the United States.* 3rd Imp. Chicago: University of Chicago Press, 1935.

Bremner, Robert. *From the Depths.* New York: New York University Press, 1956.

Brooks, John G. "Report on German Workingmen's Insurance," NCOCC, *Thirty-Second Annual Report* (1905).

——. "A New Hope for Charity," *Lend A Hand,* XII (January 1894), 6–13.

——. "Insurance of the Unemployed," *Quarterly Journal of Economics,* X (April 1896), 341–348.

——. "The Tragedy of Industry," *Journal of Social Science,* No. 40 (December 1902), 12–18.

——. "The Future Problem of Charity," *Annals of the American Academy of Political and Social Science,* Vol 5 (July 1894), 1-27.

Brooks, Phillips. "Need of an Enthusiasm for Humanity on the Part of the Churches," Evangelical Alliance, 1889. *National Needs and Perils.* New York: The Boker and Taylor Co., 1890.

Brown, Mary Wilcox. "Child Insurance," *The Charities Review,* Vol. XIII (April 1898), 71–73.

Bruno, Frank. *Trends in Social Work: As Reflected in the Proceedings of the National Conference on Social Work.* New York: Columbia University Press, 1957.

Burnet, James R. "Critical Opinions Upon Recent Employer's Liability Legislation in the United States," *Journal of Social Science,* No. 40 (December 1902), 52–69.

Butler, Amos W. "Government and Municipal Pensions," NCOCC. *Thirty-Third Annual Report (1906),* 470–487.

Carroll, Mollie Ray. *Labor & Politics:* The Attitude of the AFL Toward Legislation and Politics. Boston: Houghton-Mifflin Co., 1923.

Carstens, C. C. "Public Pensions to Widows with Children," *The Survey,* XXIX (January 4, 1913), 459–466.

Cawcroft, Ernest. "Workingmen's Compensation," *American Federationist,* XX (November 1913), 914–918.

Cheyney, Howell. "Employers and Compensation Systems," *Annals of the American Academy,* Vol. 38 (July 1911), 271–273.

Coit, Stanton. "Necessity of State Aid to the Unemployed," *Forum,* Vol. 17 (May 1894), 276–286.

Commons, John R. "The Christian Minister and Sociology," *Lend A Hand,* VIII (February 1892), 119–128.

Comstock, Anthony. "The Foes of Society, Church and State," Evangelical Alliance. *Christianity Practically Applied.* New York: Baker & Taylor, 1893, 428–444.

Creeck, Margaret. *Three Centuries of Poor Law Administration.* A study of Legislation in Rhode Island. Chicago: University of Chicago Press, 1936.

Cummings, John. "Poor Laws in Massachusetts and New York." American Economic Association, *Proceedings,* X (1895).

de Schweinitz, Karl. *England's Road to Social Security, 1349–1947.* 3rd ed. Philadelphia: University of Pennsylvania Press, 1947.

Devine, Edward T. "A Trip to England," *Charities,* Vol. I (November 1898), 1–4.
——. "Pensions for Mothers," *American Labor Legislation Review,* III (June 1913), 191–201.
——. "Public Outdoor Relief, I," *The Charities Review,* Vol. VIII (May 1898), 129–137.
——. "Social Forces," *Charities and Commons,* XVII (January 11, 1908), 1377–1378.
——. *Misery and Its Causes.* New York: The Macmillan Company, 1909.
Dewey, Davis R. "Irregularity of Employment," American Economic Association, *Proceedings,* IX, 525–539.
Diller, Luther. "Causes and Prevention of Pauperism," *National Conference of Charities and Correction, Seventh Annual Report* (1880), 242–249.
Dugdale, Robert L. *The Jukes: A Study in Crime, Pauperism, Disease and Heredity.* 4th Ed. New York: G. P. Putnam's Sons, 1910.
Edmonds, J. J., and Maurice B. Hexter. "State Pensions to Mothers in Hamilton County, Ohio," *The Survey,* XXX (December 12, 1914), 289–290.
Ely, Richard. "The Church and the Labor Movement," Evangelical Alliance, *Christianity Practically Applied.* New York: The Baker & Taylor Co., 1893.
Emery, James A. "Legislative Facts and Tendencies," NAM, *Proceedings of the Fifteenth Annual Convention* (1910), 115–132.
Fay, Lucy Atwood. "The Experience of Massachusetts," *The Charities Review,* Vol. VIII (April 1898), 68–71.
Feder, Leah Hannah. *Unemployment Relief in Periods of Depression.* New York: Russell Sage Foundation, 1936.
Fetter, Frank A. "The Need of Industrial Insurance," NCOCC, *Thirty-Third Annual Report* (1906), 464–470.
Fiske, Haley, "Industrial Insurance," *The Charities Review,* Vol. VIII (March 1898), 26–48.
——. "Industrial Insurance by Private Companies," National Civic Federation, *Ninth Annual Meeting* (1908), 96–104.
Flanigan, John D. "Benevolent Features of Trade Unions," NCOCC, *Twenty-Third Annual Report* (1896), 154–160.
Frankel, Charles. *The Democratic Prospect.* New York: Harper & Row, 1962.
Frankel, Lee K. "Facts in Connection with Workingmen's Insurance in the United States," NCF, *Ninth Annual Meeting,* 1909, 72–79.
Frankel, Lee K. and Dawson, Miles M. *Workingmen's Insurance in Europe.* New York: Russell Sage Foundation, 1910.

Friedensburg, Ferdinand Dr. *The Practical Results of Workingmen's Insurance in Germany* (Translated from German by Louis H. Gray). The Workmen's Compensation Service and Information Bureau, October 1911.

Friedlander, Walter A. *Introduction to Social Welfare,* 2nd Ed. Englewood Cliffs, New Jersey: Prentice Hall, 1963.

Gimckel, Lewis. "Outdoor Relief in Ohio," *The Charities Review,* Vol. VII (November 1897), 755–763.

Gompers, Samuel. "On the Attitude of Organized Labor Toward Organized Charity," *American Federationist,* VI (June 1899), 79–82.

——. *Seventy Years of Life and Labor.* Vol. II. New York: E. P. Dutton & Co., 1925.

Green, Marguerite. *The National Civic Federation and the American Labor Movement 1900–1925.* Washington: The Catholic University of America Press, 1956.

Hale, Edward Everett. "Universal Life Endowments," *Lend A Hand,* V (August 1890), 521–526.

——. "The Prevention of Pauperism," *Charities Review,* I (November 1891), 39–41.

Hard, William. *Injured in the Course of Duty.* New York: The Ridgeway Company, 1910.

——. "The Moral Necessity of 'State Funds to Mothers,' " *The Survey,* XXIX (March 1, 1913), 769–773.

——. "Pensions for Mothers," *American Labor Legislation Review,* III (June 1913), 229–234.

——. "Pensioners of Peace," *Everybody's Magazine,* XIX (October 1908), 522–533.

Hastings, Hugh. "Dangers of State Insurance," *North American Review,* Vol. 195 (May 1912), 630–640.

Hays, Samuel P. *The Response to Industrialism 1885–1914.* Chicago: The University of Chicago Press.

Hazard, Rowland. "What Social Classes Owe to Each Other," *Andover Review,* Vol. I (February 1884), 159–174.

Heisterman, Carl A., and Paris F. Keene. "Further Poor Law Notes," *Social Service Review,* VIII (1934), 43–49.

Henderson, Charles R. "Workingmen's Accident Insurance," *Charities and Commons,* XVII (1907), 823–825.

——. "Logic of Social Insurance," *Annals of the American Academy,* XXXIII (March 1909), 265–277.

——. *Industrial Insurance In the United States.* Chicago: The University of Chicago Press, 1908.

——. *Modern Methods of Charity*. New York: The Macmillan Company, 1904.

——. "Recent Studies in Sociology," *The Charities Review*, IV (November 1894), 46–50.

Hoffman, Frederick L. "The Progress of Private Companies," NCF, *Ninth Annual Meeting*, 1908, 116–122.

——. "Fatal Accidents in Coal Mines of North America," *The Engineering and Mining Journal*.

Hofstadter, Richard. *The Age of Reform*. New York: Alfred A. Knopf, 1955.

Holder, Arthur, and Thomas Tracy. "How Labor Fared in the 59th Congress," *American Federationist*, XIV (April 1907), 245–252.

Hopkins, Charles Howard. *The Rise of the Social Gospel in American Protestantism, 1865–1915*. New Haven: Yale University Press, 1940.

Howe, Frederic C., and Marie Jenny Howe. "Pensioning the Widow and the Fatherless," *Good Housekeeping*, LVII (September 1913), 282–291.

Howe, Stanley H. "Adequate Relief to Needy Mothers in Pennsylvania," NCOCC, *Forty-First Annual Report*, 1914, 447–450.

Hoxie, Robert Franklin. *Trade Unionism in the United States*. New York: D. Appleton & Company, 1917.

Hunter, Robert. "Outdoor Relief in the West," *The Charities Review*, VII (October 1897), 687–692.

Hutchinson, Woods. "Darwinism and Philanthropy," *The Charities Review*, VII (January 1898), 897–913.

Insurance Commissioners Convention of 1910. *Report*. 1910.

International Association of Factory Inspectors. *Proceedings*, 12th Annual Convention, 1898. (Reported in New York 13th Annual Report of Factory Inspectors.)

Irwin, Will. "Industrial Indemnity," *Century*, LXXXII (May 1911), 118–122.

Joint Conference on Workmen's Compensation Rates. *Proceedings of 1915*. Albany: J. B. Lyon Co., 1916.

Kelso, Robert W. *History of Public Poor Relief in Massachusetts, 1620–1920*. Boston: Houghton, Mifflin Co., 1922.

Kingsley, Darwin P. *Life Insurance and the Moral Obligation of Employers*. Address at Tenth Annual Dinner, NCF, November 23, 1909.

Laring, Augustus P. "Pension Funds of Individual Employers," NCF, *Ninth Annual Meeting*, 1908, 123–130.

Lewis, Frank W. *State Insurance*. Boston: Houghton Mifflin and Co., 1909.

Lindsey, Ben B. "The Mother's Compensation Law of Colorado," *The Survey*, XXIX (February 15, 1915), 714–716.

Low, Maurice. "The English Workingmen's Compensation Act," *Journal of Social Science,* No. 40 (December 1902), 19–30.

Low, Seth. "Relation of the Church to the Capital and Labor Question," in Evangelical Alliance, *National Perils and Opportunities.* New York: The Baker & Taylor Co., 1887.

Lowell, Josephine S. *Public Relief and Private Charity.* Putnam, 1884.

——. "The Evils of Investigation and Relief," *Charities,* I (July 1898).

McCarthy, Charles. *The Wisconsin Idea.* New York: The Macmillan Company, 1912.

McCash, James. "Relation of the Church to the Capital and Labor Question," in Evangelical Alliance 1887, *National Perils and Opportunities.* New York: The Baker and Taylor Co., 1887.

McCook, J. J. "The Tramp Problem," NCOCC, *Twenty-Second Annual Report* (1895), 288–301.

Mack, Julian. "Social Progress," NCOCC, *Thirty-Ninth Annual Report* (1912), 1–11.

MacVeagh, Franklin. "Opening Speech," National Civic Federation, *Industrial Conciliation,* Chicago Conference 1900, 91–98.

Mark, Clarence H. "The Industrial Scrap Heap," *American Federationist,* Vol. XIV (February 1907), 89–91.

Marks, G. Croydon (M.P.). "Lessons in Labor Legislation," *American Federationist,* Vol. XV (January 1908), 17–22.

Marks, Marcus M. "Postal Savings Banks," NCF, *Ninth Annual Meeting,* 1908, 86–91.

Mason, Alpheus Thomas. *The Brandeis Way: A Case Study in the Workings of Democracy.* Princeton: Princeton University Press, 1938.

Matthews, William H. "Widows' Families, Pensioned and Otherwise," *The Survey,* XXXII (June 6, 1914), 270–275.

Mayo-Smith, Richmond. "Workingmen's Insurance," *Charities Review,* I (December 1891), 49–54.

Means, D. McG. "The Dangerous Absurdity of State Aid," *Forum,* XVII (May 1894), 287–296.

Miller, Joseph Dana. "The Mask of Charity," *The Arena,* Vol. 28 (September 1902), 258–263.

Millis, Harry A., and Montgomery, Royal E. *Labor's Risks and Social Insurance.* New York: McGraw-Hill Book Company, 1938.

——. "The Relief and Care of Dependents, I," *American Journal of Sociology,* III (November 1897), 378–391.

Mitchell, John. "Should the Industry Bear the Cost?" National Civic Federation, *Ninth Annual Report,* 1908, 168.

Monroe, Paul. "An American System of Labor Pensions and Insurance,"
   American Journal of Sociology, II (January 1897), 501–514.
Moran, William J. "Unbinding the Eyes of Justice," National Civic
   Federation, *Ninth Annual Meeting,* 1908, 157–168.
More, Louise Balard. *Wage Earners' Budgets.* New York: Henry Holt and
   Company, 1907.
National Civic Federation. *The National Civic Federation: Its Method and
   Its Aim.* New York, 1905. Pamphlet. (Originally published November
   26 by *Harper's Weekly.)*
——. *Industrial Conference (of) 1902.* New York: The Winthrop Press,
   1903.
——. *Industrial Conciliation: Report of the Proceedings of the Conference,*
   December 16 and 17, 1901. New York and London: G. P. Putnam's &
   Sons, 1902.
Newell, Mary O'Connor. "Four Counties That Prefer Mothers to Orphan
   Asylums," *Delineator,* LXXX (August 1912), 85–86.
Nichols, Walter S. "Argument Against Liability," *Annals of the American
   Academy,* Vol. 38 (July 1911), 159–165.
O'Brien, Joseph J. "Shall We Provide for the Faithful Retired Labor
   Leader?" *American Federationist,* XV (July 1908), 522–523.
Oppenheimer, Moses. "Employers Liability Agitation," *American Feder-
   ationist,* III (January 1897), 233.
Oppenheimer, Moses. "Employers Liability Agitation," *American
   Federationist,* III (January 1897), 233.
Packer, Launcelot. "Accidents of Industry," National Civic Federation,
   Ninth Annual Meeting, 1908, 140–150.
Paine, Robert Treat. "Pauperism in Great Cities," *Lend a Hand,* XII
   (1894), 196–203.
Paulding, J. K. "Democracy and Charity," *The Charities Review,* IV (April
   1895), 281–290.
Persons, Frank W. *A Serious Step Backward.* New York: Charity
   Organization Society, 1912.
Pierson, Arthur T. (D.D.). "Estrangement of the Masses from the Church,"
   in Evangelical Alliance of 1889, *National Needs and Remedies.* New
   York: The Baker and Taylor Co., 1890, 112–123.
Pinckney, Merrit W. "Public Pensions to Widows; Experiences and
   Observations Which Lead Me To Favor Such a Law," *Child,* I (July
   1912), 43–50.
Post, C. W. "Who is the Owner?" NAM, *Proceedings of the Tenth Annual
   Convention,* 1905, 282–294.

Pumphrey, Ralph E., and Muriel W. Pumphrey (Eds.). *The Heritage of American Social Work.* New York: Columbia University Press, 1961.

Reynolds, James B. "Some Other Aspects," *The Charity Review,* VIII, No. 3 (May 1898), 142–155.

Rezneck, Samuel. "Patterns of Thought and Action in an American Depression, 1882–1886," *American Historical Review,* LXI (January 1956), 284–307.

Richmond, Mary. "Pensions and the Social Worker," *The Survey,* XXIX (February 15, 1913), 665–666.

——. "Motherhood and Pensions," *The Survey,* XXIV (March 1, 1913). 774–780.

Richmond, Mary E. "Married Vagabond," NCOCC, *Twenty-Second Annual Report* (1895), 514–519.

——. *Social Diagnosis.* New York: Russell Sage Foundation, 1917.

Rogers, E. H. "Relation of the Church to the Capital and Labor Question," in Evangelical Alliance, *National Perils and Opportunities.* New York: The Baker & Taylor Co., 1887, 234–246.

Ross, Edward Alsworth. "Social Control," *American Journal of Sociology,* Vol. VI, No. 5 (1896), 513–535.

Schneider, David M., and Albert Deutsch. *The History of Public Welfare in New York State, 1867–1940.* Chicago: University of Chicago Press, 1941.

Seager, Henry Rogers. *Social Insurance: A Program of Social Reform.* New York: The Macmillan Co., 1921.

——. "Outline of a Program of Social Reform," *Charities and Commons,* XVII (1907), 828–832.

Searing, Edward W. "Employers Liability Law," *American Federationist,* Vol. I (July 1894), 43–95.

Sherman, P. Tecumseh. "Compensation Law and Private Justice," *Annals of the American Academy,* Vol. 38 (July 1911), 151–158.

Singleton, Evelyn E. *Workmen's Compensation in Maryland.* Baltimore: The Johns Hopkins Press.

Smith, Hal. "Workmen's Compensation in Michigan," *Michigan Law Review* (1912), 290.

Speirs, Fred W. "An Experiment on Behalf of the Unemployed," *Charities Review,* Vol. I, No. 7 (May 1892), 304–310.

Stebbins, Roderick. "Some Social Problems of a Country Town," *Lend A Hand,* X (February 1893), 96–103.

Stewart, Bryce M. *Unemployment Benefits in the United States.* New York: Industrial Relations Counselors, Inc., 1930.

Stewart, William R. *The Philanthropic Work of Josephine Shaw Lowell.* New York: The Macmillan Company, 1911.

Strong, Josiah. "The Needs of the City," in Evangelical Alliance, *National Needs and Remedies.* New York: The Baker and Taylor Co., 1890, 57–67.

Taylor, Graham. "Sociological Training of the Ministry," in Evangelical Alliance, *Christianity Practically Applied.* New York: Baker and Taylor, 1893, 396–413.

Taylor, H. C. "A Plea for Better Methods in Charity Work," New York State, *Proceedings of the County Superintendents of the Poor,* XXII (1894), 47–67.

Taylor, W. Irving. *Employer's Liability.* Ph.D. Dissertation. New York: Vanden Houten & Co. [1889?]

Thaw, A. Blair. "Notes from New York," *Lend a Hand,* VIII (February 1892), 114–117.

Thurston, Henry W. *The Dependent Child.* New York: Columbia University Press, 1930.

Tonge, Thomas (Secretary of Colorado's Manufacturer's Exchange). "A Comparison of the Condition of European and American Labor," *Proceedings.* National Association of Officials of Bureaus of Labor Statistics Ninth Convention, 1892. Topeka: Hall and O'Donald Litho Co.

Tracy, Thomas F., and Arthur Holder. "How Labor Fared in the 59th Congress," *American Federationist,* Vol. XIV, No. 4 (April 1907), 245–252.

Tucker, Gideon J. "Last Drop of the Constitutional Convention," *American Federationist,* I (November 1894), 197–198.

Tyler, Morris F. "Workmen's Compensation Acts," *Yale Review,* VII (February, 1899), 421–433.

Vaile, Gertrude. "Administering Mothers' Pensions in Denver," *The Survey,* XXXI (February 28, 1914), 673–675.

Vanderlip, E. A. "Insurance From the Employers Standpoint," NCOCC, *Thirty-Third Annual Report,* 1906, 457–464.

Vreeland, Herbert H. "Welfare Work," National Civic Federation, *Welfare Work in Mercantile Houses, 1905.* Address delivered before New England Cotton Manufacturers Association, Atlantic City, September 20, 1905.

Walker, Francis. "The Tide of Economic Thought," American Economic Association, *Proceedings,* VI (1891), 15–38.

Warner, Amos G. *American Charities: A Study in Philanthropy and Economics.* New York: Thomas Y. Crowell and Company, 1894.

———. "Notes on the Statistical Determination of the Causes of Poverty," American Statistical Association, *Publications*. New Series I, No. 5 (1889), 183–201.

———. "Some Experiments on Behalf of the Unemployed," *The Quarterly Journal of Economics.* V (October 1890), 1–23.

Watson, Frank Dekker. *The Charity Organization Movement in the United States: A Study in American Philanthropy.* New York: The Macmillan Company, 1922.

Wayland, Rev. H. L. "A Scientific Basis of Charity," in Evangelical Alliance, *Christianity, Practically Applied,* New York: Baker and Taylor Co., 1893, 446–456.

Webber, Wm. L. "The Poor Laws," *Fourth Biennial Report, Michigan Board of State Commissioners . . . 1877–78,* 1879, 102–108.

Weber, Adna I. "Public Policy in Relation to Industrial Accidents," *Journal of Social Science,* No. 40 (December 1902), 31–45.

Wilensky, Harold L. and Charles N. Lebeaux. *Industrial Society and Social Welfare.* New York: Russell Sage Foundation, 1958.

Willoughby, William F. *Workingmen's Insurance.* New York: Thomas Y. Crowell, 1898.

Woodroofe, Kathleen. *From Charity to Social Work: In England and the United States.* London: Routledge and Kegan Paul, 1962.

Woods, Robert A. "Extracts from a Report on Andover House," *Lend A Hand,* XI (September 1893), 183–191.

INDEX

215